BIRMINGHAM METROPOLITAN COLLEGE

207549

D0541634

access to

British Foreign Affairs: Saving Europe at a Cost? 1919–60

FOURTH EDITION

Alan Farmer

HODDER
EDUCATION
AN HACHETTE UK COMPANY

Study guides written by Sally Waller (AQA) and Angela Leonard (Edexcel).

The publishers would like to thank the following individuals, institutions and companies for permission to reproduce copyright illustrations in this book: © Bettmann/CORBIS, pages 82, 151, 158; © CORBIS, pages 32, 137; Getty Images, page 200; © Hulton-Deutsch Collection/CORBIS, pages 15, 69; David Low, *Evening Standard*, 7th January 1929/British Cartoon Archive, University of Kent/Solo Syndication, page 37; David Low, *Evening Standard*, 2nd October 1933/British Cartoon Archive, University of Kent/Solo Syndication, page 57; David Low, *Evening Standard*, 20th September 1939/British Cartoon Archive, University of Kent/Solo Syndication, page 109; Popperfoto/Getty Images, page 167; Punch Ltd, pages 83, 103; Three Lions/Stringer, page 184; Time & Life Pictures/Getty Images, page 171; © Underwood & Underwood/CORBIS, page 17. The publishers would also like to thank the following for permission to reproduce material in this book: Curtis Brown Ltd. for an extract from *The Gathering Storm* by Winston Churchill, 1950; reproduced with permission of Curtis Brown Ltd, London on behalf of The Estate of Winston Churchill Copyright © Winston S. Churchill; Oxford University Press for an extract from *English History 1914–1945* by A.J.P. Taylor, 1977. The publishers would like to acknowledge use of the following extracts: Collins for an extract from *Britain 1914–2000* by D. Murphy, 2000; Hodder Murray for an extract from *Britain 1945–2007* by M. Lynch, 2008; Methuen for an extract from *British Foreign Policy Since Versailles 1919–1963* by W.N. Medlicott, 1968; Palgrave Macmillan for an extract from *The Illusion of Peace: International Relations in Europe, 1919–1933* by Sally Marks, 2003; Pimlico for an extract from *Now the War is Over* by P. Addison, 1985.
Every effort has been made to trace all copyright holders, but if any have been inadvertently overlooked the Publishers will be pleased to make the necessary arrangements at the first opportunity.

Hachette Livre UK's policy is to use papers that are natural, renewable and recyclable products and made from wood grown in sustainable forests. The logging and manufacturing processes are expected to conform to the environmental regulations of the country of origin.

Orders: please contact Bookpoint Ltd, 130 Milton Park, Abingdon, Oxon OX14 4SB. Telephone: (44) 01235 827720. Fax: (44) 01235 400454. Lines are open 9.00–5.00, Monday to Saturday, with a 24-hour message answering service. Visit our website at www.hoddereducation.co.uk

© Alan Farmer 1992, 2009
First published in 1992 by
Hodder Education,
An Hachette UK Company
338 Euston Road
London NW1 3BH

Second Edition published 1994.
Third Edition published 2006.
This Fourth Edition published 2009.

SUTTON COLDFIELD CAMPUS

Birmingham
Metropolitan
College LRC

Accession
207549

Class
942.08

Date Catalogued
25/05/10

Impression number   5 4 3 2 1
Year   2013 2012 2011 2010 2009

All rights reserved. Apart from any use permitted under UK copyright law, no part of this publication may be reproduced or transmitted in any form or by any means, electronic or mechanical, including photocopying and recording, or held within any information storage and retrieval system, without permission in writing from the publisher or under licence from the Copyright Licensing Agency Limited. Further details of such licences (for reprographic reproduction) may be obtained from the Copyright Licensing Agency Limited, Saffron House, 6–10 Kirby Street, London EC1N 8TS.

Cover photo of Sir Winston Churchill making the Victory sign as he greets well-wishers from his automobile, © Bettmann/Corbis.
Typeset in 10/12pt Baskerville and produced by Gray Publishing, Tunbridge Wells
Printed in Malta

A catalogue record for this title is available from the British Library.

ISBN: 978 0340 984 970

Contents

Dedication

Keith Randell (1943–2002)

The *Access to History* series was conceived and developed by Keith, who created a series to 'cater for students as they are, not as we might wish them to be'. He leaves a living legacy of a series that for over 20 years has provided a trusted, stimulating and well-loved accompaniment to post-16 study. Our aim with these new editions is to continue to offer students the best possible support for their studies.

The Making of British Foreign Policy

POINTS TO CONSIDER
This introductory chapter aims to provide you with a framework for understanding the making of British foreign policy in the years 1919–60. It will do this by considering the following questions:

- What was Britain's position in 1919?
- What problems did British statesmen face post-1918?
- Who made British foreign policy?
- What were Britain's main interests in foreign policy?

Key dates
1918   End of the First World War
1919   Signing of the Treaty of Versailles
1939   Start of the Second World War

1 | Britain's Position in 1919

> **Key question**
> How great was Britain in 1919?

> **Key date**
> End of the First World War: 1918

> **Key terms**
>
> **Armistice**
> A truce: the suspension of hostilities.
>
> **RAF**
> The Royal Air Force, formed in 1918, was the youngest of Britain's armed services.

In November 1918 an **armistice** finally brought the First World War to an end. In Britain, as in other victorious countries, there was great rejoicing and hope of a golden era of peace and prosperity.

Britain seemed to have emerged from the First World War in a strong position. It had lost only five per cent of its male population, whereas France had lost 10 per cent and Germany 15 per cent. In 1918:

- the British army numbered 5.5 million men
- the Royal Navy had 58 battleships, over 100 cruisers, and a host of lesser craft
- the **RAF** had over 20,000 planes.

The British Empire, which amounted to a quarter of the world's land surface, had greatly assisted Britain's war effort, providing vital raw materials and some 2.5 million troops. The war seemed to provide proof of the Empire's unity and utility.

The lack of major rivals
Britain's strong position in 1918 was enhanced by the weakness of its traditional rivals:

- Germany was defeated; its army had ceased to exist as a major fighting force, its fleet was in the hands of Britain, and its empire was lost.
- Russia, Britain's ally in the First World War but a rival for much of the nineteenth century, was in chaos. Civil war was raging and several provinces had taken advantage of the turmoil to declare independence.

Britain also appeared to have little to fear from the other victorious powers:

- France had been hard hit by the war.
- Common ties of language, culture and tradition meant that there was already talk of a 'special relationship' between the USA and Britain.
- Japan and Britain had been allied since 1902.

Britain's economic and financial strength

The First World War had less economic impact on Britain than many had feared. Britain's enormous reserves of wealth and its established hold on many overseas markets cushioned the blow. There was no great trade deficit: indeed Britain's **balance of payments** remained in the black for the war years as a whole. The elimination of German competition helped British manufacturers. In spite of millions of men being mobilised for the armed forces, industrial output had hardly fallen. Britain had been able to finance the war largely out of its own resources and had even been able to loan vast sums of money to other Allied governments, especially Russia. Although Britain owed money to the USA, most of this debt had been contracted by Britain on behalf of its Allies, who owed Britain far more money than it owed the USA.

Key terms

Balance of payments
The difference between a nation's total receipts from foreign countries and its total payments to foreign countries.

Industrial Revolution
The economic and social changes arising out of the change from industries carried on in the home with simple machines to industries in factories with power-driven machinery.

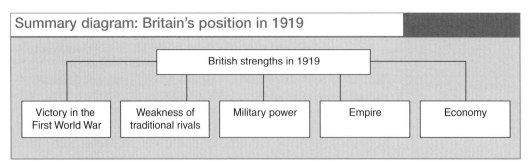

Summary diagram: Britain's position in 1919

British strengths in 1919 — Victory in the First World War — Weakness of traditional rivals — Military power — Empire — Economy

2 | Problems Facing British Statesmen

British statesmen, however, faced serious problems as they struggled to preserve both peace and Britain's status.

The threat from Germany and the USA pre-1914

Britain's influential position in world affairs in the nineteenth century was due to a number of interrelated factors:

Key question
What were the main problems facing Britain after 1918?

Key terms

Workshop of the world
Britain had produced most of the world's industrial goods before 1870.

Banking house of the world
Britain had surplus capital (money) to invest in projects around the world in the nineteenth century.

National debt
Money borrowed by a government and not yet repaid.

Right
Those who are inclined towards conservatism or who are strongly nationalist.

Left
Those who want to change society and who might incline to socialism or communism.

League of Nations
A global organisation, set up in 1919, to resolve international disputes.

Treaty of Versailles
One of the peace treaties that ended the First World War.

- The **Industrial Revolution** had ensured that Britain was both the **workshop of the world** and the **banking house of the world** before 1870.
- Throughout the eighteenth and nineteenth centuries the Royal Navy had ensured that Britain was secure from attack.
- Economic and naval supremacy had helped Britain acquire the most extensive Empire the world had ever seen (see Figure 1.1).

However, by 1900 Britain's economic position was threatened by Germany and the USA, who had become serious industrial rivals.

Economic and financial problems after 1918

The First World War had imposed serious strain on the British economy. The financial costs had been massive: £7 million a day. The war resulted in an 11-fold increase in the **national debt**, the annual interest payments of which consumed a large percentage of government expenditure post-1918. Moreover Britain had been forced to sell off some of its overseas investments, which had a damaging effect on its balance of payments. The war had also damaged Britain's industrial capacity. In many cases normal replacement and improvement of industrial plant and machinery had been postponed, as Britain struggled to produce the military materials it needed to wage war. To make matters worse, Britain had lost lucrative markets, especially in Latin America and the Far East, to the USA and Japan. Britain's share of world trade steadily declined after 1918.

Defence problems

Britain was a great imperial power with global commitments. Indeed, many politicians on both the **right** and the **left** saw the country as the policeman of the world:

- Those on the right believed Britain could and should maintain British interests wherever and whenever they were challenged.
- Those on the left thought Britain should enforce the decisions of the **League of Nations**, an organisation that was set up after the **Treaty of Versailles** (see pages 14–22).

Indeed at no time in the inter-war years could British ministers free themselves from the popular assumption that on them rested the responsibility for defending the victims of aggression in any part of the world.

Economic and financial problems meant there was a growing disparity between Britain's global commitments and its capacity to meet them. British military spending was massively reduced after 1918. In 1913, 30 per cent of Britain's government expenditure had been on defence. By 1933 this had fallen to 10 per cent. By the 1930s the fleet was growing old, the army was under 400,000 strong and the RAF was only the fifth largest in the world.

Key date

Signing of the Treaty of Versailles: 1919

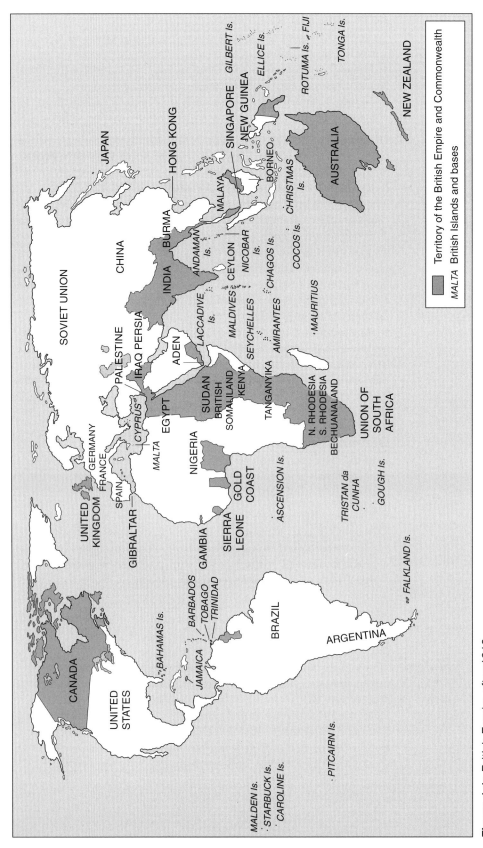

Figure 1.1: British Empire after 1918.

Lack of allies

Britain could not rely on others to help in its peacekeeping role:

- The First World War alliance with France soon wore thin. In 1921 Foreign Secretary Lord Curzon wrote that 'in almost every quarter of the globe ... the representatives of France are actively pursuing a policy which is either unfriendly to British interests or, if not that, is consecrated to the promotion of a French interest which is inconsistent with ours'.
- The USA emerged from the First World War as potentially the world's greatest power. Without US help it is unlikely that Britain and France would have won the war. But after 1919 the USA was reluctant to involve itself in international affairs, especially in the 1930s when its assistance was most needed. Most US presidents were not indifferent to Europe (or Asia), but their willingness and ability to exert themselves was severely constrained by US public opinion, which was strongly **isolationist**.

Imperial weakness

Nor could Britain depend on its Empire, which was not as strong as it seemed. In many ways it was a hotchpotch of independent, semi-independent and dependent countries held together by economic, political or cultural links that varied greatly in strength and character:

- There were growing **nationalist** movements in some colonies, especially in India.
- The **Dominions** were anxious to achieve greater autonomy and to develop their own foreign policies, rather than be committed to the consequences of British diplomacy.

The foreign threat

British statesmen had to face the fact that several potentially very strong nations had grievances and ambitions that might well threaten world peace and even Britain's security. Germany, Russia, Italy and Japan, for a variety of reasons, were dissatisfied with the peace settlement of 1919 (see pages 19–27) and the **status quo**.

Key terms

Isolationist
One who supports avoiding political entanglements with other countries.

Nationalist
A person who favours or strives after the unity, independence or interests of a nation.

Dominions
Countries within the British Empire that had considerable – in some cases almost total – self-rule.

Status quo
The existing condition.

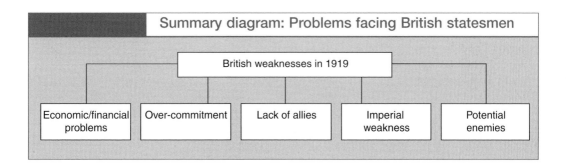

Summary diagram: Problems facing British statesmen

British weaknesses in 1919

Economic/financial problems — Over-commitment — Lack of allies — Imperial weakness — Potential enemies

3 | Who Made British Foreign Policy?

Key question
Who determined
British foreign policy?

In the making of British external policy, the relationship between Prime Minister and Foreign Secretary was (and still is) crucial. The relative power and influence of Foreign Secretaries in relation to Prime Ministers varied according to the personalities involved. Some Prime Ministers chose Foreign Secretaries whom they could trust and to whom they felt able to delegate substantial authority. Others tried to run their own foreign policies, sometimes coming into conflict with their Foreign Secretaries.

Table 1.1: British governments, Prime Ministers and Foreign Secretaries 1919–39

Governments	Prime Ministers	Foreign Secretaries
War Cabinet Dec. 1916–Jan. 1919	D. Lloyd George	A.J. Balfour
Coalition Jan. 1919–Oct. 1922	D. Lloyd George	A.J. Balfour (until Oct. 1919) then Lord Curzon
Conservative Oct. 1922–May 1923	A. Bonar Law	Lord Curzon
Conservative May 1923–Jan. 1924	Stanley Baldwin	Lord Curzon
Labour Jan. 1924–Nov. 1924	Ramsay MacDonald	Ramsay MacDonald
Conservative Nov. 1924–June 1929	Stanley Baldwin	Austen Chamberlain
Labour June 1929–Aug. 1931	Ramsay MacDonald	Arthur Hendrson
National Aug. 1931–June 1935	Ramsay MacDonald	Marquess of Reading then Sir John Simson
National (Conservative) June 1935–May 1937	Stanley Baldwin	Sir Samuel Hoare then Sir Anthony Eden
National (Conservative) May 1937–May 1940	Neville Chamberlain	Anthony Eden then Lord Halifax

The Cabinet

The shaping of foreign policy did not totally depend on the decisions of Prime Ministers and Foreign Secretaries. All Prime Ministers and Foreign Secretaries had to consider the views of other members of the **Cabinet**. Relatively few diplomatic issues actually reached Cabinet level and when they did most Prime Ministers were able to have the last word. Nevertheless, all Prime Ministers realised the necessity of having the support of the Cabinet on key foreign issues and even strong Prime Ministers heeded the advice of their Cabinets, sometimes against their better judgement.

Cabinet
Senior ministers of the government who meet regularly to discuss policy.

Key term

The role of Parliament

Prime Ministers and their Cabinets were ultimately responsible to Parliament. Although Parliament rarely intervened in day-to-day foreign affairs, many individual MPs were interested in external developments and often questioned the wisdom of government policy. In the last resort Parliament could force governments to take particular courses of action. For example, given the feeling in the House of Commons, Chamberlain would have found it difficult not to have declared war on Germany on 3 September 1939 (see pages 112–13).

British public opinion

Parliament, in turn, represented public opinion. After 1918 British statesmen no longer had quite the same room for manoeuvre as their counterparts in earlier generations. The 1918 general election in Britain was the first to be conducted on the basis of full **manhood suffrage** and there was also a limited **franchise for women**. (The franchise was finally extended to women on the same terms as men in 1928.) Politicians could now gain and preserve power only by winning the support of a far larger electorate than in the past.

While the public as a whole was rarely interested in the details of foreign policy, public opinion did set the broad ideological framework within which foreign policy operated. The fact that most people preferred governments in peacetime to spend money on health, social services and education rather than on armaments and adventures abroad was something that governments, anxious to win elections, could not ignore.

The mass media

The public were influenced by the mass media, particularly by the press but increasingly in the 1930s by radio and **newsreels**. (Only a small percentage of the population could afford a television set before the mid-1950s.) The extent to which the media were influenced by – or influenced – both the government and public opinion is keenly debated by historians and social scientists in general. The various media were certainly in a position to shape the agenda of public debate by focusing on certain news items and giving them particular colouring and significance.

Developments in communications meant that statesmen now negotiated in the full glare of publicity. Day-to-day dealings with foreign countries were subject to much greater scrutiny, sometimes with disastrous effects on difficult and delicate negotiations – for example, the Hoare–Laval Pact in 1935 (see pages 61–2). However, governments have invariably found ways of managing the media, not least during wartime.

The press

By 1937 there were over 1500 newspapers and over 3000 **periodicals**. Virtually every family took a national newspaper and most local newspapers enjoyed good circulations. *The Times*, although not the most widely read, remained the most influential

Key terms

Manhood suffrage
The right of all men to vote.

Franchise for women
The right of women to vote.

Newsreels
Short news programmes shown between feature films at cinemas.

Periodicals
Journals or magazines that are usually published weekly or monthly.

paper: it was viewed abroad as the voice of the government and its editor was regarded as one of the four most powerful figures in Britain (along with the King, Prime Minister and Archbishop of Canterbury). *The Times* prided itself on the breadth and depth of its foreign coverage and employed a vast team of foreign correspondents. The *Daily Express*, owned by Lord Beaverbrook, claimed the world's largest daily circulation (three million). A radical right-wing paper, it was popular with most income groups. It faced competition from Lord Rothmere's *Daily Mail*. The *Daily Telegraph*, another pro-Conservative newspaper, also had a rising circulation. The *News Chronicle*, a liberal paper, sold over one million copies daily. The *Daily Mirror* and *Daily Herald* supported the Labour Party. Press freedom ensured that there was always critical comment of government actions from one paper or another.

Radio's influence

By the late 1930s some nine million homes owned a radio. Controlled by the British Broadcasting Corporation (the BBC), radio was heavily regulated by the government. Sir John Reith, the BBC's director general, aware that the BBC was perceived abroad as the mouthpiece of the government, operated with great caution. Thus, BBC coverage of international events rarely offered critical comment and opponents of government action were given little opportunity to air their views.

Cinema's influence

In the mid-1930s there were over 4300 cinemas in Britain and some 23 million people went to the cinema at least once a week. Cinemas showed newsreels between the feature films. The newsreels were produced by five companies – three British and two American owned. All the companies provided a highly sanitised view of foreign policy – if they provided anything at all.

The Civil Service

It is possible to argue that foreign policy-making was as much in the hands of professional career civil servants in the Foreign Office as politicians. The most senior Foreign Office civil servant, the Permanent Under-Secretary, was in a strong position to exert influence on Foreign Secretaries and thus determine overall policy.

Other government departments also had some control over overseas policy. In the imperial sphere, the dominant force before 1947 was the India Office, linking the British government with the Indian sub-continent. The Colonial Office dealt with Britain's other overseas territories. There was also a Dominions Office to handle relations with Canada, Newfoundland, Australia, New Zealand, South Africa and Eire.

Inevitably, the War Office, the Admiralty and the Air Ministry influenced foreign policy-making. Treasury officials, because they were in a position to scrutinise any proposal involving government spending, also had considerable authority. Therefore, foreign policy-making was handled by a plethora of civil service departments, each with its own specialists, who remained at their post whatever party was in office. The harmonising of different and often conflicting viewpoints swallowed up time and energies. The lack of effective machinery for policy review was particularly serious.

Many of the senior civil servants came from similar backgrounds to most politicians. They attended the same public schools (especially Eton and Harrow) and the same universities (overwhelmingly Oxford and Cambridge), and often frequented the same London clubs. Some historians think that this élite controlled foreign policy in their own 'class' interests. This conclusion, which does not account for the fact that members of this élite had very different views on many policy issues, is far too sweeping.

Foreign influence

The final – and obvious – point is that British foreign policy was largely shaped and determined by the actions of non-Britons. As Herbert Morrison, Labour Foreign Secretary in 1951, put it: 'Foreign policy would be OK except for the bloody foreigners.' Prime Ministers, Foreign Secretaries, Cabinets, Parliaments, public opinion, media or civil servants had limited control over the policies of the USA, the USSR, Germany, Japan, etc., and British policy-makers had, of necessity, to respond to the actions of a variety of powers, both friendly and hostile.

Conclusion

For most of the period Prime Ministers, Foreign Secretaries and Cabinets took the essential decisions. Governments usually gave the impression that they were more in control of events than was often the case. In reality, decisions were often knee-jerk reactions to surprise crises and were often taken on the basis of poor information and in the context of a mass of conflicting problems.

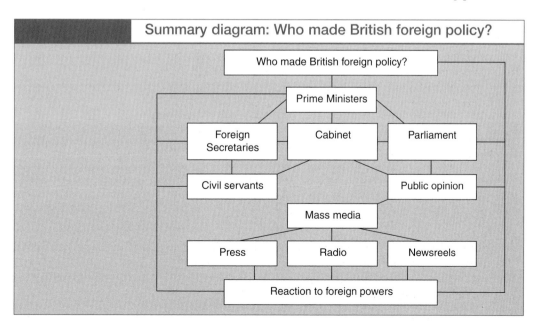

Summary diagram: Who made British foreign policy?

4 | British Interests in Foreign Policy

Political differences

While there were differences of emphasis, most governments, whether Conservative or Labour, tended to adopt similar policies. In part, this reflected the political situation. On two occasions when the Labour Party was in power (1924 and 1929–31) it depended on Liberal support.

   Throughout this period there was strong continuity in Foreign Office personnel. Experienced Foreign Office officials had considerable influence over most Prime Ministers and Foreign Secretaries. This helped to ensure continuity in style and purpose. Prudence, pragmatism, moderation, a tendency to understatement and irony tended to be features of the British government's style, almost regardless of which party was in power.

Key question
Did different political parties have different foreign policy interests?

British concerns

Preserving peace

The maintenance of peace seemed Britain's greatest national interest. The terrible losses of the First World War made both politicians and public recoil from the prospect of another war. There was also an awareness that Britain was vulnerable to air attack. Thus, Britain seemed to have everything to lose and nothing to gain from a major war.

Key question
What were the main British concerns?

The defence of Britain

Although governments did their best to avoid conflict, most were concerned to ensure that, if war should come, Britain was adequately defended. Defence policy was based on four main objectives:

- the security of Britain
- the protection of essential trade routes
- defence of the Empire
- a readiness to co-operate in the defence of Britain's allies.

Governments had to assess Britain's defence requirements in the light of the current international situation and in terms of what the country could afford. Successive governments in the 1920s – Conservative and Labour – decided that the country could afford very little. In 1919 Lloyd George's government decided that 'the British Empire will not be involved in any large war over the next 10 years'. This 'Ten-Year Rule', which was used to justify keeping defence spending as low as possible, continued until 1932. It made some sense: there was no serious threat to world peace in the 1920s. The threat of Hitler in the 1930s forced Britain to rearm and it did so in the nick of time.

Preserving the balance of power

Most British governments wished to maintain the **balance of power** in Europe as the best insurance against the renewal of war. Prior to 1939 most were reluctant to assume any definite commitments to further this aim. Many Britons believed the First

Balance of power
British governments had long tried to ensure that no nation was so strong that it could dominate Europe and thus threaten Britain.

Key term

Key term

Alliance system
Before 1914 Europe had been divided into two armed camps: the Triple Entente (Britain, France and Russia) against the Triple Alliance (Germany, Austria-Hungary and Italy).

World War had been caused by a rigid **alliance system** and fixed military plans. As a result, most British governments opposed binding the country to France or any other nation. This was to remain a cardinal tenet of British policy until 1939.

World power
While most politicians appreciated the importance of Europe, few considered Britain a fully fledged European state. British interests were global rather than just continental. The preservation of the Empire was essential if Britain was to remain a great world power. Although politicians claimed that self-government was the ultimate destiny of every part of the Empire, most were determined to preserve the imperial union in some form.

The importance of the USA
A key British aim was to remain on good terms with the USA. This was the case before 1939. It was even more important thereafter.

Appeasement
Most British politicians hoped that sensible policies of compromise, conciliation and concession would prevent conflict. In the 1930s such policies were called appeasement. The meaning of the word has been so stretched and distorted since 1939 that some scholars believe the word should no longer be used. Appeasement can be used to cover all aspects of British diplomacy between the two world wars. Or it can be used more specifically to describe Chamberlain's policies towards Germany in 1937–8 (see pages 68–84). Since the Second World War appeasement has tended to have a derogatory meaning, and the word is often used to mean a craven surrender to force. But for most of the inter-war years, appeasement was seen as a positive concept: the continuation of a long diplomatic tradition of trying to settle disputes peacefully. Those who opposed appeasement were seen as cranks or war-mongers. Only the failure of Chamberlain's policies in 1939 (when he actually abandoned appeasement!) turned appeasement into a pejorative term. After 1945, British and US statesmen, learning (they believed) the lessons of the 1930s, were determined to stand firm against – and not appease – Russian leaders.

Key date

Start of the Second World War: 1939

Conclusion
In 1919 most Britons assumed that the First World War had been the war to end all wars. Few envisaged that two decades later their country would become involved in a second world war and that when this war ended Britain would no longer be a first-class power, unable to compete with the two superpowers of the USA and Russia. So what went wrong? Was Britain already in retreat pre-1914 – a retreat that continued through the inter-war years? Did the Second World War seriously weaken Britain, thus instigating its decline, or did the conflict simply accelerate already established trends? Was Britain's decline almost

inevitable, whoever was in power and whatever they did? Or were individual statesman responsible for Britain's demise?

It should be said that few historians today would accept that events in history are inevitable. Therefore, most would accept that the policies of individual statesmen did have considerable effect. But perhaps it is wrong to blame the statesmen. Perhaps it is better to see the period, in historian W.N. Medlicott's words, as 'a long process of adaptation to the realities of the modern world', rather than as a period of decline. Perhaps most – if not all – the British governments of the period acted for good and rational reasons. Perhaps Britain's position in 1945 might have been worse but for their actions.

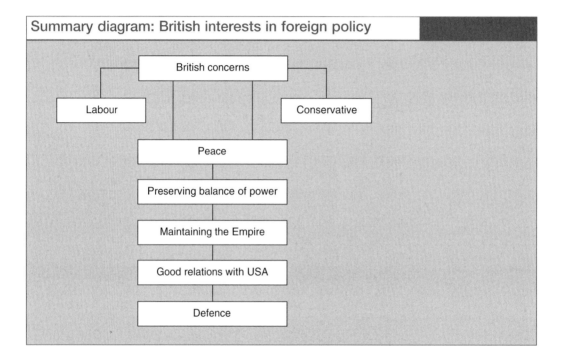

Summary diagram: British interests in foreign policy

2 The Illusion of Peace 1919–31

POINTS TO CONSIDER
This chapter examines the aims of the 1919 peacemakers (especially Lloyd George), the problems they faced and the results of their work. An understanding of the peace settlement is essential if you are to make sense of Anglo-German relations in the inter-war period. You must think carefully about the criticisms of the peace settlement which were made at the time and which have been made since. Try to decide whether the peacemakers (particularly Lloyd George) should be blamed or praised for their efforts. You must also try and evaluate the success of Lloyd George's successors: Bonar Law, Baldwin and MacDonald. From 1919 to 1931 there was no real challenge to the status quo and thus no serious threat of war. But how well did British statesmen deal with the problems that arose? To help your understanding, the chapter has been divided into the following themes:

- The problems of peacemaking
- The aims of the peacemakers
- The main terms of the Treaty of Versailles
- The settlement of Eastern Europe and Turkey
- Anglo-Soviet relations
- The problem of Italy
- The German question in the 1920s
- The League of Nations
- Disarmament

Key dates

1918	December	General election: victory for Conservative–Liberal coalition. Lloyd George continued as Prime Minister
1919	January	Paris Peace Conference began
	June	Treaty of Versailles (with Germany)
	September	Treaty of St Germain (with Austria)
	November	Treaty of Neuilly (with Bulgaria)
1920	June	Treaty of Trianon (with Hungary)
	August	Treaty of Sèvres (with Turkey)
1922	February	Washington Naval Agreement
	October	Lloyd George resigned: Bonar Law became Prime Minister

	October	Mussolini seized power in Italy
1923	January	French and Belgium troops occupied the Ruhr
	May	Bonar Law resigned: Baldwin became Prime Minister
	July	Treaty of Lausanne (with Turkey)
1924	January	MacDonald became Prime Minister
	February	Britain recognised the Soviet government
	August	Dawes Plan
	October	Baldwin became Prime Minister
1925		Locarno Conference
1926		Germany joined the League of Nations
1929		MacDonald became Prime Minister

1 | The Problems of Peacemaking

In January 1919 the leaders of 32 countries, representing some 75 per cent of the world's population, assembled in Paris to make peace with the defeated **Central Powers**. Many criticisms have been made of the way the conference was conducted. These include:

- the decision of the Allied leaders to participate in the work of detailed negotiation personally
- the '**secret diplomacy**'
- the fact that representatives of Russia, Germany and the other defeated powers were excluded from the peacemaking process
- the fact that no agreement had been reached on the programme to be followed or how the conference was to be organised.

Criticisms of the peacemaking process have sometimes been exaggerated. However, it would be difficult to exaggerate the seriousness of the problems which the peacemakers faced:

- They somehow had to cope with a whole series of conflicting treaty commitments, promises and pronouncements which had been made during the war.
- The breakdown of the German (Hohenzollern), Russian (Romanov), Austro-Hungarian (Habsburg) and Turkish (Ottoman) empires had resulted in economic chaos, famine and outbursts of nationalism – sometimes violent – throughout Central and Eastern Europe and the Near East.
- There was the fear that **Bolshevism** might spread from Russia and threaten the whole of Europe.
- The peacemakers were aware that the peace settlement would need to reflect the intense popular feeling within their own countries.
- Decisions would have to be made quickly.

Key question
What problems did the peacemakers face in 1919?

Key date
Paris Peace Conference began: January 1919

Key terms

Central Powers
Germany, Austria-Hungary, Turkey and Bulgaria were known as the Central Powers in the First World War.

Secret diplomacy
Negotiations taking place behind closed doors.

Bolshevism
The Bolshevik Party seized power in Russia in November 1917. Led by Lenin, the Bolsheviks supported communism. The word 'Bolshevism' became a derogatory term for communism.

Key term

Big Three
Lloyd George
(Britain),
Clemenceau
(France) and
Woodrow Wilson
(USA) dominated
the peacemaking
process. They
represented the
strongest countries
that had defeated
the Central Powers.

The **Big Three** each had large supporting teams of experts. All three were concerned with the main question: how to provide security for the future. All had different views on that issue.

The conclusion of a satisfactory peace treaty with Germany was the major concern of the Big Three. Once the Treaty of Versailles had been signed (in June 1919), Lloyd George, Wilson and Clemenceau returned home. The completion of treaties with Germany's allies was left to less eminent representatives.

The Big Three at Versailles. From left to right: Georges Clemenceau, Woodrow Wilson and David Lloyd George.

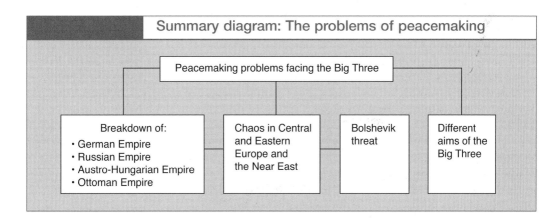

Summary diagram: The problems of peacemaking

Peacemaking problems facing the Big Three

| Breakdown of:
• German Empire
• Russian Empire
• Austro-Hungarian Empire
• Ottoman Empire | Chaos in Central and Eastern Europe and the Near East | Bolshevik threat | Different aims of the Big Three |

2 | The Aims of the Peacemakers

When Germany had sought peace terms in the autumn of 1918, it had assumed these would be based on President Wilson's **Fourteen Points** that it had initially rejected when it was still hopeful of victory.

Wilson, seeking to distance himself from traditional European diplomatic dealings, had talked in terms of a peace based on justice, equality and democracy. He had later stated that the eventual peace should contain 'no annexations, no contributions, no punitive damages'. Wilson's Fourteen Points, which suggested that Germany would be treated leniently, were regarded as idealistic pipe dreams by most hard-headed European statesmen. But they could not be rejected out of hand. If they were to defeat Germany, Britain and France had to retain the support of the USA, the world's strongest economic power. However, both Lloyd George and Clemenceau did express serious reservations about some of Wilson's ideas. They were aware that most people in Britain and France wanted a harsh peace. By November 1918 even Wilson accepted that Germany should make compensation 'for all damage done to the civilian population of the Allies'.

Clemenceau vs Wilson

Clemenceau was determined on a punitive peace. Twice in his lifetime France had been invaded by Germany. In 1871 France had lost Alsace-Lorraine and been forced to pay massive **reparations**. French casualties between 1914 and 1918, in proportional terms, were the highest sustained by the Allied powers. Clemenceau wanted German power reduced so that all prospect of a future military threat was eliminated. In demanding security and compensation for the losses France had endured, he was asking no more than every French citizen expected.

Wilson was less interested in punishing Germany. The USA had no territorial or even overt economic aims. Wilson was primarily concerned with establishing a fair and lasting system of international relations. In particular, he wanted to set up a League of Nations and favoured the principle of **self-determination** for all subject peoples.

Lloyd George's aims

Although Britain had no territorial claims in Europe, Lloyd George was anxious to preserve Britain's naval supremacy and also prepared to enlarge the British Empire – time-honoured British objectives. Aware of the strong anti-German feeling in Britain, he had announced in the 1918 election campaign that he expected Germany to pay 'to the limit of her capacity' for the damage she had inflicted. Lloyd George was anxious to destroy **German militarism** and even supported demands that **Kaiser Wilhelm II** should be hanged.

However, he distinguished between the old German leaders and the German people as a whole. Germany was now ruled by parliamentary leaders. It seemed unwise to persecute them for

Key question
What were the main aims of the peacemakers?

Key terms

Fourteen Points
Wilson's peace programme, the Fourteen Points, was announced to the US Congress in January 1918.

Reparations
Compensation paid by defeated states to the victors.

Self-determination
The right of people, usually of the same nationality, to set up their own government and rule themselves.

German militarism
The German army had been a major force in Europe since 1870. German generals had exerted great political influence, particularly during the First World War.

Key question
Was Lloyd George the main architect of the Treaty of Versailles?

Key figure

Kaiser Wilhelm II
German Emperor, 1888–1918. When it was clear that the First World War was lost, he abdicated and fled to the Netherlands.

Profile: David Lloyd George 1863–1945

1863 – Born in Manchester
1864 – Moved to Llanystumdwy in Wales
1890 – Elected as Liberal MP
1905 – President of the Board of Trade
1908 – Became Chancellor of the Exchequer: responsible for introducing old age pensions and national insurance
1915 – Became Minister for Munitions
1916 – Became Prime Minister
1918 – Widely regarded as 'the man who won the war', he also won the December election but was now dependent on Conservative support
1919 – Attended Paris Peace Conference
1922 – Resigned as Prime Minister when the Conservatives left his coalition government: never again held office
1945 – Died

Lloyd George had critics at the time, and since. J.M. Keynes, the economist, portrayed him as a political chameleon, 'rooted in nothing', 'void and without content'. Some historians have concluded that his principal aim at Versailles was simply to win popularity at home. Others have argued that he was devious, unscrupulous and delighted in improvisation; so much so that for him, the means justified themselves almost irrespective of the ends.

However, Lloyd George also had and has his supporters. Some regard him as the most inspired and creative British statesman of the twentieth century. Historian A.J.P. Taylor thought him, 'The greatest ruler of Britain since Oliver Cromwell'. Many historians see him as charting a tricky and skilful course in 1919 between the opposing views of Clemenceau and Wilson, while at the same time trying (with great success) to preserve British interests. His defenders claim that, of all the peacemakers, he had the most realistic post-war vision to reinforce his spell-binding skills as a negotiator.

Key date

General election: victory for Conservative–Liberal coalition. Lloyd George continued as Prime Minister: December 1918

the sins of the Kaiser. Conscious of the danger of leaving an embittered Germany, he was inclined to leniency. In the Fontainbleu memorandum of March 1919, Lloyd George wrote:

> I cannot imagine any greater cause for future war than that the German people who have proved themselves one of the most powerful and vigorous races of the world, should be surrounded by a number of small states, many of them consisting of peoples who have never previously set up a stable government for themselves, but each containing large masses of Germans clamouring for reunion with their native land.

Lloyd George also feared that if Germany was excessively humiliated it might be driven into the arms of the Bolsheviks. While he talked 'hard' for home consumption, he was prepared to act 'soft' and do all he could to ease some of the harsher terms that Clemenceau was intent on imposing.

Lloyd George has often been seen as the main architect of the Versailles settlement. It is claimed that he was in a strong position because he found himself able to mediate between Clemenceau and Wilson. However:

- arguably Lloyd George, rather than Wilson, was the main opponent of most of the extreme French demands
- the process of bargaining among the Big Three was highly complex, with attitudes by no means fixed.

Certainly the final treaty was the result of a series of compromises on many issues. It would be wrong, therefore, to single out Lloyd George as the main arbiter of the peace settlement.

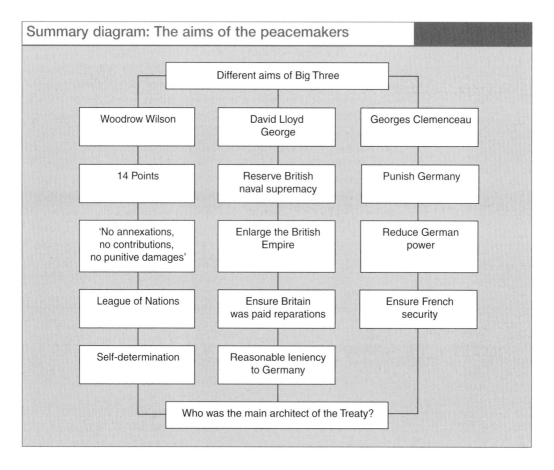

Summary diagram: The aims of the peacemakers

Different aims of Big Three

Woodrow Wilson	David Lloyd George	Georges Clemenceau
14 Points	Reserve British naval supremacy	Punish Germany
'No annexations, no contributions, no punitive damages'	Enlarge the British Empire	Reduce German power
League of Nations	Ensure Britain was paid reparations	Ensure French security
Self-determination	Reasonable leniency to Germany	

Who was the main architect of the Treaty?

3 | The Main Terms of the Treaty of Versailles

Key question
Was Germany harshly treated?

Key date
Treaty of Versailles: June 1919

The Treaty of Versailles was completed in great haste at the end of April 1919. The Germans, allowed only three weeks to make written observations, attacked nearly every provision. In the end, however, Germany had no option but to accept the terms or face the threat of invasion. The treaty was finally signed on 28 June 1919.

Territorial changes

Negotiations about Germany's frontiers were highly contentious. Clemenceau demanded that Germany's western frontier should be fixed on the River Rhine. The area on the left bank would go to France or become an independent **buffer state**. Lloyd George and Wilson both opposed this idea, believing it would become a cause of constant German resentment. Clemenceau failed to get his way. He was appeased by the promise of an Anglo-American defensive guarantee whereby both countries would provide military support for France.

It was agreed that Germany should return Alsace-Lorraine to France, Northern Schleswig to Denmark, and Eupen and Malmedy to Belgium. Though the **Rhineland** was not divorced from Germany, it was to be occupied by Allied troops for 15 years and was to remain permanently **demilitarised**. The Saar region was placed under League of Nations control for 15 years, during which time the French could work its coal mines. A **plebiscite** would then be held to decide the area's future.

Key terms

Buffer state
A neutral country lying between two others whose relations are, or may become, strained.

Rhineland
The part of Germany to the west of the River Rhine.

Demilitarised
Not occupied by military forces.

Plebiscite
A vote by the people on one specific issue – like a referendum.

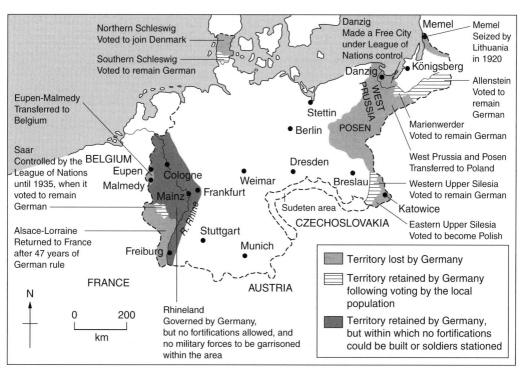

Figure 2.1: The Treaty of Versailles.

The settlement of Germany's eastern border caused even more problems. The Fourteen Points had promised to create an independent Poland that would be given access to the sea. Germany could, therefore, expect to lose land to Poland. However, it was difficult to determine which land this should be because there was no clear-cut division between areas of German and Polish majority population in eastern Germany. Clemenceau wanted a strong Poland and supported the most extreme Polish territorial claims. But Lloyd George, fearful of incorporating millions of embittered Germans within the new state, fought to keep Poland as small as possible. His pressure ensured that:

- the key port of Danzig was made a Free City under the League of Nations
- a plebiscite was held (in 1921) in Upper Silesia, with the result that only about one-third of the area went to Poland.

The Germans were outraged by the loss of land to Poland, especially the loss of the **Polish Corridor**. Germany also lost Memel to Lithuania. Moreover, it was forbidden to unite with the Germanic 'rump' state of Austria. Had it been allowed to do so, Germany would have been greater in area and population (and thus in potential military strength) than in 1914. However, this decision seemed to confirm the fact that the principle of self-determination would not be applied to Germans.

Germany's colonies

Germany lost all its colonies. Britain gained German East Africa and the Cameroons; Australia took New Guinea; South Africa acquired South-West Africa; New Zealand got Samoa; and Japan took all German possessions in China and in the Pacific north of the Equator. On Wilson's insistence, these areas were to be ruled as **mandates**. This meant that the ruling powers had to bear in mind the wishes of the colonial inhabitants who should eventually be prepared for self-government under the supervision of the League. Lloyd George was not opposed to this principle which he described as 'virtually a codification of existing British practice'.

Armaments

The Allies agreed that:

- Germany was to have no heavy artillery, tanks or aeroplanes
- the German army was limited to 100,000 men
- Germany was to have no **capital ships** and no submarines.

Reparations and war guilt

Germany was forced to sign the War Guilt clause (Article 231 of the Treaty of Versailles) accepting blame for causing the war and therefore responsibility for all losses and damage. This provided a moral basis for the Allied demands for Germany to pay reparations. In reality, the War Guilt clause, which was hated by the Germans, had little practical effect as Germany had already accepted in the Armistice terms that it would make compensation

Key terms

Polish Corridor
A stretch of land which gave Poland access to the Baltic Sea but which cut off East Prussia from the rest of Germany.

Mandates
The system created in the Peace Settlement for the supervision of all the colonies of Germany (and Turkey) by the League of Nations.

Capital ships
Warships of the largest and most heavily armoured class, for example, battleships.

for 'all damage done to the civilian population of the Allies'. The main difficulty was deciding how much Germany should pay.

Wilson wanted a reparations settlement based on Germany's ability to pay. However, the French and British public wanted, in the words of Sir Auckland Geddes, 'to squeeze the German lemon till the pips squeaked'. This would serve the dual purpose of helping the Allied countries meet the cost of the war and also keep Germany financially weak for years to come.

Lloyd George was pulled several ways. He was determined that Britain should get its fair share of reparations and insisted (successfully) that 'damage' should include merchant shipping losses and the costs of pensions to those disabled, widowed or orphaned by the war. Like Wilson, however, he thought that Germany should pay only what it could reasonably afford and he accepted the view that if Germany was hit too hard it would no longer be a good market for British goods. Whatever his own feelings, Lloyd George could not afford to ignore the prevailing mood in Britain or the fact that in the 1918 election, he had promised to screw Germany 'to the uttermost farthing'.

PEACE AND FUTURE CANNON FODDER

Peace and future cannon fodder. What point is the cartoonist intending to make?

The Tiger: "Curious! I seem to hear a child weeping!"

Eventually, at Lloyd George's suggestion, a Reparations Commission was set up to determine the amount. In 1921 the Commission recommended a sum of £6600 million (of which Britain was to get some 22 per cent). Although this was far less than originally envisaged, some economists and most Germans claimed (probably wrongly) that it was more than Germany could afford.

The League of Nations

The League of Nations was written into the Treaty of Versailles. This was Wilson's obsession. He had believed (quite wrongly) that Britain and France would oppose the idea. Although neither Lloyd George nor Clemenceau was an enthusiastic advocate, both were prepared to support the concept of the League in return for US friendship. Indeed, Britain had prepared a concrete scheme for the League, whereas Wilson had come to Paris 'armed' only with rather vague ideas. The British scheme thus became the framework for the League. Germany was not allowed to join until it had given solid proof of its intention to carry out the peace terms.

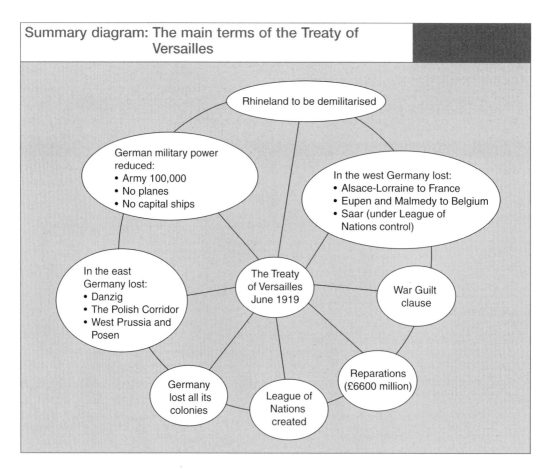

Summary diagram: The main terms of the Treaty of Versailles

Rhineland to be demilitarised

German military power reduced:
• Army 100,000
• No planes
• No capital ships

In the west Germany lost:
• Alsace-Lorraine to France
• Eupen and Malmedy to Belgium
• Saar (under League of Nations control)

In the east Germany lost:
• Danzig
• The Polish Corridor
• West Prussia and Posen

The Treaty of Versailles June 1919

War Guilt clause

Germany lost all its colonies

League of Nations created

Reparations (£6600 million)

4 | Key Debate

How justified are the criticisms of Versailles?

In 1919 the Treaty of Versailles was well received in Britain and passed through Parliament with huge majorities. On the whole Britain seemed to have gained what it wanted:

- German naval power had been destroyed (the German fleet had scuttled itself in **Scapa Flow** in June 1919)
- Britain and its Dominions had acquired German colonies
- Germany had agreed to pay reparations.

The prevailing British view was that the treaty was firm but fair.

Criticism of the treaty

Germans of all political persuasions claimed that the treaty was punitive and unfair, and a major departure from Wilson's Fourteen Points which they had been led to believe would be the basis of the peace settlement. Radical opinion in Britain soon reached the same conclusion. In 1919 the economist J.M. Keynes wrote a devastating critique of the treaty in an influential book, *The Economic Consequences of the Peace*. He argued that a naive Wilson had been forced by a vindictive Clemenceau and the scheming Lloyd George to agree to an over-harsh peace, and particularly condemned the reparations clauses. Ironically, even Lloyd George had doubts about the treaty and suspected that Germany had been treated unfairly. These doubts were to be echoed by many British politicians in the years ahead.

However, most of the French considered the treaty far too soft. After a long and costly war, for which it was largely responsible, Germany had lost only 13 per cent of its pre-war territory and 10 per cent of its population. Surrounded by small, unstable states on its southern and eastern borders, Germany remained potentially the strongest state in Europe. Clemenceau had accepted the treaty only because Wilson and Lloyd George had offered France a defensive alliance. The US Senate, however, refused to sanction this alliance. The British government then did likewise. Most French people, in consequence, felt betrayed.

Historians have echoed these contemporary criticisms. Some have claimed that the treaty was the worst of all worlds: too severe to be permanently acceptable to most Germans, and too lenient to constrain Germany for long. Historian A.J.P. Taylor claimed that it was the Allies' failure to solve the **German problem** in 1919 that laid the foundation of the Second World War.

Defence of the treaty

Some historians, such as Paul Kennedy and Anthony Adamthwaite, have been prepared to defend both the peacemakers and the treaty. While agreeing that the German problem was not solved, they have pointed out that, even with hindsight, it is difficult to suggest realistic solutions to that

Key terms

Scapa Flow
A major British naval base in the Orkney Islands.

German problem
Since 1871, Germany had been the strongest nation in Europe. The Treaty of Versailles reduced but did not destroy Germany's potential power. The German problem was essentially Germany's power.

problem. Arguably, the overriding problem was not so much the terms of Versailles, but rather German hostility to the treaty because it represented a defeat which most Germans were not willing to acknowledge. Even a treaty based on the Fourteen Points would not have been acceptable to Germany because it would have involved the loss of land to Poland. Thus, Adamthwaite sees Versailles as a 'brave attempt to deal with intractable, perhaps insoluble problems'.

The Big Three, jumping from question to question and under severe domestic pressures, were not unaware of the deficiencies in their handiwork. But this was precisely why, so far as Lloyd George was concerned, the League of Nations was created. In 1919 he said that it would 'be there as a Court of Appeal to readjust crudities, irregularities, injustices'. This was perhaps putting too much faith in an organisation which lacked enforcement powers. Moreover, the League also lacked the USA. The US Senate refused to ratify the Treaty of Versailles and thus America did not become a member of the League – something unforeseen by the peacemakers.

Conclusion

Perhaps the Versailles settlement fell between two stools in that it was both too harsh and too soft. While giving Germany a sense of grievance, it left it with the potential strength to redress those grievances in the future. It is thus possible to blame the Versailles peacemakers for the Second World War. But is this fair? It is clear that Lloyd George, Wilson and Clemenceau faced a host of – possibly intractable – problems. They did their best, in difficult circumstances, to resolve them. Is it fair to blame them for something that happened two decades later?

Some key books in the debate
A. Adamthwaite, *The Making of the Second World War* (Routledge, 1977).
M.L. Dockrill, *Peace without Promise: Britain and the Peace Conferences 1919–23* (Batsford, 1981).
P. Kennedy, *The Realities Behind Diplomacy* (Fontana, 1981).
A. Lentin. *Guilt at Versailles: Lloyd George and the Pre-History of Appeasement* (Methuen, 1985).
A. Sharp, *The Versailles Settlement: Peacemaking in Paris, 1919* (Macmillan, 1991).

Key term

Habsburg Empire
Until 1918 the Austro-Hungarian Empire, ruled for centuries by the Habsburg family, had controlled much of Central and Eastern Europe.

5 | The Settlement of Eastern Europe and Turkey

Key question
How successful was the settlement of Eastern Europe?

Eastern Europe posed severe difficulties for the peacemakers. By late 1918 the **Habsburg Empire** had fallen apart. Countries such as Poland and Czechoslovakia already effectively existed. Russia, in the hands of the Bolsheviks and in the throes of civil war, had no representatives at the peace conference, and little involving the country could be settled.

Figure 2.2: The settlement of Eastern Europe.

France, Britain and the USA had divergent, but not completely dissimilar, aims in Eastern Europe:

- Some British and French statesmen would have liked to retain the Habsburg Empire in some form, as a potential counter-weight to Russia and Germany. But given the intense

nationalist feeling among the peoples of the former empire, this was impossible.
- France supported the creation of sizeable, economically viable and strategically defensible states, which they hoped would be strong enough to withstand either German or Russian pressure.
- Britain was unwilling to produce a settlement that left large numbers of Germans outside Germany.
- Most Allied statesmen supported the principle of self-determination and efforts were made to redraw the frontiers of Eastern Europe along ethnic lines.

The mixture of national groups meant that the establishment of frontiers was certain to cause massive problems. To make matters worse, while the peacemakers in Paris tried to redraw national boundaries, various ethnic groups in Eastern Europe battled it out in a series of military confrontations. The borders that finally came into existence owed as much to the outcome of these clashes as to the negotiations at Paris.

The Eastern European treaties

Ultimately, treaties were signed with Austria (the Treaty of St Germain), Hungary (the Treaty of Trianon), and Bulgaria (the Treaty of Neuilly). All the defeated powers had to pay reparations and lost large slices of territory. Austria, for example, lost land to Poland, Czechoslovakia, Italy and Yugoslavia, with the result that its population was reduced from 28 million to fewer than eight million.

The treaties, combined with various settlements along the Russian borderlands, ultimately created a string of new states from Finland to Yugoslavia (see Figure 2.2 on page 25). Disputes over exact frontiers continued well into the 1920s. Although the peacemakers did their best to apply the principle of self-determination, large communities found themselves governed by people of a different ethnic group. Czechoslovakia, for example, had a population made up of Czechs, Slovaks, Germans, Hungarians, Ruthenians and Poles. Nothing short of massive population transfers could have resolved the problem.

The results

British politicians throughout the 1920s shared Lloyd George's view that the eastern frontiers were unsound and the new (or enlarged) states were unstable and unreliable. Bulgaria, Hungary and Austria were left bitter and resentful and there were social, economic and political tensions in almost every Eastern European state. The fact that many of the new states contained large minorities of discontented Germans was a further problem. It seemed likely that Germany, at some stage, would press for territorial modifications. British governments, therefore, were reluctant to commit themselves to defend the settlement in Eastern Europe. The best that could be hoped for was that the flawed settlement could be revised peacefully.

Key dates

Treaty of St Germain (with Austria): September 1919

Treaty of Neuilly (with Bulgaria): November 1919

Treaty of Trianon (with Hungary): June 1920

Key question
How satisfactory was the Turkish settlement?

Key dates

Treaty of Sèvres: August 1920

Treaty of Lausanne: July 1923

Key terms

Ottoman Empire
Ottoman rulers controlled Turkey and much of the Middle East.

The Straits
Comprising the Bosphorus and the Dardanelles, these form the outlet from the Black Sea to the Mediterranean.

The Turkish settlement

Britain played a major role in deciding the fate of the **Ottoman Empire**. The Treaty of Sèvres satisfied most of Britain's concerns:

- **The Straits** were to be demilitarised and placed under international supervision.
- Large parts of the Arab areas of the Ottoman Empire were given (as mandates) to Britain and France. France acquired what is today Syria and Lebanon. Britain acquired present-day Israel, Jordan and Iraq.
- Eastern Thrace, the Gallipoli peninsula, Smyrna and several Aegean islands were given to Greece.

The Chanak crisis

In 1919–20 Mustafa Kemal led a national uprising. His aim was to liberate his country from continuing Allied military control and Greek occupation in the west. He rallied the various movements for Turkish liberation and by 1920 controlled Turkey. Lloyd George, who had no love for the Turks, saw no reason to recognise Kemal's authority. In March 1921, Greece, with Lloyd George's tacit approval, declared war on Kemal's government. Britain confined its aid to moral support, and the Greeks failed to make much headway. Kemal meanwhile came to terms with Italy, France and the USSR. In 1922 Turkish forces launched a major offensive. Greek resistance collapsed and the Turks threatened the British forces occupying the international zone of the Straits.

Lloyd George seemed prepared to go to war to defend the Straits, even though Britain could expect no help from France and only lukewarm support from the Dominions. At the end of

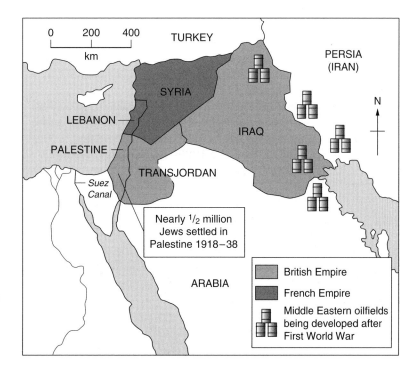

Figure 2.3: The Middle East Mandates shared by Britain and France (former possessions of the Ottoman Empire).

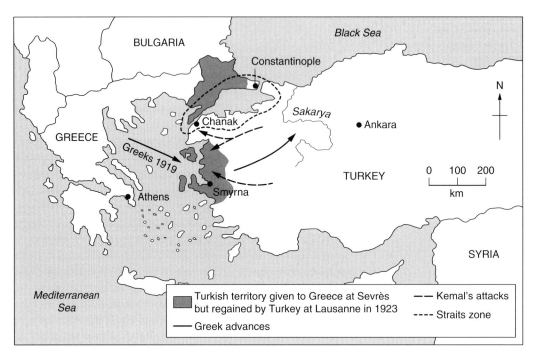

Figure 2.4: War between Greece and Turkey 1920–2.

September 1922 Turkish forces reached Chanak, the British base. Military confrontation was only avoided because of the cool judgement of the commanders on the spot. The Turks, who had no wish to go to war with Britain, agreed to respect the international zone. Some saw the Chanak crisis as an example of successful firmness in the face of aggression. But others saw the whole affair as unnecessary war-mongering on Lloyd George's part and the Chanak crisis contributed to his downfall in October 1922. Bonar Law now became Prime Minister.

Lloyd George resigned: Bonar Law became Prime Minister: October 1922 · *Key date*

The Treaty of Lausanne
Negotiations with Kemal's government were handled skilfully by Lord Curzon, the Foreign Secretary, and a new agreement, the Treaty of Lausanne, was signed in 1923. This was the first significant revision of the **peace settlement**:

Peace settlement This term comprises all the different peace treaties, including the Treaty of Versailles. · *Key term*

- Turkey retained Eastern Thrace, Smyrna and the Aegean islands it had won back from Greece.
- Turkey accepted the loss of its Arab territories and agreed that the Straits should remain demilitarised and open to the ships of all nations in time of peace.

Britain's main interests were thus preserved. Given that relations with Turkey now improved, Britain had good reason to be satisfied.

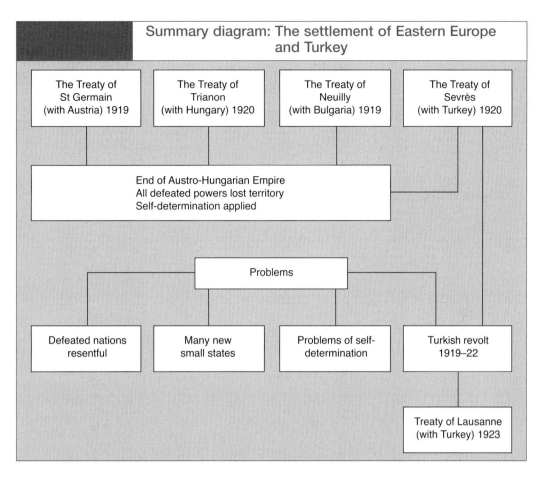

Summary diagram: The settlement of Eastern Europe and Turkey

The Treaty of St Germain (with Austria) 1919 — The Treaty of Trianon (with Hungary) 1920 — The Treaty of Neuilly (with Bulgaria) 1919 — The Treaty of Sevrès (with Turkey) 1920

End of Austro-Hungarian Empire
All defeated powers lost territory
Self-determination applied

Problems

Defeated nations resentful — Many new small states — Problems of self-determination — Turkish revolt 1919–22

Treaty of Lausanne (with Turkey) 1923

Key question
How far did a fear of Bolshevism influence British policy in the period 1917–31?

Key term

Communism
A social theory according to which society should be classless, private property should be abolished, and the means of production and distribution should be collectively owned and controlled.

6 | Anglo-Soviet Relations 1917–31

British hostility to Bolshevism 1918–20

The coming to power of Lenin and the Bolshevik Party in November 1917 was greeted with a mixed reaction in Britain. While many on the left sympathised with **communism**, public opinion in general seems to have been hostile, especially when Lenin made peace with Germany at Brest-Litovsk in March 1918, enabling the Germans to concentrate all their forces on the Western Front. This anger intensified when the Bolshevik government nationalised all foreign enterprises in Russia and refused to repay war debts due to Britain.

Most Conservative and Liberal MPs were implacably opposed to Lenin and agreed with Minister of Munitions, Winston Churchill, when he spoke of 'the foul baboonery of Bolshevism'. Churchill was all for sending British forces to Russia to destroy the Bolsheviks before they could sow the seeds of revolution elsewhere in the world. From 1918 to 1920 British policy was one of outright hostility to the Bolshevik regime.

In March 1918 Britain sent troops to Murmansk and Archangel to ensure that war supplies which had been sent there did not fall into Bolshevik hands. As Russia plunged into civil war, British troops began to co-operate with '**White**' forces that were trying to topple Lenin and his '**Reds**'. Although Churchill and other Cabinet ministers fully supported this interventionist policy, Lloyd George was more cautious, particularly after the armistice with Germany. He tended to the view that the Russians should resolve their own internal crisis. Nevertheless, he did send some military help (about 30,000 troops in all) and provided some financial assistance to the Whites. However, by the end of 1919 the Bolsheviks had established control in Russia and British forces were withdrawn.

The British left and Bolshevik Russia

Left-wing opinion, including the Labour Party and the **Trades Union Congress (TUC)**, had condemned British intervention in Russia, representing it as a capitalist attack on the working class.

In 1920 Polish forces tried to take over the Ukraine from Russia. The Bolsheviks fought back and the Red Army looked as though it might capture Warsaw, the Polish capital. The British government considered sending help to Poland. The Labour movement opposed British intervention. London dockers refused to load a ship carrying munitions purchased by Poland. Some 350 Councils of Action sprang up throughout Britain and even moderate Labour supporters seemed ready to support a **general strike** in a 'Hands off Soviet Russia' campaign. However, the Poles, with French assistance, succeeded in driving back the Red Army and Russia and Poland now made peace. British intervention, therefore, was no longer an issue and the domestic crisis ended.

Some Britons sympathised with the communist 'experiment' in Russia. Although the British Communist Party was very small (it had only 4000 members in 1920), many trade unionists, rank and file Labour supporters and radical intellectuals (such as H.G. Wells and George Bernard Shaw) were ready to applaud the Russian 'workers' state', especially at a time of industrial unrest at home. However, Ramsay MacDonald and other Labour leaders were highly suspicious of the anti-democratic and violent nature of Bolshevism and drew a clear distinction between **socialism** and communism.

Lloyd George and Russia 1920–1

By 1920–1 MacDonald held not dissimilar views to Lloyd George. The latter still had little enthusiasm for Lenin. But he now believed that wooing Russia back into a commercial relationship with Europe would have far more effect in softening the Bolshevik regime than a policy of armed intervention. In a Commons debate in 1920 he went so far as to say that the moment trade was established 'Communism would go'.

However, many Conservatives wished to see the **USSR** (as Russia was renamed in 1922) kept in diplomatic isolation and remained deeply suspicious of Bolshevik intentions. There was some substance to these fears. Lenin hoped that other European countries would follow Russia's example. The **Comintern** was

Key terms

Whites
Various opponents of the Bolsheviks.

Reds
Bolshevik supporters.

Trades Union Congress (TUC)
The main organisation of the British trade union movement.

General strike
When workers in all industries refuse to work.

Socialism
A social and economic system in which most forms of private property are abolished and the means of production and distribution of wealth are owned by the community as a whole.

USSR
The Union of Soviet Socialist Republics.

Comintern
Communist International (also known as the Third International), founded in 1919 in Moscow, in an effort to co-ordinate the actions of communist parties globally.

Key terms

Spartakist rising
An attempt by communists to seize power in Germany over the winter of 1918–19.

New Economic Policy (NEP)
In 1922 Lenin backed down from the notion of total communism. His NEP allowed some private ownership.

founded in 1919 precisely to achieve this objective. The (failed) **Spartakist rising** in Germany, the establishment of (short-lived) communist regimes in Hungary and Bavaria in 1919 and the (failed) attempts to impose a communist government in Poland in 1920 lent some credibility to Lenin's hopes and British Conservatives' fears. Conservatives also believed that Russian agents were at work stirring up anti-British feeling in India, Afghanistan and Iran.

Changes in the USSR

After 1920 Anglo-Soviet relations very much depended on which party was in power in Britain, with Conservative governments far less willing to do business with the USSR than Labour. However, policy also shifted in response to changes in Soviet objectives. In 1921 Russia suffered appalling famine which provoked something of a U-turn in Lenin's thinking and the adoption of the **New Economic Policy (NEP)**. Soviet foreign policy began to speak with two voices:

- The first, that of the Comintern, preached world revolution and claimed that Britain was the spearhead of capitalist–imperialist aggression which was aiming to destroy communism in Russia.
- The second, that of the Soviet government, urged the need for normal relations with those countries – including Britain – whose economic co-operation they needed.

British diplomats had difficulty adjusting to this double-speak.

Conciliatory moves

In 1921–2 Lloyd George pressed ahead with negotiations with the USSR, hoping that the re-establishment of trade relations would help the British economy. He also feared that if the USSR continued to be treated as an outcast it might well ally with the other European pariah – Germany. Such an alliance would threaten Europe's peace and stability.

In March 1921 an Anglo-Soviet trade agreement was signed. Under its terms each side agreed to refrain from hostile propaganda. The Soviet government recognised in principle its obligations to private citizens in Britain who had not yet been paid for goods supplied to Russia during the war. However, Britain (along with many other nations) was still unwilling to grant full recognition to Lenin's government.

In 1922 Lloyd George tried to widen the scope of the trade agreement and to bring Russia back into the mainstream economic system at the World Economic Conference at Geneva. He had a series of secret discussions with Soviet delegates, but made little progress. The chief stumbling block was the USSR's refusal to pay compensation for the substantial pre-war Western investment in Russia.

Lloyd George's worst fears seemed to have been realised when, in the middle of the conference, the USSR and Germany

Profile: James Ramsay MacDonald 1866–1937

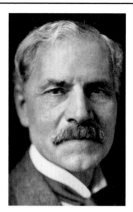

1866	–	Born, the illegitimate son of a Scottish farmgirl
1894	–	Joined the Independent Labour Party
1906	–	Elected MP
1906–12	–	Secretary of the Labour Party
1911	–	Elected leader of the parliamentary Labour Party
1914	–	Resigned as Labour leader because of his pacifist opposition to the First World War
1918	–	Lost his seat in the Commons
1922	–	Returned to head the Labour Party
1924	–	Led Labour's first short-lived government as well as serving as Foreign Secretary
1929–31	–	Prime Minister of Labour government
1931–5	–	Prime Minister of the National Government
1937	–	Died

MacDonald was Britain's first Labour Prime Minister and the first Prime Minister to have no previous ministerial experience. A moderate, he believed that socialism would only come by gradual stages and for much of his political career tried to show that the Labour Party was respectable. His decision in August 1931 to accept the leadership of the National Government, with Conservative and Liberal support, led to his being branded a traitor by many in the Labour Party (from which he was expelled). After 1931 his health deteriorated and in his final period as Prime Minister, up to 1935, he was in some ways a figure of fun. (He was known in the Commons as 'Ramshackle Mac'.)

MacDonald was opposed to war, supported disarmament and tried to develop collective security through the League of Nations. Like many others, he did not see Nazi Germany as a particular threat to Britain (page 56).

announced they had signed the Treaty of Rapallo. This brought economic and military benefits to both countries:

- Germany was able to produce and test new weapons in the USSR – weapons which it was banned from producing in Germany.
- The USSR received useful German technical expertise.

However, despite this pact of 'mutual friendship', both the USSR and Germany (to Britain's relief) continued to regard each other with suspicion.

After the fall of Lloyd George in October 1922, Foreign Secretary Lord Curzon played a more prominent role in foreign affairs. He was much less committed to economic co-operation with the USSR and threatened to end the trade agreement because of repeated Soviet violation of the undertaking to refrain from hostile propaganda. The Russian reply was conciliatory and

Key terms

Policy of rapprochement
To renew or improve relations with someone.

Seditious activities
Actions against the state which are intended to cause disorder and trouble.

General Strike of 1926
In May 1926 British workers, from a variety of industries, went on strike in support of the coal miners. In the face of resolute government action, the TUC called off the strike after nine days.

Key dates

MacDonald became Prime Minister: January 1924

Britain recognised the Soviet government: February 1924

Baldwin became Prime Minister: October 1924

MacDonald became Prime Minister: 1929

the agreement survived. But Curzon would take no further steps towards recognising the legitimacy of the Bolshevik regime.

Ramsay MacDonald and the USSR

In 1924 the Labour Party came to power. Ramsay MacDonald, who was both Prime Minister and Foreign Secretary, immediately resumed full diplomatic relations with the USSR and was soon negotiating for a new trade treaty which he hoped would provide an increased market for Britain. The main obstacle was still the question of debts to British creditors. In August an Anglo-Soviet Agreement was reached. There were promises of friendship and the cessation of propaganda. In the event of a satisfactory arrangement over the settlement of British debts, Britain agreed to guarantee a loan of £30 million. The agreement, said one contemporary, was merely an agreement to agree if and when the parties could agree to agree. However, many Conservatives and Liberals, suspicious of the **policy of rapprochement** with the USSR, saw the agreement as more important and more threatening. The Liberals withdrew their support from the minority Labour government and in the general election which followed, Labour was charged with being susceptible to communist pressure.

The Zinoviev letter

On 25 October 1924, just a few days before the general election, the *Daily Mail* published a letter, purporting to be from Gregory Zinoviev, head of the Comintern. This letter urged the British Communist Party to work for the proposed Anglo-Soviet Agreement because of the opportunities for subversion which it would provide. It also issued instructions for all types of **seditious activities**. The Conservatives immediately denounced Labour as accomplices or dupes of the communists. The forged Zinoviev letter probably made no substantial difference to the election result. Even before the letter was published, the Conservatives had succeeded in tarring the Labour Party as pandering to communism. Due largely to the collapse of the Liberal vote, the Conservatives won a resounding victory.

Anglo-Soviet problems 1924–31

Not surprisingly, Anglo-Soviet relations now deteriorated. Prime Minister Baldwin did not ratify the Anglo-Soviet Agreement. A large USSR donation to the Miners' Federation during the **General Strike of 1926** led to angry protests by the British Cabinet.

The Arcos affair caused a further rift. Arcos – the All Russian Co-operative Society – was the main organisation through which Anglo-Soviet trade was conducted. A raid on its London premises in 1927 led to Baldwin accusing the USSR of using Arcos as a means of directing 'military espionage and subversive activities throughout the British Empire and North and South America'. Britain broke off diplomatic relations and ended all trade agreements.

The Labour government, which came to power in 1929, restored diplomatic contacts and signed a new commercial treaty with the USSR in 1930. However, it proved impossible to reach agreement over Russian debts and the possibility of British loans. No intimacy developed between the two countries. Stalin, who was now in control in the USSR, was primarily concerned with economic development. MacDonald's government was content to see the USSR remain on the periphery of Europe.

Summary diagram: Anglo-Soviet relations 1917–31

1917	Bolshevik Revolution
1918	Bolsheviks quit First World War, nationalised foreign enterprises and refused to pay war debts
1918–9	Britain sent troops to support the Whites
1920–1	Russo-Polish War: British government against British trade unions
1921	Anglo-Soviet trade agreement
1922	Creation of USSR
1924	British Labour government resumed full diplomatic relations with USSR
1924	Zinoviev letter
1924	Conservatives won general election. Anglo-Soviet relations deteriorated
1927	Arcos affair: Britain broke off diplomatic relations
1929	Labour government restored diplomatic contacts

---

7 | The Problem of Italy

Key question
How great a threat was Mussolini in the 1920s?

Italy had looked to the peace settlement to give it large amounts of territory which had been promised in 1915 when it had entered the war. This would compensate for its heavy losses in the war and help to make Italy the great power it had so long yearned to be. However, the peace settlement failed to provide all the promised territory, and caused resentment in Italy.

In 1922 Benito Mussolini, leader of the **Fascist Party**, seized power in Rome. He demanded revision of the peace settlement and talked of making Italy a great imperial power. He soon showed he was prepared to involve himself in dramatic foreign policy escapades. His ambitions in the Mediterranean, which he regarded as an Italian lake, seemed to pose a direct threat to the British Empire. The Mediterranean, which provided access to the Suez Canal, was regarded by Britain as a vital link in its world-wide communication chain.

However, for most of the 1920s Mussolini kept a relatively low profile, only involving himself in adventures where some glory could be won on the cheap. He won some modest gains in Africa, succeeded in annexing the port of Fiume on the border with Yugoslavia, and strengthened Italy's hold over Albania. Neither

Fascist Party
A nationalist, authoritarian, anti-communist movement developed by Mussolini in Italy after 1919. The word fascism is often applied to authoritarian and National Socialist movements in Europe and elsewhere.

Key term

Key date

Mussolini seized power in Italy: October 1922

Mussolini nor fascism, which appeared to be a uniquely Italian phenomenon, posed a serious threat in the 1920s. Indeed, some British statesmen, including Churchill and Lloyd George, expressed admiration for Mussolini's achievements in Italy.

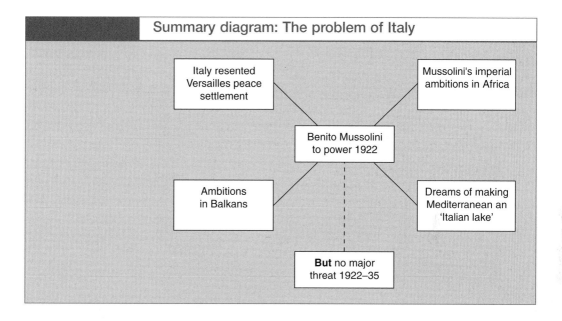

Summary diagram: The problem of Italy

- Italy resented Versailles peace settlement
- Mussolini's imperial ambitions in Africa
- Benito Mussolini to power 1922
- Ambitions in Balkans
- Dreams of making Mediterranean an 'Italian lake'
- **But** no major threat 1922–35

Key question
Why did Britain and France disagree about how to treat Germany?

8 | The German Question in the 1920s

British foreign policy in the 1920s was dominated by the German question. In 1919 it had been assumed that Germany would honour the Treaty of Versailles as other defeated nations had honoured peace treaties in the past. But most Germans were determined to avoid carrying out the peace settlement's terms. In consequence, the enforcement of the treaty required the same determination and co-operation among the victorious powers as winning the war had done. The reverse occurred. By the start of the 1920s Britain and France disagreed on most issues, while the USA divorced itself from events in Europe.

Allied disagreement

French leaders were particularly concerned about Germany's efforts to undo the treaty. France had a land border with an embittered Germany: a country with 50 per cent more people and four times France's heavy industry. In this situation the French response was to insist on the most stringent enforcement of the peace terms. French governments also searched for alternative means of security:

- They sought a firm military alliance with Britain.
- They concluded military agreements with Eastern European states, such as Poland (1921) and Czechoslovakia (1924).

British governments opposed most aspects of French policy. Few British statesmen actually trusted France. In 1920 a Channel tunnel project was rejected by the Foreign Office on the grounds that 'our relations with France never have been and are not, and probably never will be, sufficiently stable and friendly to justify the building of a Channel tunnel'. Indeed, in the 1920s British Foreign Office officials feared French domination of Europe as much as they feared the possibility of a German revival of strength.

Moreover, many British politicians soon expressed misgivings about Germany's treatment in 1919. There was unease about the one-sided application of self-determination (see page 20), about Germany's exclusion from the League of Nations (see page 22) and about reparations. Many influential people thought that a revision of the treaty was urgently needed if there was to be a lasting peace.

The reparations problem

In the early 1920s international relations were dominated by two topics: reparations and security. No fewer than 23 conferences were held between 1920 and 1922. Most followed a similar pattern. British representatives urged France to relax the provisions of Versailles, but to little effect. French leaders feared that any treaty revision would lead to German dominance in Europe and the spectre of a German war of revenge.

In 1920 and 1921 French troops occupied several German cities when Germany violated the reparation and disarmament clauses of Versailles (pages 20–2). Britain opposed French action. First Lloyd George, then Bonar Law and Baldwin (who succeeded Bonar Law as Prime Minister in May 1923), were inclined to support policies which would appease Germany. They particularly wished to reduce reparation payments and to promote Germany's economic recovery in the belief that this would help British trade. France might have been prepared to take a more conciliatory line had Britain been ready to sign a military alliance. But most British politicians opposed this idea.

In 1922 Britain tried to resolve the reparations issue by proposing a cancellation of both reparations and the payments of war debts to the USA. This idea received little favour in the USA, France or even in the City in London (Britain, owed four times as much as she owed the USA, would have been a net loser if the scheme had been adopted.) Reparations, therefore, continued to sour Anglo-French and Franco-German relations.

The occupation of the Ruhr

By December 1922 Germany had fallen hopelessly behind in its reparation payments. Poincaré, the new anti-German French leader, decided that enough was enough. In January 1923 French and Belgian troops occupied the Ruhr, the industrial heart of Germany, with the intention of forcing Germany to meet its financial obligations. German authorities adopted a policy of **passive resistance**, with the result that industrial production in the Ruhr ground to a halt, the German economy collapsed, and Germany suffered **hyperinflation**.

Key dates

Bonar Law resigned: Baldwin became Prime Minister: May 1923

French and Belgium troops occupied the Ruhr: January 1923

Key terms

Passive resistance Deliberate refusal to co-operate with the authorities. Those who support such action adopt peaceful, not violent, protest.

Hyperinflation A huge increase in the amount of (almost worthless) money in circulation, resulting in a massive increase in prices. In Germany in 1923 an egg cost hundreds of millions of marks.

The British government disliked but did not openly condemn French policy. It adopted what one contemporary described as a policy of 'surly neutrality', trying without success to resolve the crisis. Some British officials thought the Ruhr occupation was an economic disaster for Britain. In fact just the opposite was the case. British exports soared and unemployment fell as German competition disappeared. Although Poincaré faced strong British and US financial pressure, he held out stubbornly for several months, opposing any reform of the reparations settlement. Finally, Germany abandoned its policy of passive resistance.

The Dawes Plan

In April 1924 a reparations committee (known as the Dawes Committee after its US chairman) proposed that payments should be reduced and phased over a longer period. MacDonald, the new British Prime Minister, worked hard to secure French and German acceptance of the Dawes Plan. The replacement of Poincaré by Herriot in May helped MacDonald's cause and agreement was reached in August:

- Germany agreed to meet the new reparation payments.
- France agreed to withdraw its forces from the Ruhr within a year.

Both countries kept their side of the bargain. For the next few years Germany met its reparations almost in full, thanks largely to

Key date

Dawes Plan: August 1924

GERMANY:
"ACH! AINDT IT TOO FAR?"
PARKER GILBERT:
"THE FIRST SEVEN MILLION MILES ARE THE HARDEST. AFTER THAT YOU GET USED TO IT." (gives a hollow chuckle)

LOAN

DEBT

FINANCIAL EXPERTS

LOW

IN REPARATIONS DREAMLAND.

'In Reparations Dreamland', a cartoon by David Low published in the *Evening Standard*, 7 January 1929. Why in the cartoon are loans shown as balloons and the financial experts shown as sinister figures? Why should a British cartoonist be sympathetic to Germany?

extensive US loans. Thus began a bizarre triangular flow of money between the USA and Europe. US loans enabled Germany to pay reparations to France and Britain which in turn helped Britain and France to repay their US war debts.

Most historians consider the occupation of the Ruhr as a defeat for France. Ultimately it had been forced to accept a substantial revision of reparations and had gained nothing in return.

The Locarno Pact

The Ruhr occupation convinced French leaders that in future they should not attempt to enforce the Treaty of Versailles single-handedly. Worried by Germany's growing strength, they looked to Britain for guarantees of security. However, both Labour and Conservative governments were opposed to binding Britain to France and were opposed to French efforts to strengthen the coercive powers of the League of Nations. Balfour thought France's obsession with security was 'intolerably foolish … They are so dreadfully afraid of being swallowed up by the tiger that they spend all their time poking it.' Even the pro-French Austen Chamberlain, who became Foreign Secretary in November 1924, failed to persuade his Conservative Cabinet colleagues to accept anything in the way of an Anglo-French alliance.

However, in 1925 Chamberlain took up an offer from Gustav Stresemann, the German Foreign Minister. Stresemann said he was prepared to enter into an agreement with France for a joint guarantee of their frontiers in Western Europe. Thanks largely to Chamberlain's efforts, representatives from Britain, France, Germany, Italy, Poland, Czechoslovakia and Belgium met at Locarno in Switzerland in September 1925. Chamberlain, Stresemann and Aristide Briand, the French foreign minister, were all anxious to see an improvement in Franco-German relations. Therefore Locarno was a far cry from the grim tension of earlier conferences.

The Locarno Pact consisted of a number of agreements:

- Germany was to be welcomed into the League of Nations in 1926.
- Germany's western frontiers with France and Belgium were accepted as final and were guaranteed by Britain and Italy.
- Stresemann, while not agreeing to Germany's eastern boundaries, accepted that the frontiers should not be altered by force.

The results of Locarno

At the time, the Locarno Pact was seen as a diplomatic triumph and a great landmark. Austen Chamberlain regarded it as 'the real dividing line between the years of war and the years of peace'. It seemed that Germany had been readmitted to the community of nations and that France and Germany had been reconciled. People talked of the 'spirit of Locarno', and Chamberlain, Briand and Stresemann were awarded the Nobel Peace Prize for their efforts.

Key question
How important was the Locarno Pact?

Locarno Conference: 1925

Germany joined the League of Nations: 1926

Key dates

However, many historians now tend to view Locarno in a less positive light. They point out that Germany did not abandon any of its ambitions in the east and that perhaps Britain encouraged these ambitions by indicating its unwillingness to guarantee Germany's eastern frontier. Britain's guarantee of the western borders can also be seen as little more than an empty gesture. The British Chiefs of Staff had no plans and few forces to give substance to the new obligations. From France's point of view, Locarno was worrying. It represented the furthest extent Britain was prepared to go in terms of supporting the Versailles settlement – and by simply giving a general pledge against German aggression in the west Britain had not gone far. Indeed the British pledge was as much a guarantee to Germany as to France: a new French move into the Ruhr was now impossible without France breaking the Locarno Pact. In reality the pact did not denote any fundamental change in British policy. The British government had no intention of being drawn into military talks with France.

Moreover, Locarno did not end Germany's sense of grievance or its attempts to secure revision of the Treaty of Versailles. France retained its distrust of German intentions, so much so that in 1927 it began the construction of the **Maginot Line**. Regular meetings between Stresemann, Briand and Chamberlain after 1926 yielded little in the way of agreement. Chamberlain, in private, grumbled over Germany's ingratitude and its demands for further revision. Stresemann grumbled that further concessions to Germany took longer than he had anticipated.

Key term

Maginot Line
French defensive fortifications stretching along the German frontier.

Improved relations

The Locarno Pact did improve the international atmosphere of the late 1920s. Although Stresemann was determined to dismantle the Versailles settlement, he saw the advantage of collaboration with the Western powers and was prepared to work with Chamberlain and Briand through the League of Nations. In the late 1920s there seemed no prospect of major conflict. In 1928 all the major powers signed the Kellogg–Briand Pact, renouncing war as a means of settling international disputes. (Frank Kellogg was the US Secretary of State.) The British government was happy to sign, although some Conservatives thought the pact idealistic nonsense.

In 1929 the Young Plan extended the period of reparation payments by 60 years, thus further easing the burden on Germany. As part of this package, Britain and France agreed to end their occupation of the Rhineland five years ahead of schedule. In 1929 it seemed, as historian William Rubinstein has written, 'literally inconceivable that a second world-wide general war, far deadlier than the last, could break out only 10 years later'.

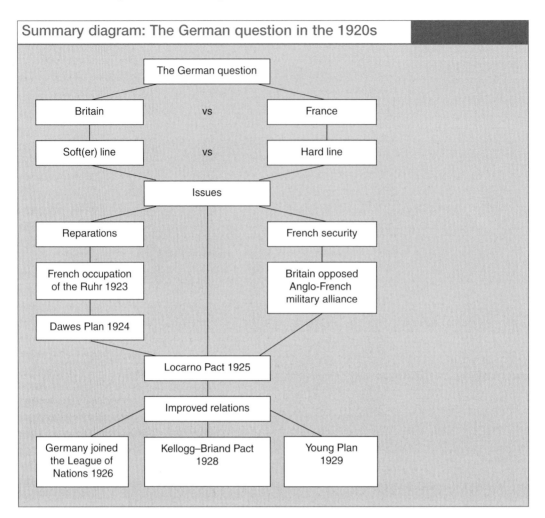

Summary diagram: The German question in the 1920s

9 | The League of Nations

One result of the Treaty of Versailles was the creation of the League of Nations. This had its headquarters in Geneva. The Assembly of the League, composed of representatives of all the member states, met yearly and each state had one vote. Britain, France, Italy and Japan had permanent seats on the Council of the League. The Assembly could then elect four (later six) further members of the Council. The Council made most of the League's decisions. By the Covenant of the League, member states agreed to a number of (somewhat vague) Articles. Perhaps the most important was Article 16 which stated that if any member of the League resorted to war, the other states should impose **economic sanctions** and, if necessary, take appropriate military action.

Britain and the League
Although the League owed its inception largely to US President Woodrow Wilson, it soon evoked enthusiastic support in Britain, especially from the left. British public opinion came to believe

Key question
How effective was the League of Nations in the 1920s?

Economic sanctions
Refusing to trade with a particular country.

Key term

that the League was an institution which could solve all international problems peacefully. Many thought that no aggressor would dare to risk war with the 50 or so League states and that in consequence force would not be needed to uphold the principles of the League. British Foreign Ministers faithfully attended the meetings of the Assembly and the Council, aware that support for the League often brought popularity at home. The **League of Nations Union** soon proved to be an effective pressure group. Its chairman claimed in 1928 that 'All parties are pledged to the League ... all Prime Ministers and ex-Prime Ministers support it.'

But while they might support the League in principle, few Conservative politicians really believed in its efficacy as an instrument for solving international disputes. They realised that its existence did not automatically prevent aggression and that without the USA and the USSR it was hardly a truly global organisation. Military leaders pointed out that the League had no armed forces of its own and warned that it created a dangerous sense of security. In reality it depended on Britain and France resisting those countries bent on aggression.

From the start, France hoped to fashion the League into a force to preserve the Versailles boundaries. It continued to try to strengthen the League's obligations and to make them more binding on member states. Britain, by contrast, favoured a looser, less binding arrangement and thought the League should function as an instrument for the peaceful adjustment of international boundaries and other disputed matters, not as a force committed to oppose all change.

The impact of the League

The League did have some successes in the 1920s, establishing itself as an international organisation capable of resolving disputes between minor powers and promoting a wide range of humanitarian and economic activities. It was a useful talking shop and its meetings provided opportunities for statesmen to meet and discuss outside the formal sessions. However, the League had little real influence. The important questions of the day were settled in the hotel rooms of the Foreign Ministers of Britain, France, Italy and (after 1926) Germany. The small states were helpless in the face of the reality of great power politics.

Key term

League of Nations Union
A British organisation set up to support the League.

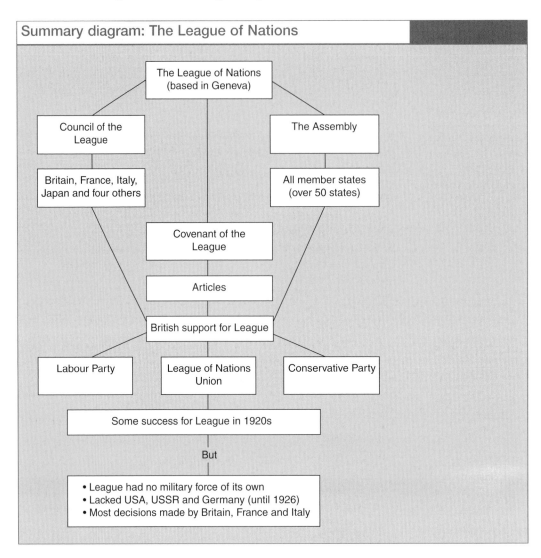

Summary diagram: The League of Nations

The League of Nations (based in Geneva)

Council of the League

Britain, France, Italy, Japan and four others

The Assembly

All member states (over 50 states)

Covenant of the League

Articles

British support for League

Labour Party

League of Nations Union

Conservative Party

Some success for League in 1920s

But

• League had no military force of its own
• Lacked USA, USSR and Germany (until 1926)
• Most decisions made by Britain, France and Italy

10 | Disarmament

In 1919 the Allies had disarmed Germany, a move seen by some as the first step in the process of general world disarmament. Members of the League of Nations agreed to disarm to 'the lowest point consistent with national safety'. Most British governments in the 1920s favoured disarmament for political and economic reasons. By 1932 Britain was spending only £102 million on defence, compared with £760 million in 1919–20. The army reverted to its pre-war role of imperial police force and, although the RAF preserved its separate identity, it remained small in numbers. The most interesting developments surrounded the Senior Service – the Royal Navy.

Key question
How successful were efforts to achieve disarmament in the 1920s?

Naval disarmament

Although the war had brought about the destruction of the German fleet, in 1919 there seemed every prospect of there being

Key date

Washington Naval
Agreement: February
1922

Key term

Admiralty
The government
board that
administered the
Royal Navy.

a naval race between the USA and Britain. The **Admiralty** was furious that the US naval building programme aimed to create a fleet larger than the Royal Navy. There was also the problem of a growing Japanese fleet in the Pacific. The USA, more suspicious of Japan's intentions than Britain, was anxious to end the Anglo-Japanese treaty of 1902.

In November 1921 representatives of the main naval powers met in Washington. This conference resulted in the 1922 Washington Naval Agreement under which capital ships allowed to the countries concerned would be in the following ratios: USA 5; Britain 5; Japan 3; Italy 1.75; and France 1.75. No new capital ships were to be constructed for 10 years. Britain also agreed not to renew its alliance with Japan. It was replaced by a Four Power Treaty signed by Britain, the USA, France and Japan, guaranteeing the status quo in the Far East.

There was considerable British opposition to the Washington agreement:

- Britain no longer had naval superiority. The size of its fleet would now be determined by the treaty, not by an assessment of Britain's strategic needs.
- The halt in capital ship building would leave Britain with an obsolescent fleet by the time construction was allowed again.
- British interests in the Far East would no longer be protected by the Japanese alliance.

While some historians still argue that the Washington agreement was a catastrophe for Britain, there were some advantages:

- It avoided a wasteful and unnecessary naval race with the USA.
- Although Britain had sacrificed its old relationship with Japan and thus weakened its position in the Far East, it had at least remained on good terms with the USA – and at the end of the day this was more important than remaining on good terms with Japan.

For many politicians at the time, the Washington naval disarmament system seemed to be a constructive and forward-looking act. However, it was not totally successful. Throughout the 1920s there was a naval race of sorts as Britain, the USA and Japan all set about constructing non-capital ships. In 1927 an attempt to limit the number of cruisers broke down. Eventually, in 1930 the USA, Britain and Japan agreed to limit their cruisers in a fixed ratio (10:10:7) and to prolong the agreement on the building of capital ships for a further five years.

Military disarmament

Securing agreement about land armaments proved far more difficult. The main problem was the relationship between France and Germany. French leaders, aware that Germany was not even complying with the disarmament terms of the Treaty of Versailles, realised it would be national and political suicide to reduce its own large forces without watertight guarantees of security.

Germany, on the other hand, demanded to be treated as an equal. A Preparatory Commission on Disarmament, set up in 1926, failed to make headway because of mutual suspicion. German demands for equality were incompatible with French demands for security. Thus, the German army continued to be limited to 100,000 men.

Britain continued to cut back spending on its army. After 1918 the **General Staff** hoped to maintain a small, professional and well-equipped, mechanised and motorised army. The army was small and professional but unfortunately it was not well equipped, mechanised or motorised. There seemed little point in spending huge sums of money on the army when there was no serious threat to Britain.

General Staff
The body which administers the British army.

Key term

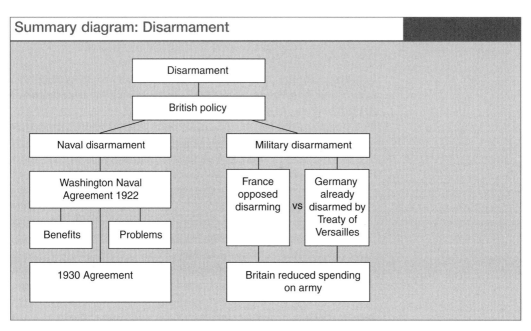

Summary diagram: Disarmament

11 | Key Debate

> Was British foreign policy-making in the 1920s a success or failure?

Historians have conflicting views about British foreign policy-making in the 1920s.

A success?

By 1930 there seemed good reason for optimism. Although many outstanding questions still menaced Franco-German relations, both countries seemed ready to settle disputes by negotiation rather than by force. Mussolini's oratory was occasionally war-like, but his escapades were minor. The USSR had turned out to be more an embarrassment than a serious problem. No great power in the 1920s had threatened Britain's security or that of its

Empire. In consequence, it had been able to run down its armed forces. Almost all the major powers had agreed to renounce war and the League of Nations seemed an effective organisation that would ensure peace.

In 1929 Viscount D'Abernon, British Ambassador to Germany in the mid-1920s, wrote that the lesson of the post-war years was not:

> … negative … but positive. It is not a recital of unfortunate events which led up to a great catastrophe. It is the narrative rather of a historical period in which immense progress has been made towards pacification, and during which the international suspicion diminished, and the cause of co-operation between nations appreciably advanced.

Winston Churchill, writing in 1948, summed up the 1920s in generally favourable terms:

> [In 1929] the state of Europe was tranquil, as it had not been for 20 years, and was not to be for at least another 20. A friendly feeling existed towards Germany following upon our Treaty of Locarno, and the evacuation of the Rhineland by the French Army and Allied contingents at a much earlier date than had been prescribed at Versailles. The new Germany took its place in the truncated League of Nations … France and its system of alliances also seemed secure in Europe. The disarmament clauses of the Treaty of Versailles were not openly violated. The German Navy was non-existent. The German Air Force was prohibited and still unborn. There were many influences in Germany strongly opposed, if only on the grounds of prudence, to the idea of war, and the German High Command could not believe that the Allies would allow them to rearm.

A failure?

Sally Marks, a historian, writing in 1976, had a different view:

> A few men knew that the spirit of Locarno was a fragile foundation on which to build a lasting peace. After all, the real spirit at Locarno, behind the facade of public fellowship, was one of bitter confrontation between a fearful France flanked by the unhappy East Europeans, trying to hide their humiliation and panic, and a resentful, **revisionist** Germany demanding even more alterations in the power balance to its benefit. Since Germany was potentially the strongest power on the continent, the private fears of its neighbours could only deepen.
>
> Yet the public faces remained serene and smiling, and the ordinary European did not know about the clashes behind closed doors … The public facade of the Locarno conference and the treaties themselves had created an illusion of peace, and ordinary men rejoiced. Misled by a false front, Europe thankfully entered upon the Locarno years, thinking that real peace had arrived at

Key term

Revisionist
Keen to change or overthrow the status quo.

last. Of all the inter-war years these were perhaps the best years, but none the less they were years of illusion.

Just as contemporaries saw good reason for optimism, so historians, like Marks (with, it should be said, the benefit of hindsight), have seen good reason for pessimism. By 1931 Germany had secured substantial revision of the Treaty of Versailles. But most Germans were still not satisfied with Stresemann's achievements. Indeed, after his death in 1929, German statesmen adopted a more confrontational style. It was clear that future German governments, of whatever political complexion, were likely to seek further revision, especially in Eastern Europe.

Praise or blame?

It is possible to criticise the British statesmen of the 1920s for their complacency and lack of foresight. Some condemn them for not supporting French efforts to maintain the Treaty of Versailles. Some argue that if Britain had given France the assurances of support which it sought, French policy towards Germany might not have been so intransigent. Others claim that Britain should have tried to meet some of Germany's more reasonable complaints in the hope of consolidating the German 'moderates' in power.

However, it is possible to defend British policy. Even with the benefit of hindsight, historians cannot agree whether a consistent 'hard' or 'soft' approach to Germany would have been the more effective. In the circumstances British efforts to find a 'middle way' made sense. British statesmen appreciated French fears, but did their best to appease Germany whenever possible. After the experience of the First World War it was only natural that Britain was determined to avoid entanglements on the Continent.

British policy-makers did not have a crystal ball. Few people in the 1920s – not even Churchill – foresaw the dark days ahead. Neither Germany, Italy nor Japan seemed to pose a serious threat to world peace. Britain's relations with all three countries had been reasonably amicable throughout the 1920s. It is not easy to see, even now, what rational actions the politicians of the 1920s could have taken which would have prevented the threat of Hitler, Mussolini and the Japanese militarists in the 1930s. The great world-wide depression of the 1930s came out of the blue. Few had predicted it. Fewer still could foresee its political repercussions and the effect they would have on British foreign policy.

Some key books in the debate
W.S. Churchill, *The Second World War: Vol. 1 The Gathering Storm* (Cassell, 1948).
P.W. Doerr, *British Foreign Policy, 1919–1939* (Manchester University Press, 1998).
S. Marks, *The Illusion of Peace: International Relations in Europe, 1918–1933* (Palgrave Macmillan, 2003).

Study Guide: AS Questions

In the style of AQA

(a) Explain why the Locarno Treaties were signed in 1925.

(b) 'Between 1919 and 1928, promising steps were taken towards disarmament.' Explain why you agree or disagree with this view.

Exam tips

The cross-references are intended to take you straight to the material that will help you to answer the questions.

(a) To answer this question, you will need to consider a range of reasons to explain the Locarno Treaties. You should try to present your reasons in a way which emphasises the links between them and you should show some evaluation of the most important or identify an overarching theme. You will need to refer to:

- French worries about growing German strength (pages 35–8)
- British opposition to a strengthening of the League of Nations (pages 40–1)
- Stresemann's ambitions (pages 38–9).

You may also wish to refer back to the problems of the Treaty of Versailles (pages 19–24) which lay beneath the decision to hold new talks. Try to show some judgement in your conclusion.

(b) You will need to start with a short plan identifying the evidence which agrees and that which disagrees with the statement. Before you begin to write, decide whether, on balance, you will agree or disagree and try to maintain your view through the answer so as to arrive at a substantiated judgement in the conclusion. You will need to comment on:

- the disarmament of Germany at the Treaty of Versailles (page 20)
- the 'no-army' League of Nations Washington treaty of 1922 (pages 42–3)
- the Kellogg–Briand Pact of 1928 (page 39).

You might also mention voluntary cutbacks in armament for example in Britain (pages 42–4). However, this should be balanced against the fact that the only country made to disarm had been Germany and that the agreements were all limited in extent. French concerns and the difficulties of achieving consensus could also be discussed (pages 43–4) in order to arrive at a substantiated conclusion.

Study Guide: A2 Question

In the style of Edexcel

'Complacent and ultimately harmful to British interests.' How far do you agree with this opinion of British foreign policy in the years 1925–9?

Exam tips

The cross-references are intended to take you straight to the material that will help you to answer the question.

An analysis of the question indicates that there are two linked element to assess. 'Complacent' will require you to explore whether policy-makers underestimated the threat to British interests; 'ultimately harmful' will require you to explore the consequences of the decisions which were taken.

To address 'complacent' you should consider:

- the lack of threat to Britain in the 1920s from another major power (page 46)
- the perception of the spirit of Locarno and the effectiveness of the League of Nations (pages 38–9)
- the policy of disarmament (pages 42–4).

To address 'ultimately harmful' you should consider:

- whether Locarno gave encouragement to Germany's ambitions (pages 38–9)
- whether disarmament represented a saving of expenditure at too great a cost to Britain's interests and prestige (pages 42–4).

In coming to a conclusion which explores how far Britain's interests were actually harmed, keep the two elements of the question in mind. You should take care not to judge the complacency of the policy-makers of the 1920s with the benefits of hindsight. Note the optimistic signs in 1928 and 1929 indicated by the Kellogg–Briand Pact (page 39) and the Young Plan (page 39).

3 The Gathering Storm 1931–8

POINTS TO CONSIDER

Between 1931 and 1938 British governments faced problems with regard to Germany, Italy and Japan. British foreign policy in the period was criticised at the time (most notably by Winston Churchill) and has been criticised by historians since. The main charge is that Britain should have taken stronger action against Hitler, Mussolini and Japan rather than try to appease them. Indeed, few issues in British foreign policy in the twentieth century have been more controversial than appeasement and few Prime Ministers more vilified than Neville Chamberlain. This chapter will examine why British governments acted as they did, by focusing on the following themes:

- Depression and disarmament
- The problem of Japan 1931–3
- The problem of Germany 1933–5
- The problem of Italy 1935–6
- The Rhineland, Spain and rearmament
- Chamberlain's aims in foreign policy
- Chamberlain's concerns 1937–8
- The *Anschluss*
- The problem of Czechoslovakia
- The Munich Conference

Key dates

1931	August	National Government formed in Britain
	September	Japanese troops began military operations in Manchuria
1932	February	Import Duties Act
	October	Lord Lytton's Commission reported on the Manchuria situation
1933	January	Hitler became German Chancellor
	October	Germany left the Disarmament Conference and the League of Nations
1935	March	Hitler announced German rearmament
	June	Anglo-German Naval Agreement
	October	Italy invaded Abyssinia
	November	Baldwin's National Government won the general election
1936	March	German troops reoccupied the Rhineland

	July	Start of the Spanish Civil War
1937	May	Chamberlain became Prime Minister
	July	Start of Chinese–Japanese war
1938	March	Hitler annexed Austria
	September	Munich Conference

1 | Depression and Disarmament

Key question
What impact did the Depression have on British foreign policy 1931–3?

At the start of the 1930s, there seemed every chance that the peace and stability of the 1920s would continue. However, the global economic depression that followed the 1929 **Wall Street Crash** was to have serious effects on foreign policy.

The Great Depression
Britain was hit hard by the Depression. By 1932 over 20 per cent of the British work force was unemployed. In an effort to save the economy, MacDonald split the Labour Party and joined forces with the opposition in a National Government. In the October 1931 general election the National Government gained the biggest majority in modern history: 554 MPs against 61 for all the other groups combined. MacDonald remained Prime Minister, but the National Government was essentially Conservative and increasingly dominated by Tory leader Stanley Baldwin.

Imperial preference
The Depression encouraged all countries to think primarily of themselves. In order to protect its industries, Britain abandoned **free trade** and turned to **imperial preference**. The Import Duties Act in February 1932 imposed a 10 per cent tax on most imported goods, except those from the British Empire. The Ottawa Conference in July 1932 led to Britain and the Dominions agreeing to establish an imperial economic bloc, protecting their trade by a system of **quotas** and import duties.

Support for disarmament
The National Government, committed to restoring sound finances, was anxious to reduce defence spending. Many on the left saw no point in spending money on armaments, believing they were more likely to cause a war than prevent one. Indeed most Labour and Liberal politicians rejected the use of force as an instrument of policy and pressed for disarmament. A spate of anti-war literature – poems, plays and autobiographies – in the 1920s and 1930s condemned the futility and wastefulness of the First World War. A number of anti-war organisations – the National Peace Council, the League of Nations Union and the Peace Pledge Union – sprang up and seemed to be gaining in strength. In October 1933 in the East Fulham by-election, a Conservative candidate who advocated increased defence spending was defeated by a pacifist Labour opponent. The

Key terms

Wall Street Crash
In October 1929 share prices on the New York Stock Exchange (on Wall Street) collapsed. Many US banks and businesses lost money. This event is often seen as triggering the Great Depression.

Free trade
The interchange of all commodities without import and export duties.

Imperial preference
Britain tried to ensure that countries within the Empire traded first and foremost with each other.

Quotas
Limits of goods allowed in the country.

Key dates

National Government formed in Britain: August 1931

Import Duties Act: February 1932

Conservative majority of 14,000 was transformed into a Labour majority of 5000.

The National Government, intending to ward off Labour and Liberal attack, adhered to the principles of disarmament and international co-operation through the League of Nations. Almost all British politicians regarded the League as an alternative to armaments. No one believed in rearming in order to support the League.

Key question
Why did hopes of disarmament not materialise?

The World Disarmament Conference

MacDonald pinned great hopes on the World Disarmament Conference which met at Geneva in 1932. Arthur Henderson, an ex-British Foreign Secretary, was the conference president. The main problem was Germany's claim for parity of treatment. Britain was prepared to accept this claim, but France, still fearing Germany, was not prepared to reduce its forces without watertight guarantees of security. It proved impossible to find a compromise between Germany's demand for equality and France's demand for security.

The end of reparations

Despite failure on the disarmament front, MacDonald continued to hope that the just grievances of Germany could be settled by negotiation. Given Germany's dreadful economic position (over five million people unemployed in 1932), a conference meeting in June 1932 at Lausanne in Switzerland agreed that reparation payments should be abolished.

The impact of Depression

The Great Depression had different effects in different countries:

- It made some countries, like the USA, more peaceful than ever.
- Elsewhere it undermined democracy and led to governments coming to power which favoured foreign conquest as a means of acquiring new lands, markets and raw materials to help alleviate the economic situation.

As a result the international climate became more threatening and Britain faced potential challenges from Japan, Germany and Italy. As a result of cutbacks in military spending, Britain was not best prepared for the dangers that lay ahead.

Summary diagram: Depression and disarmament

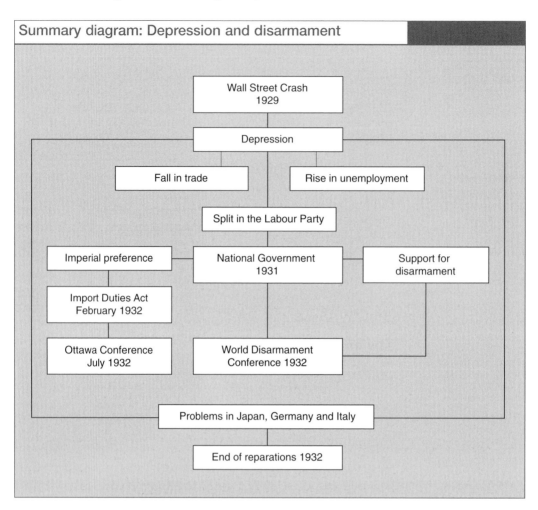

2 | The Problem of Japan 1931–3

By the 1920s Japan was a major economic, military and imperial power, securing Formosa (present-day Taiwan) from China in 1895, Korea from Russia in 1905, and all Germany's colonies in China and the Pacific north of the Equator by 1919. Japan also had substantial interests in Manchuria, a large province which it leased from China.

Japan was nominally a **constitutional monarchy**, under the Emperor Hirohito, and during the 1920s had been governed by a succession of liberal coalitions, most of which supported international co-operation. The onset of the Depression, which hit Japan hard, had a destabilising political effect. A growing number of radical nationalists, especially strong in the army, wanted Japan to pursue a policy of territorial expansion. The turmoil in China and the often provocative policies of the Chinese government provided an incitement to Japan to intervene.

Key question
Why was Japan a problem?

Key date

Japanese troops began military operations in Manchuria: September 1931

Key term

Constitutional monarchy
Government where the powers of the monarch are defined and limited.

Manchuria

In September 1931 units in the Japanese army, acting without orders from their government, seized a number of points in Manchuria. Aware of popular support for the occupation of Manchuria, the Japanese government did little to halt the army.

Japan's action was the first challenge by a major power to the 'new international system' and there was concern that Article 16 of the Covenant of the League might be invoked. This article declared that if any member of the League should resort to war in disregard to its obligations, this would amount to an act of war against all other members of the League. The League was then empowered to subject the aggressor to economic sanctions.

However, it was not clear that Japan had committed a 'resort to war': incidents between Chinese and Japanese soldiers were commonplace in Manchuria. Moreover, China did not immediately attempt to invoke Article 16 and so initially the League did little except appeal to China and Japan to refrain from action which might worsen the situation. But the Japanese army was in no mood to be coerced by verbal warnings. By February 1932 it had occupied the whole of Manchuria and set up the puppet state of Manchukuo.

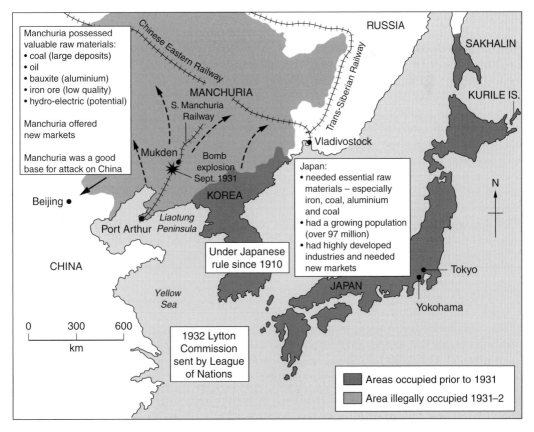

Figure 3.1: The Japanese occupation of Manchuria 1931–2.

Britain's reaction

Most British politicians were critical of Japan's action, and Britain did not recognise Manchukuo. However, it had no intention of risking a major war with Japan:

Key question
What action should Britain have taken?

- Britain had serious economic problems in 1931–2.
- British forces in the Far East were small.
- There was some sympathy for Japan. Anglo-Japanese relations had been friendly for many years. Japan (like Britain) had suffered considerable provocation from Chinese Nationalists throughout the 1920s. Much of China was in a state of political chaos. Japan had at least brought relative prosperity to the part of Manchuria it had previously controlled, might well restore order in the whole of Manchuria, and would provide a bulwark against Soviet aggression.

The Lytton Commission

The League of Nations set up a commission under Lord Lytton to look into the rights and wrongs of the Manchuria situation. The Lytton Commission's report in October 1932 declared that many of Japan's grievances were justified, but condemned its methods of redressing those grievances. It recommended that Manchuria should have autonomous status under Chinese supervision. The League accepted Lytton's recommendations by 42 votes to 1. Japan, the only nation to vote against the findings, withdrew from the League in protest and ignored its rulings.

Key date

Lord Lytton's Commission reported on the Manchuria situation: October 1932

Anglo-Japanese relations 1932–7

Britain condemned Japan's action but did little else. Given its weak military position, there was much to be said for caution. If action was to be taken, US support was vital, but that support was not forthcoming. Japanese imperialism, although a potential threat to British interests in the Far East, was not an immediate danger. Indeed Japanese expansion in northern China could be seen as reducing the risk of Japanese expansion in other, more sensitive, areas (for example, Southeast Asia).

Key question
How troubled were Anglo-Japanese relations after 1932?

Economic sanctions were unlikely to achieve much. The Royal Navy was not strong enough to enforce a trade embargo, and the USA, Japan's biggest trading partner, made it clear it would not support any League action. The best policy, therefore, seemed to be to accept Japan's takeover of Manchuria and to hope that the Japanese threat did not develop. A few limited precautions were taken:

- Work was resumed on the Singapore naval base.
- The 'Ten-Year Rule', the diplomatic and military assumption that no major war would occur in the next 10 years, was abandoned. However, in practice, this meant very little. Britain did not yet embark on a serious programme of rearmament.

Some politicians, such as Neville Chamberlain, were keen to restore friendly relations with Japan, if needs be at the expense of China. This seemed a good way to protect British possessions and investments in the Far East as well as reducing the amount of money that Britain would have to spend on improving its defences to combat Japan. But others realised that an Anglo-Japanese pact would have little moral justification and would do untold damage to Britain's relations with China and the USA (which distrusted Japan).

Relations between Britain and Japan remained uneasy. Throughout the 1930s different military and political factions in Japan often pursued conflicting policies and Britain found it hard to accept that confusion, rather than duplicity, frequently lay behind the twists and turns of Japanese policy. But Japanese nationalists stressed that Japan regarded the whole of China and East Asia as its **sphere of influence**. This was worrying. So was the fact that Japan made it clear that it intended to end the existing naval agreements and to increase its navy. The Anti-Comintern Pact, signed by Germany and Japan in November 1936, further alarmed Britain. This pact was aimed primarily against the USSR, but might be a potential threat to Britain.

Key term

Sphere of influence
A state under the control of another, more powerful, state.

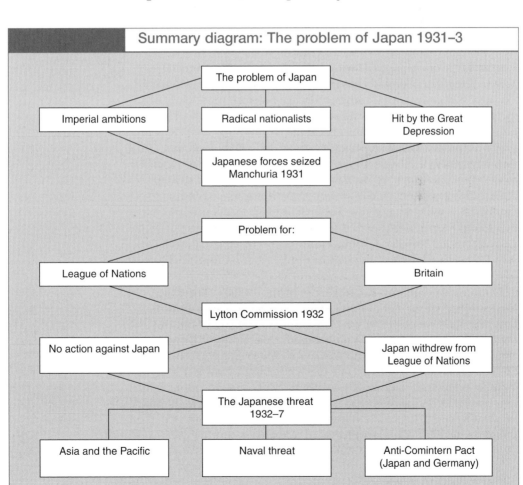

Summary diagram: The problem of Japan 1931–3

- The problem of Japan
  - Imperial ambitions
  - Radical nationalists
  - Hit by the Great Depression
- Japanese forces seized Manchuria 1931
- Problem for:
  - League of Nations
  - Britain
- Lytton Commission 1932
  - No action against Japan
  - Japan withdrew from League of Nations
- The Japanese threat 1932–7
  - Asia and the Pacific
  - Naval threat
  - Anti-Comintern Pact (Japan and Germany)

3 | The Problem of Germany 1933–5

Adolf Hitler

In 1933 Adolf Hitler came to power in Germany. This was a cause for alarm in many countries, not least Britain. It seemed certain that Hitler's **Nazi** government would challenge the existing European balance of power. Hitler was clearly intent on freeing Germany from the shackles of the Versailles settlement. He wanted to see an end to the restrictions on Germany's rearmament. He also favoured the inclusion within Germany of all the German-speaking people in Europe, especially the Austrians and the Germans in Czechoslovakia and Poland. In his book *Mein Kampf* ('My Struggle'), written in the mid-1920s, he had also talked about winning *lebensraum*.

Was *Mein Kampf* an early folly or a blueprint for the future? Even assuming it was a blueprint, did Hitler actually pose a threat to Britain? In his book, Hitler spoke of Britain as a potential ally. His main ambitions seemed to be in Eastern not Western Europe. His chief enemy seemed likely to be the USSR. A stronger Germany would be a useful bulwark against Soviet expansion. Nor was the prospect of a German–Russian war necessarily a bad thing from the point of view of British interests.

In 1961, historian A.J.P. Taylor, in his book *The Origins of the Second World War*, claimed that Hitler was really a rather ordinary German statesman with a rather ordinary mission, that of increasing Germany's standing among the world's nations. He was, said Taylor, no different to previous German leaders. He took advantage of situations as they arose and rarely took the initiative himself. He was no more wicked or unscrupulous than most other statesmen. Taylor's book sparked off a major debate among historians. Few today accept Taylor's arguments in their entirety. But many accept that Hitler had no detailed programme in 1933 and simply improvised as events unfolded. Given the debates among historians about Hitler's objectives, it is hardly surprising that British politicians in the 1930s were unsure about how to deal with the German leader.

There were some who feared the worst. Sir Robert Vansittart, the leading civil servant at the Foreign Office, warned ministers from the start about the threat of Nazism. So did Churchill. But the fact that some people distrusted Hitler did not give Britain the right – nor did it have the power – to intervene in Germany. Some British observers expected that Hitler would not last long. If he failed to solve Germany's economic problems, he might well lose power. Others hoped that he might become less extreme now he was German Chancellor. There remained considerable sympathy for German grievances and many thought that greater efforts should be made to redress those grievances.

Hitler's first moves 1933–4

Hitler's first moves were relatively cautious. He went out of his way to express admiration for Britain and to voice the hope that 'the two great Germanic nations' could work together. However,

Key question
To what extent was Hitler a threat in 1933?

Key date

Hitler became German Chancellor: January 1933

Key terms

Nazi
Short for National Socialist German Workers Party.

Lebensraum
'Living space': Hitler hoped to expand Germany's territory in the east, at the expense of Poland and the USSR.

Key question
What were Hitler's aims in 1933–4?

'Well – What are you going to do about it now?' A cartoon by David Low published in the *Evening Standard*, 2 October 1933. From left to right: Simon, Mussolini, Daladier and Hitler. Sir John Simon was British Foreign Secretary, Daladier was French minister of War and Defence, Mussolini was the fascist ruler of Italy. How has the cartoonist represented a) Hitler and b) the League of Nations?

" WELL – WHAT ARE YOU GOING TO DO ABOUT IT NOW ? "

in October 1933 Germany withdrew from both the Disarmament Conference at Geneva (page 51) and the League of Nations. Hitler's justification was that the great powers would not treat Germany as an equal. This action destroyed the Disarmament Conference. Without German participation, no useful agreement could be reached.

In 1933–4 most British MPs were aware that Germany was secretly rearming and thus becoming an increasing threat. In March 1934 Churchill said:

> Germany is arming fast and no one is going to stop her. That seems quite clear. No one proposes a preventive war to stop Germany breaking the Treaty of Versailles. She is going to arm; she is doing it; she has been doing it. I have no knowledge of the details, but it is well known that those very gifted people with their science and with their factories … are capable of developing with great rapidity the most powerful Air Force for all purposes, offensive and defensive, within a very short period of time. I dread the day when the means of threatening the heart of the British Empire should pass into the hands of the present rulers of Germany.

Sir John Simon, the Foreign Secretary, admitted that:

> German civil aviation is now the first in Europe. Germany already has in effect a fleet of 600 military aeroplanes and facilities for its very rapid expansion. She can already mobilise an army three times as great as that authorised by the Treaty.

In 1934 Britain began to spend more money on the RAF. But few people in Britain yet feared war. Indeed the Labour Party censured the government for increasing defence spending and thus 'jeopardising the prospects of international disarmament'.

German caution

Hitler continued to be cautious. In 1934 he signed a non-aggression pact with Poland, previously regarded as Germany's arch-enemy. A Nazi-inspired **putsch** in Austria in 1934 led to the assassination of the Austrian Chancellor, Dollfuss. Mussolini regarded Austria as an Italian satellite state and rushed 100,000 Italian troops to the Austrian border as a warning in case Hitler tried to take advantage of the confusion in Vienna. Mussolini's action enabled the Austrian authorities to stabilise the internal situation. Hitler did nothing to help the Austrian Nazis and their *putsch* failed.

Key terms

Putsch
An attempt to seize power, usually by force.

Conscription
Compulsory enrolment for military service.

Germany rearms

In March 1935 Hitler declared that Germany had an air force and announced the introduction of **conscription**, forbidden under the terms of the Treaty of Versailles. The German army would be increased to 500,000 men: five times the permitted number. Although everyone was aware that Germany had been violating the military clauses of Versailles for many years, Hitler's announcement was a diplomatic challenge which could not be ignored.

The heads of government and foreign ministers of Britain, France and Italy met at Stresa in Italy in April 1935. They condemned Hitler's action and resolved to maintain the existing treaty settlement of Europe and to resist any future attempt to change it by force. This agreement was known as the Stresa Front.

France also strengthened its ties with the USSR. In May 1935 France and the USSR concluded a treaty of mutual assistance. This was reinforced by a Soviet–Czechoslovakian agreement. It seemed as though Europe intended to stand firm against Hitler.

Key question
What action should Britain have taken against Germany in 1935?

Key dates

Hitler announced German rearmament: March 1935

Anglo-German Naval Agreement: June 1935

The Anglo-German Naval Agreement

Britain still did not consider itself to be particularly threatened by Hitler, who so far had said nothing about naval rearmament. In June 1935 Britain signed a naval agreement with Germany:

- Germany was to have the right to build up to 35 per cent of Britain's capital ships.
- Germany was to be allowed parity in submarines.

This agreement, signed without prior discussion with France or Italy, damaged the Stresa Front. Britain, by sanctioning a much larger German navy than was permitted by the Treaty of Versailles, seemed to be condoning Germany's rearmament immediately after the Stresa Front's condemnation.

Although the Anglo-German Naval Agreement was criticised by some at the time and by many historians since, in 1935 it had the approval of the Admiralty, Foreign Office and the entire Cabinet. They thought it was a realistic contribution to peace. Given the Japanese threat in the Far East, Britain had no wish to face a greater danger in home waters. The naval agreement ensured that Britain maintained a naval superiority twice as great as in 1914.

Key question
Was the Anglo-German Naval Agreement a mistake?

Moreover, many British politicians were angry at France's flirtation with the USSR. The French seemed to be doing their best to encircle Germany, a move that might encourage rather than avert war.

Hitler hoped that the agreement would lead to a fully fledged alliance with Britain. However, British public opinion was opposed to such a move. The Nazi dictatorship was unpopular in many quarters in Britain, especially on the left.

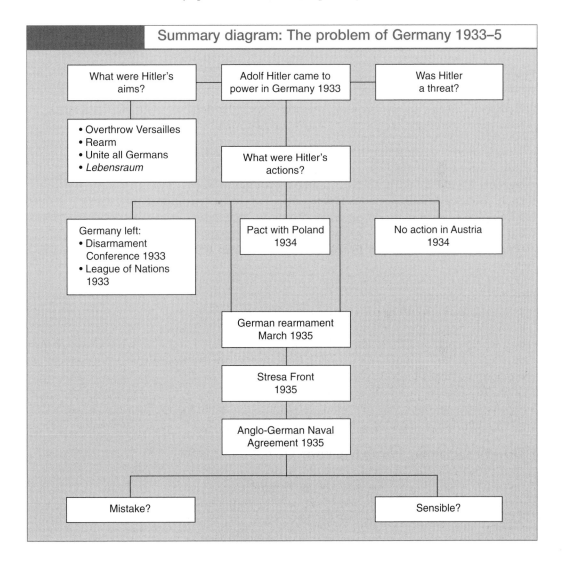

Summary diagram: The problem of Germany 1933–5

Key question
Why did Anglo-Italian relations deteriorate in 1935–6?

4 | The Problem of Italy 1935–6

Mussolini's ambitions to build up an empire in Africa and make the Mediterranean an 'Italian lake' meant that there was potential for Anglo-Italian rivalry. However, for most of the 1920s and early 1930s Mussolini had done little to upset things and had generally sought prestige by remaining within the bounds of international society. In 1933 Britain saw Italy as a friendly power. Indeed many British and French politicians hoped that Mussolini might be a useful ally against Hitler. There was some basis for these hopes. Italy, like France, was fearful of the consequences of Germany once again becoming a major power. In particular, the prospect of a union between Germany and Austria, which would result in a powerful German state along its northern border, horrified Italy. In April 1935 Italy had joined with France and Britain in the Stresa Front (page 58).

The problem of Abyssinia

However, by 1935 trouble was brewing. Mussolini wanted to take over Abyssinia (now known as Ethiopia), one of the last countries in Africa that was free from European control. In the early 1930s there were a number of incidents along the borders of Abyssinia and Italian Somaliland and Eritrea. These gave Mussolini a convenient excuse to build up his forces and prepare for an attack in October 1935.

Italy invaded Abyssinia: October 1935

Mussolini, recognising that Italian action might damage relations with Britain and France, tried to ensure that they would accept his Abyssinian adventure. In January 1935 Laval, the French Foreign Minister, anxious to keep on good terms with Italy because of the German threat, in effect promised Mussolini a free hand in Abyssinia. It also seemed that Britain was prepared to accept Italian expansion. The British were well aware of the Italian military build-up and yet no 'formal' mention of Abyssinia occurred at the Stresa meeting. Britain's silence, in Mussolini's view, implied consent.

However, as the summer progressed, Britain made it clear that it would not approve of Italian annexation of Abyssinia. Britain's reaction surprised and then angered Mussolini, but he determined to go through with his plan. Throughout the summer the world was presented with the spectacle of a crisis in slow motion. It was clear that Italy was planning to attack in the autumn when the rainy season ended. Attempts were made to reach a compromise settlement but without success.

Baldwin becomes Prime Minister

In June 1935 Conservative leader, Stanley Baldwin, replaced Ramsay MacDonald as Prime Minister. Sir Samuel Hoare became Foreign Secretary and Anthony Eden entered the Cabinet as Minister for League of Nations Affairs. Hoare had relatively little experience in foreign affairs. This may have given top civil servants like Vansittart more influence than usual. Vansittart, who considered Germany the main threat, was keen to appease Italy. On balance, however, the change of government made little difference to British policy.

War

In October 1935 Italy invaded Abyssinia. Haile Selassie, Emperor of Abyssinia, immediately appealed to the League of Nations. Britain and France were now faced with a difficult choice. Haile Selassie was hardly a model ruler and Abyssinia was hardly a good

Key question
What action should Britain have taken following the Italian invasion of Abyssinia?

neighbour. Abyssinia had caused Britain as much trouble on the Sudanese frontier as Italy had experienced on the Eritrean frontier. To take action against Mussolini would wreck the Stresa Front and, even worse, might force Italy into an agreement with Hitler.

But serious principles were at stake. The main one was whether Britain should honour its obligations under the League covenant (see page 40). Public opinion in Britain was strongly opposed to the Italian invasion. The results of the peace ballot, held in 1934 but not declared until June 1935, showed massive support for the League. Over 11.5 million people had voted in the ballot, held at the behest of the League of Nations Union; 95 per cent thought Britain should remain in the League and large majorities had voted in favour of supporting economic and, if necessary, military measures against aggressor states. Public opinion could not be ignored, if only because a general election was in the offing.

Despite its previous readiness to consider concessions, the British government now took a moral stand. It condemned the Italian invasion and supported League of Nations' action against Italy. France, anxious not to drive Mussolini into the German camp but equally anxious to keep in step with Britain, did likewise.

League of Nations action

In October the League denounced Italy as the aggressor and imposed economic sanctions. All imports from Italy and some exports were banned. Seventy per cent of Italy's trade was with League members and it was assumed that economic pressure would bring Italy to a negotiated settlement.

The 1935 general election

In October Baldwin announced a general election. The National Government's sanctions policy – cheap, popular and avoiding war – was neatly tailored to the requirements of the election campaign. As far as foreign policy was concerned, both Labour and the National Government said much the same thing; both committed themselves to the principle of collective security and both talked of the benefits of disarmament. Baldwin, although promising to 'remedy the deficiencies which have occurred in our defences', refused to emphasise new rearmament plans for fear of losing support. With the economy improving, the National Government won a handsome victory, winning 432 seats to Labour's 154.

The Hoare–Laval Pact

The League sanctions, which did not include an embargo on oil, had a limited effect on Italy's war effort. Closure of the **Suez Canal** would have damaged the Italian war effort even more than oil sanctions, but this might have led Mussolini to the 'mad dog act' of declaring war on Britain – a war that was likely to benefit Germany.

Key term

Suez Canal
The canal, which ran through Egyptian territory, joined the Mediterranean to the Red Sea. It was controlled by Britain.

Key date

Baldwin's National Government won the general election: November 1935

Key question
Was the Hoare–Laval Pact a sensible solution to the crisis?

In December 1935 the British and French Foreign Ministers, Hoare and Laval, met in Paris to discuss the Abyssinian situation. They proposed a compromise settlement:

- Italy would receive about one-third of Abyssinia.
- Haile Selassie would be ceded a strip of Italian territory, giving Abyssinia access to the Red Sea.

Baldwin's Cabinet approved the plan and Mussolini was ready to agree to it. However, when details of the Hoare–Laval Pact were leaked to the press, there was a storm of indignation, not least among Conservative MPs, who felt the government was breaking its election promises and betraying its commitment to the League. In the face of this outburst, the Cabinet decided to abandon the Hoare–Laval Pact.

Hoare resigned, claiming that his policy offered the best solution that Abyssinia could now hope for. However, Eden, the new Foreign Secretary, distrusted Mussolini and thought Britain should stand firm and support the League. In March 1936 Britain voted for oil sanctions but refused to impose a full-scale naval blockade, and oil from the USA continued to flow into Italy.

Italian victory

Meanwhile the Italians fought well. In May 1936 Haile Selassie fled and Abyssinia became part of the Italian Empire. Mussolini's prestige in Italy soared.

In June 1936 Chancellor of the Exchequer Neville Chamberlain described the continuation of sanctions as the 'very midsummer of madness'. A week later the sanctions were withdrawn by Britain and the League. Chamberlain, like several other Cabinet members, was prepared to forgive Italian 'crimes' in the hope that Anglo-Italian friendship could be restored. But Britain infuriated Mussolini by refusing to recognise the Italian conquest.

> **Key question**
> What were the main consequences of the Abyssinian war?

The results of the Abyssinian war

The Abyssinian crisis had several important results:

- It was a death blow to the League of Nations, which had again failed to deter or halt an aggressor. This was a shock to British public opinion. Collective security and the League, those concepts that had seemingly guarded British and world peace without the necessity to spend vast sums on armaments, had failed.
- The crisis had caused a major split between Italy and Britain and France. Mussolini felt bitter at the way he had been treated by the Western powers.
- Although Mussolini still regarded Hitler with some suspicion, he began to move closer to the German dictator, who had supported Italy's actions in Abyssinia.

Churchill believed that the failure to check Mussolini in 1935–6 was an important step on the way to world war. Arguably Britain and the League should have been prepared to fight Mussolini. Churchill assumed that Italy would have been easily defeated and that this would have strengthened collective security and helped to deter later German aggression. But recently this argument has been questioned. Almost certainly Britain would have defeated Italy; but victory would have left an embittered Italy and might not have been as easy as many have assumed. Italy was reasonably well prepared for war in 1935–6, unlike Britain.

Most historians are agreed that British policy in 1935–6 was weak and inept. It fell between two stools: the search for a compromise with Italy on the one hand and the need to stand firm against Italian aggression on the other. In the end nothing was achieved. Britain had failed to appease Mussolini or to uphold collective security.

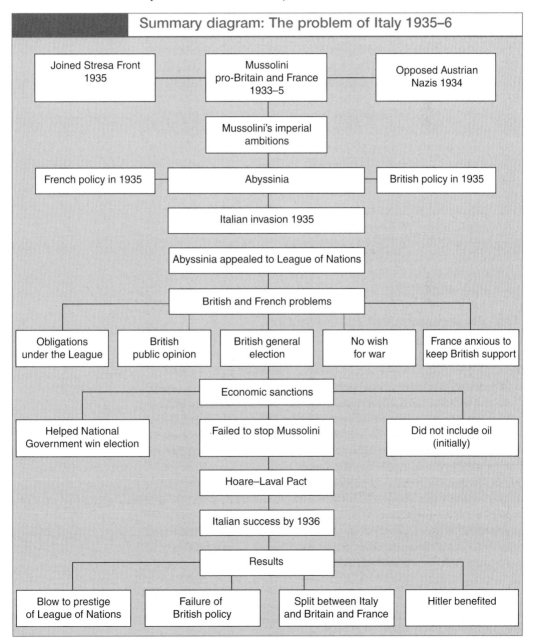

Summary diagram: The problem of Italy 1935–6

- Joined Stresa Front 1935
- Mussolini pro-Britain and France 1933–5
- Opposed Austrian Nazis 1934
- Mussolini's imperial ambitions
- French policy in 1935
- Abyssinia
- British policy in 1935
- Italian invasion 1935
- Abyssinia appealed to League of Nations
- British and French problems
  - Obligations under the League
  - British public opinion
  - British general election
  - No wish for war
  - France anxious to keep British support
- Economic sanctions
  - Helped National Government win election
  - Failed to stop Mussolini
  - Did not include oil (initially)
- Hoare–Laval Pact
- Italian success by 1936
- Results
  - Blow to prestige of League of Nations
  - Failure of British policy
  - Split between Italy and Britain and France
  - Hitler benefited

5 | The Rhineland, Spain and Rearmament

In March 1936 Hitler sent German troops into the demilitarised Rhineland. In doing so he was clearly violating both the Treaty of Versailles and the Treaty of Locarno (see page 38). Hitler's excuse was the ratification by the French Senate of the 1935 Franco-Soviet alliance (see page 58), which he claimed was a threat to Germany. Hitler knew he was taking a considerable gamble. Germany was not strong enough to fight a long war and the token German forces that marched into the Rhineland had orders to withdraw at the first sign of French opposition.

Key question
Should Britain have taken action against Hitler in 1936?

Key date

German troops reoccupied the Rhineland: March 1936

Britain and France's reaction

Neither the French nor the British government had been altogether surprised by Hitler's action. Both governments had expected that Hitler would raise the issue of the Rhineland as a topic for negotiation and both had a number of prior warnings from their intelligence staffs about the German move. Unlike Britain, France had forces available to take action but the fact that the country had a **caretaker government** made a French call to arms unlikely. In the event, France did nothing, except pass the problem to Britain by asking if it would support French action.

Baldwin's government made it clear that it had no intention of risking war against Germany. British opinion saw Hitler's move into the Rhineland as regrettable in manner but not particularly threatening in substance. Most MPs probably agreed with Lord Lothian's remark that Germany had every right to walk into its own 'backyard'. Some French politicians later claimed that France did not take action because Britain failed to offer support. In reality, there was no will in France to risk war with or without British support.

Key term

Caretaker government
A temporary government. The French political situation was highly unstable. Coalitions of various parties formed governments but then quickly fell. The result was weak government.

The consequences of Hitler's action

Hitler had again gambled and won. His troops remained in the Rhineland and began to build fortifications along the French frontier. Henceforward it would be even more difficult for Britain or France to take action against Germany.

In retrospect, many historians have claimed that Germany's march into the Rhineland offered 'the last chance' to stop Hitler without the risk of a major war. It is possible that the threat of force might have forced him to back down and that he might, as a consequence, have suffered a disastrous blow to his prestige. However, it was far from clear to French leaders at the time that Hitler would have pulled out of the Rhineland, and some historians have questioned the long-held view that he would have retreated if France and Britain had stood firm. In 1936 Germany might not have been the easy push-over that most historians have assumed. Certainly there was little that Britain could have done to help France.

Only a few British politicians, most notably Churchill, pressed for a resolute stand against Germany. Most MPs thought that there was still insufficient evidence to suggest that Hitler's ambitions were entirely open-ended and violent. Eden, for example, believed that there might be much to be gained by accepting the German move and taking seriously Hitler's new proposals for a 25-year non-aggression pact. Through the summer of 1936 attempts were made to reach a stronger Anglo-German agreement. These attempts failed, but at least Britain and Germany remained on reasonably good terms throughout most of 1936–7. Hitler declared that he had no territorial claims in Europe, and for nearly two years maintained a remarkably low profile. Germany continued to rearm, but not on the scale that many in the West later believed.

The Spanish Civil War

Key question
What were the consequences of the Spanish Civil War?

Key date

Start of the Spanish Civil War: July 1936

In July 1936 the attention of most British statesmen changed from Germany to Spain. Right-wing nationalists, led by General Franco and supported by **monarchists**, the Catholic Church and most of the armed forces, tried to overthrow the newly elected Republican government. The Republicans, supported by the industrial working class, liberals, socialists and communists, fought back.

British public opinion was excited and divided by the Spanish Civil War. The Labour Party and the left saw Franco as a fascist 'puppet' and strongly supported the Republicans. About 2000 people from Britain went to Spain to join the **International Brigade** and fight against Franco, convinced that they were waging war against fascism. But some Britons, regarding the Republicans as communist-inspired, sided with Franco.

Key terms

Monarchists
In terms of Spain, those who supported the return of a Spanish king.

International Brigade
A left-wing military force made up of volunteers from a number of different countries.

Baldwin's main aim was to prevent the war becoming a general European conflict between the great powers. Accordingly he supported the setting up of a Non-Intervention Committee to discourage intervention on either side and enforce a ban on the export of war materials to Spain. Most of the powers joined the Committee but it was soon clear that its decisions were being flouted:

- Mussolini sent aircraft, armaments and nearly 100,000 men to help the Nationalists. Italian submarines sank merchant ships suspected of trading with the Republicans.
- Germany sent far fewer men, but used the war to test the value of new weapons and military techniques. The destruction of the small town of Guernica by German aircraft in April 1937 made a great impression on contemporaries.
- The USSR sent men and weapons to help the communists on the Republican side.

The impact of the Spanish Civil War

The civil war dragged on for three bloody years. British fears that it might lead to a general war proved to be unfounded. Crises occurred, but in each case agreements were cobbled together. However, many people in Britain were convinced that should a general war occur, the line-up would be on ideological grounds, rather than on grounds of perceived 'national interest'. Most on the left thought Britain should align on the anti-fascist side. Many on the right, by contrast, while having little time for fascism, had no wish to align themselves with socialists and communists. Conservative opinion, on the whole, thought it was in Britain's best interest to stay out of any future ideological conflict.

Germany probably benefited most from the Spanish Civil War. Not only did it give Hitler an opportunity to test his new weapons, but it led to improved relations with Italy. In November 1936 Mussolini proclaimed the **Rome–Berlin Axis**. In 1937 Italy joined Germany and Japan in the Anti-Comintern Pact (see page 55). Relations between Britain and Italy sank to a new low.

Rearmament

Key question
How effective was British rearmament?

By the end of 1936 Britain faced serious problems:

- Germany was rearming.
- Italy was a potential threat in the Mediterranean.
- Japan had a substantial navy in the Far East.
- The League system was defunct and Britain had few strong, reliable allies.

In the circumstances Britain seemed to have little alternative but to rearm. Baldwin's government was still hesitant. Extra military spending meant sacrificing other, more popular, programmes – housing, health and education. But already in 1935 a defence white paper had concluded that, 'Additional expenditure on the armaments of the three Defence Services can no longer be postponed.' In 1936 a Minister for the Co-ordination of Defence was appointed and Chamberlain introduced an extensive four-year plan for rearmament. The increased rearmament was deplored by Labour MPs who opposed every major initiative for increased defence funding, right through to the introduction of conscription in 1939.

Problems of rearmament

One of Britain's main problems was that it had to prepare for several different types of war. Britain had to be ready to fight a **colonial war**, a naval war in the Far East and a European war. The nightmare scenario was that it might have to fight all three potential enemies – Germany, Italy and Japan – at the same time. Priority was naturally given to those services which could defend Britain from attack. Naval strength was essential to defend vital trade routes. Air defences were also a major concern. Far less money was spent on the army. Building bombers was seen as a cheaper and better way of preventing war in Europe than building a large army. The assumption was that a major aerial bombing threat would deter Hitler or Mussolini from risking war with Britain.

Perhaps more money should have been spent on rearmament, as Churchill claimed at the time and later. But Treasury officials and military experts realised that economic strength was almost as vital as having powerful armed forces. Unfortunately, Britain was short of machine tools and skilled labour. Up to one-sixth of

Key terms

Rome–Berlin Axis
A term first used by Mussolini in 1936 to describe Italy's relationship with Germany. He envisaged European affairs being determined by, or revolving around, Italy and Germany.

Colonial war
An overseas conflict in defence of Britain's imperial interests. It could be action against insurgents seeking independence or war against a hostile power.

the 1937 arms programme had to be met from imports. Increased military spending meant running the risk of a balance of payments crisis. This would undermine Britain's ability to continue importing for rearmament. Those, like Churchill, who argued in favour of more defence spending, ignored Britain's industrial weakness. The gradual expansion of forces, which avoided the temptation to spend large sums of money on weapons which might soon be outdated, also made sense.

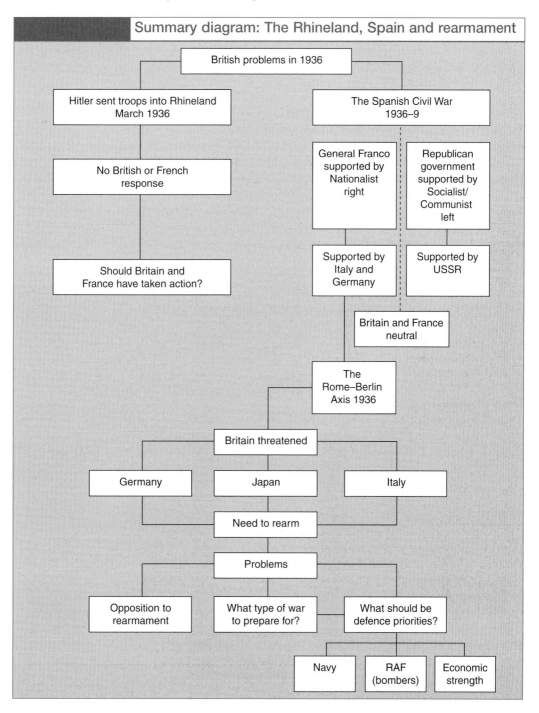

Summary diagram: The Rhineland, Spain and rearmament

- British problems in 1936
  - Hitler sent troops into Rhineland March 1936
    - No British or French response
      - Should Britain and France have taken action?
  - The Spanish Civil War 1936–9
    - General Franco supported by Nationalist right
      - Supported by Italy and Germany
    - Republican government supported by Socialist/Communist left
      - Supported by USSR
    - Britain and France neutral
    - The Rome–Berlin Axis 1936
      - Britain threatened
        - Germany
        - Japan
        - Italy
      - Need to rearm
        - Problems
          - Opposition to rearmament
          - What type of war to prepare for?
          - What should be defence priorities?
            - Navy
            - RAF (bombers)
            - Economic strength

6 | Chamberlain's Aims in Foreign Policy

In May 1937 Baldwin retired. Neville Chamberlain succeeded him as Prime Minister. Chamberlain's family was steeped in politics. His father, Joseph Chamberlain, had been a major politician and his half-brother, Austen, had been Foreign Secretary in the 1920s. Neville had come to political life late, becoming an MP in 1918 when he was nearly 50. He had made his name first as a social reformer and then as a competent Chancellor of the Exchequer who had helped to steer Britain through the Depression.

Chamberlain was the obvious choice for Prime Minister. He had experience in high office and was widely respected within the Conservative Party and in Parliament. He was, perhaps, a difficult man to like: serious, aloof and imperious. But he was an easy man to respect: tough, efficient and conscientious. Even Churchill was lavish in his praise when seconding his nomination for the Conservative Party leadership.

Few thought that the change of Prime Minister would mean dramatic changes of policy. Baldwin and Chamberlain had co-operated closely on domestic and foreign issues. Baldwin supported, and in many ways had groomed, Chamberlain as his successor. Chamberlain reshuffled the Cabinet but his team was essentially the same as Baldwin's.

However, there were to be differences. Baldwin had lacked dynamism and, after 1935, could be accused of allowing policy to drift. Chamberlain, though 68 years old (only two years younger than Baldwin), was determined to play a more vigorous role. His style contrasted sharply with that of Baldwin. He intended to control foreign policy and not be controlled by civil servants or by his Foreign Secretary. His feeble appearance belied his confidence and strength of purpose.

Chamberlain's aims

Chamberlain was not a muddler in foreign affairs as some historians have suggested. Intelligent and clear-sighted, he had been closely involved in all matters of government throughout the 1930s and, as Chancellor of the Exchequer, had recognised the interconnections between foreign and financial policy.

It was evident to Chamberlain that soon there would be enormous changes in the relative international standing of the great powers, especially Germany. He hoped that these changes could occur without war: in Chamberlain's view, war 'wins nothing, cures nothing, ends nothing'. Although British intelligence exaggerated German military power, and particularly the damage the **Luftwaffe** might do to Britain, Nazi Germany would undoubtedly be a difficult enemy to defeat in the event of war. Consequently Chamberlain was prepared to go to great lengths to preserve peace. But he was not a pacifist. If Britain's vital interests were at stake he was prepared to fight.

Convinced that the maintenance of peace could not be achieved without British participation in foreign affairs, he

Key question
What were Chamberlain's aims in foreign policy?

Key date

Chamberlain became Prime Minister: May 1937

Key term

Luftwaffe
The German air force.

Profile: Neville Chamberlain 1869–1940

1869	–	Born near Birmingham
1918	–	Elected Conservative MP
1922	–	Became Postmaster General
1923	–	Served as Paymaster General and then Minister of Health
1923–4	–	Chancellor of the Exchequer
1924–9	–	Minister of Health
1931–7	–	Chancellor of the Exchequer
1937	–	Became Prime Minister
1938	–	Attended the Munich Conference
1939	–	Declared war on Germany
1940	May –	Replaced as Prime Minister by Churchill
	Nov. –	Died of cancer

Key term

Appeasement
A policy of making concessions to another nation to avoid war. The term is primarily associated with British and French foreign policy in the 1930s.

The word now indissolubly linked to Chamberlain's name is **appeasement**. For many years after the Second World War appeasement had a bad press. Those who had supported it were seen as the 'guilty men' whose misguided policies had helped to bring about war. The appeasers were portrayed either as cynical defenders of the capitalist system who hoped to drive Germany and the USSR into mutual destruction, or as timid cowards. Chamberlain was usually seen as guilty man number one.

However, many historians now view appeasement and Chamberlain in a far more positive light. They point out that the main ideas of appeasement were not something that Chamberlain invented. For hundreds of years it has been a cardinal principle of British foreign policy that it is better to resolve international disputes through negotiation and compromise than through war. In the circumstances of 1937–8 appeasement was the only alternative to war.

determined to play a key conciliatory – or appeasing – role. He had no illusions about how difficult a task he faced, but he believed that a just settlement of many of the German, Italian and Japanese grievances was possible. He had been a businessman and liked the idea of face-to-face, business-like discussions between statesmen.

Chamberlain has been criticised for lacking an insight into the minds of the dictators. In his defence, Chamberlain did not trust Hitler, Mussolini or the Japanese. (He soon believed Hitler to be 'utterly untrustworthy and dishonest'.) For this reason he was not simply intent on appeasing the dictators. He also favoured rearmament. He was convinced that 'you should never menace unless you are in a position to carry out your threat'. But until Britain was adequately armed, he thought 'we must adjust our foreign policy to our circumstances and even bear with patience and good humour actions which we would like to treat in a very different fashion'.

Chamberlain was suspicious of the Foreign Office and claimed in private that it had 'no imagination and no courage'. He was quite prepared to use his own intermediaries and communicated directly, rather than through the Foreign Office, with some ambassadors, such as Sir Nevile Henderson in Berlin. Henderson pictured Hitler as a moderate with limited aims, a man with whom it was possible to do business. Henderson probably helped to confirm Chamberlain in his policies.

Support for Chamberlain

While Chamberlain's personal diplomacy sometimes angered the Foreign Office, there seems little doubt that the policy he pursued was supported by the great majority of the Cabinet, Parliament and the British public. Recent research has suggested that the government manipulated public opinion through a variety of propaganda techniques in order to sustain support for appeasement policies. However, this is far from proven. What is certain is that the most Britons were repelled by the prospect of war.

Key question
Why did many Britons support Chamberlain's policy while others opposed him?

Opposition to Chamberlain

Churchill was the most prominent anti-appeaser. He was later to acquire the reputation of having been right on Hitler, whereas Chamberlain had been wrong. However, there were not many in Britain who cared to go along with Churchill's hunches and prejudices in 1937–8. He had been wrong on too many occasions in the past. He was seen by many as a right-wing maverick and war-monger. Only a small cluster of Conservative MPs supported his anti-appeasement line.

The Labour Party disliked Chamberlain and hated Hitler, Mussolini and fascism. Some Labour MPs objected to Chamberlain's policy to the dictators simply because it was Chamberlain's policy. Unfortunately, most Labour MPs proposed no viable alternative course of action. They preached a strong policy but opposed every initiative for increased defence spending.

The problem of allies

Chamberlain realised he could count on little support from Britain's potential allies:

- Throughout the 1930s France was ruled by a series of weak and short-lived governments and Chamberlain had no confidence in the country or its statesmen.
- Chamberlain had even less confidence in the USSR. He feared and distrusted Stalin and communism as much as he feared and distrusted Hitler and Nazism.
- Chamberlain recognised that there was little prospect of US involvement in European or world affairs. In the 1930s the USA was overwhelmingly isolationist and had no wish for foreign entanglements.

US **President Roosevelt** had some sympathy with Britain and France. In October 1937 he called for a concerted effort to

President Roosevelt
Franklin Delano Roosevelt was elected president in 1932 (and re-elected in 1936). The USA had been badly hit by the Depression. Roosevelt's main priority was to get Americans back to work.

Key figure

oppose those countries who were creating 'a state of international anarchy'. However, such talk was not followed by action. 'It is always best and safest', thought Chamberlain, 'to count on nothing from the Americans but words'. However, aware of the importance of US help to Britain in the First World War, he was reluctant to become involved in another European conflict without some assurances of US support.

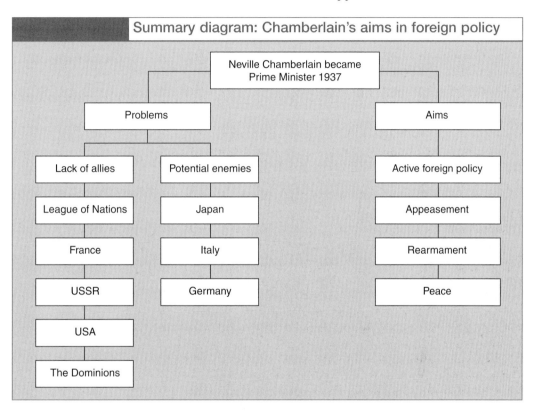

Summary diagram: Chamberlain's aims in foreign policy

Key question
Why was Japan a problem for Chamberlain?

Key date

Start of Chinese–Japanese war: July 1937

Key term

New order
Japan's aim for Asia, ending European imperialism and uniting Asians in an alliance (led by Japan) free of Western taint.

7 | Chamberlain's Concerns 1937–8

The problem of Japan

Chamberlain immediately faced problems in the Far East. In July 1937 Chinese–Japanese hostility escalated into full-scale war, destroying any possibility of Japan being reintegrated into the international community. Japanese forces quickly took over large areas of China and Japan proclaimed its intention of securing a **new order** in East Asia.

Chamberlain seemed to have little alternative but appeasement. Faced with a worsening situation in Europe, he could not risk a conflict with Japan. His government appealed for an end to the conflict, but in vain. Efforts to co-ordinate policy with the USA had limited success. In the circumstances the best British hope was that Japan would get bogged down in a war of attrition in China, which indeed was what happened.

Chamberlain's attention was focused more on Europe than the Far East. However, he could not avoid the fact that European and Far Eastern problems often interacted: policy in each area was influenced by the other. Fear of Japanese aggression was an important factor in understanding why he was keen to conciliate Italy and Germany.

Chamberlain and Hitler

In July 1937 Chamberlain explained to the Cabinet the impossibility of fighting Germany, Italy and Japan at the same time. The only solution was to find a way of separating these powers by diplomatic means. He intended to explore the prospects of a settlement with each potential enemy in turn.

Key question
How successful was Chamberlain in 1937 and early 1938?

In the autumn of 1937 Chamberlain sent Lord Halifax to Germany to find out precisely what Hitler wanted. (Foreign Secretary Eden was not happy about the visit by a colleague who had no responsibility for foreign affairs!) Halifax made it clear that Britain was prepared to accept some changes in Austria, Czechoslovakia and Poland, provided the changes came about through peaceful means. Hitler, who indicated that he still hoped for an agreement with Britain, seemed to pose no immediate threat. Germany and Britain remained important trading partners.

Chamberlain and Mussolini

In 1937 Chamberlain spent a great deal of time trying to improve relations with Italy. By-passing Eden and the Foreign Office, he sent a letter to Mussolini suggesting that Britain and Italy should make a serious effort to resolve their differences. Mussolini responded favourably, but the continuation of the Spanish Civil War made Anglo-Italian accommodation difficult. Anglo-Italian talks, initiated by Chamberlain in January 1938, were inconclusive. Mussolini wanted Italian domination of the Mediterranean and North Africa, which Britain was not prepared to concede.

Chamberlain's personal efforts to reach an agreement with Mussolini led to major discord with Eden, who felt that his authority as Foreign Secretary was being undermined. Eden was also critical of Chamberlain's attempts to appease Mussolini. In Eden's view, the Italian leader was 'the complete gangster whose pledged word means nothing'. In February 1938 Eden resigned, declaring 'I do not believe that we can make progress in European appeasement … if we allow the impression to gain currency abroad that we yield to constant pressure.'

Chamberlain appointed Lord Halifax in Eden's place. He also replaced the anti-German Sir Robert Vansittart (see page 56) with Sir Alec Cadogan. Chamberlain was now more in control of foreign affairs with compliant personnel to assist him.

In April 1938 Britain and Italy reached agreement. Britain would recognise Italy's position in Abyssinia in return for Italy's withdrawing troops from Spain. The agreement was not to come into force until the Spanish Civil War had ended. Anglo-Italian relations improved somewhat. Nevertheless, Italy remained a potentially hostile power and Mussolini continued his military build-up in the Mediterranean. However, by the spring of 1938 German actions in Central Europe had assumed a far greater significance than Italian actions in the Mediterranean.

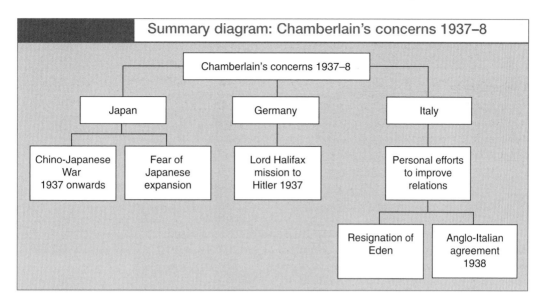

Summary diagram: Chamberlain's concerns 1937–8

8 | The *Anschluss*

Key question
What was Britain's reaction to the *Anschluss*?

Key date

Hitler annexed Austria: March 1938

Although the union of Germany and Austria had been forbidden by the Treaty of Versailles, Hitler had long harboured ambitions to annex his homeland. He was encouraged by the fact that many Austrians also favoured union with Germany and that the Austrian Nazi Party had considerable support. Since 1934 the Austrian government had struggled to keep Austrian Nazis under control and German influence at bay. Until 1936 it had the support of Italy, but, as Hitler and Mussolini drew closer together, Austria could rely less and less on Italian help.

Throughout 1937 Austrian Nazis, aided by money and advice from Berlin, increased their influence. By 1938 Schuschnigg, the Austrian Chancellor, felt he was losing control of the situation. In February 1938 he visited Hitler's home at Berchtesgaden in Bavaria, hoping to persuade him to restrain the Austrian Nazis. The meeting was a mistake. Hitler threatened the Austrian leader, insisting he should include Nazis in his Cabinet. Schuschnigg, shocked and fearful, agreed to Hitler's demands and Seyss-Inquart, the Austrian Nazi leader, became Interior Minister.

Hitler acts

It seems that Hitler planned to do little more at this stage. However, Schuschnigg again precipitated events, announcing that he intended to hold a plebiscite (on 13 March) to enable the Austrian people to decide whether they wished to become part of Germany. Hitler, fearing the vote might go against him, was outraged. He demanded the cancellation of the plebiscite, whipped up opposition among the Austrian Nazis and threatened war.

Schuschnigg resigned. His successor, Seyss-Inquart, immediately invited Hitler to send troops into Austria to preserve order. On 12 March, hastily assembled German forces crossed the frontier and were enthusiastically welcomed by the Austrians. Hitler returned in triumph to his homeland and declared the union (or **Anschluss**) of Austria and Germany. The *Anschluss*, approved by a massive majority in a plebiscite run by the Nazis, was clearly a triumph for Hitler.

Reaction to the *Anschluss*

Chamberlain was not opposed to the *Anschluss* as such, but to the way it had happened. He accepted that 'Nothing could have arrested this action by Germany unless we and others with us had been prepared to use force to prevent it.' Britain was not prepared to use the limited force it possessed. France, with a large army but without a government throughout the Austrian crisis, did nothing but protest. Mussolini, who had protected Austria in 1934, did nothing at all.

It was, in fact, hard to argue that a great crime had occurred when so many Austrians expressed their joy at joining the **Third Reich**. Perhaps the most important feature of the *Anschluss* was not that it had happened, but how it had happened. If one frontier could be changed in this way, why not others? Hitler's justification for the *Anschluss* was that there were large numbers of people of German stock in Austria demanding union with Germany. The uncomfortable fact was that there were German-speaking people in Poland, Lithuania and Czechoslovakia who also wished to join Germany.

Key terms

Anschluss
The union of Austria and Germany.

Third Reich
Hitler's Germany from 1933 to 1945. (*Reich* meaning Empire.)

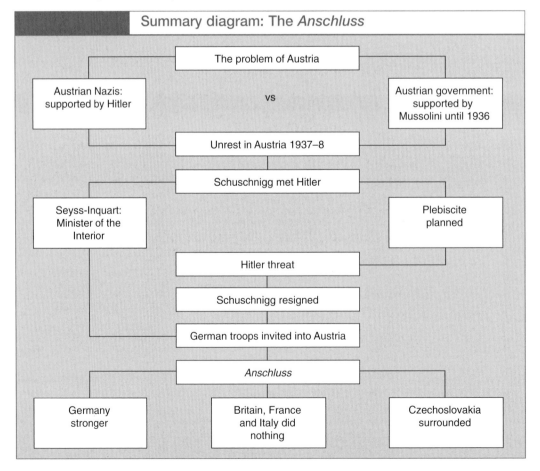

Summary diagram: The *Anschluss*

The problem of Austria

Austrian Nazis: supported by Hitler — vs — Austrian government: supported by Mussolini until 1936

Unrest in Austria 1937–8

Schuschnigg met Hitler

Seyss-Inquart: Minister of the Interior

Plebiscite planned

Hitler threat

Schuschnigg resigned

German troops invited into Austria

Anschluss

Germany stronger

Britain, France and Italy did nothing

Czechoslovakia surrounded

Key question
Why was
Czechoslovakia a
major problem in
1938?

9 | The Problem of Czechoslovakia

The *Anschluss* immediately focused international attention on Czechoslovakia, much of which was now surrounded by German territory. The creation of Czechoslovakia had been, in Churchill's view in 1919, 'an affront to self-determination'. By the 1930s only about half of its 15 million population were Czechs. The country contained over two million Slovaks, 750,000 Hungarians, 500,000 Ruthenians and 100,000 Poles.

However, the largest minority ethnic group within Czechoslovakia were some 3.25 million Germans. Most of these occupied the Sudetenland, which had been part of Austria-Hungary until 1918. By 1938 many Sudeten Germans, claiming they were victimised by the Czechs, were demanding either greater 'home rule' or, preferably, union with Germany. They received encouragement and support from Germany, where the Nazi press launched bitter attacks on the Czech government.

President Beneš, the Czechoslovakian head of state, opposed the Sudeten German demands. He realised that if all the various ethnic groups within the country were given independence or self-rule, there would be no viable Czech state left. He was therefore determined to stand firm against German pressure.

Chamberlain's views

Most British politicians had some sympathy with Czechoslovakia. While it did not treat its ethnic minorities particularly well, it had preserved a democratic constitution more successfully than most European states. A few politicians, such as Churchill, thought Czechoslovakia worth fighting for. Chamberlain was not among that number. He regarded Czechoslovakia as a 'highly artificial' creation, and had some sympathy for the Sudeten Germans. He was quite willing to see the Sudetenland handed over to Germany, provided this could be done by negotiation rather than by force.

In March 1938 Chamberlain told the Commons that British vital interests were not involved in Czechoslovakia. Britain had no treaty obligation to defend the Czech state and was in no position to offer serious military aid. In late March 1938 he wrote:

> You have only to look at the map to see that nothing France or we could do could possibly save Czechoslovakia from being overrun by the Germans if they want to do it … I have therefore abandoned any idea of giving guarantees to Czechoslovakia or the French in connection with her obligations to that country.

The Chiefs of Staff agreed. On 28 March 1938 they reported to the Cabinet that:

> We conclude that no pressure that we and our possible allies can bring to bear, either by sea, on land or in the air, could prevent Germany from invading and overrunning **Bohemia** and from inflicting a decisive defeat on the Czechoslovakian army. We should then be faced with the necessity of undertaking a war against

Key term

Bohemia
A major province in
Czechoslovakia.

Germany for the purpose of restoring Czechoslovakia's lost integrity and this object would only be achieved by the defeat of Germany and as the outcome of a prolonged struggle. In the world situation today it seems to us … Italy and Japan would seize the opportunity to further their own ends and that in consequence the problem we have to envisage is not that of a limited European war only, but of a World War.

France and Czechoslovakia

Chamberlain's main concern was not so much Czechoslovakia but France. France, unlike Britain, did have an alliance with the Czechs. Chamberlain feared that if Germany invaded Czechoslovakia, France might go to its aid. Britain might then be forced to help France. A German defeat of France would tilt the European balance so overwhelmingly against Britain that it could not be contemplated.

Unbeknown to Chamberlain, the French had no wish to be drawn into war over Czechoslovakia. Their strategic view was similar to that of the British. Czechoslovakia could not be defended. Daladier, the new French Prime Minister, and Bonnet, his Foreign Minister, were frantically looking for ways to avoid having to honour France's obligations to Czechoslovakia. They would be delighted if Britain gave them an excuse.

Chamberlain's policy, March–September 1938

Convinced that the Sudeten issue could no longer be ignored, Chamberlain determined to get ahead of events. His main aim was to extract from the Czech government concessions which would satisfy the Sudeten Germans before Hitler used force to impose a settlement. This policy had the full support of Lord Halifax, the Cabinet and the Foreign Office. The ironic thing is that in the early spring of 1938 Hitler seems to have had no immediate designs on Czechoslovakia.

Key question
What could Chamberlain have done as the Czechoslovakian crisis developed?

The May Crisis

The flaw in Chamberlain's policy was that the Czech government was in no mood to make concessions. In May, after what proved to be false reports of German troop movements, the Czechs prepared for war. Both Britain and France, fearing a German attack on Czechoslovakia, warned Hitler against making such a move.

Hitler was outraged by Czech mobilisation and by the fact that the Western powers seemed to have won a diplomatic victory because he had stepped back from invasion – an invasion which he was not actually then planning. This May Crisis seems to have been a critical factor in persuading him towards a confrontation with Czechoslovakia. He told his chief officers. 'It is my unalterable decision to smash Czechoslovakia by military action in the near future.'

Increased tension

As the summer wore on, tension increased. The German press stepped up its campaign against Czechoslovakia, claiming that the Sudetan Germans were being persecuted. The Czech government stood firm. Daladier and Bonnet, troubled by economic and political crises within France, were quite happy to allow Britain to undertake the major initiatives in an effort to preserve peace. From their perspective, this meant that, whatever happened, at least Britain would commit itself to involvement in Europe. It might also be a way by which France could escape from the responsibilities of its Czechoslovakian alliance.

Chamberlain and the USSR

Chamberlain has been criticised for ignoring the possibility of talks with the USSR. The USSR, like France, had an alliance with Czechoslovakia and might have been prepared to support the Western powers against Hitler. However, Chamberlain distrusted Stalin, suspecting that the Soviet leader hoped that Britain and France would fight Germany. The USSR, moreover, was in the midst of the **great purges** and there seemed little Stalin could or would do. Military experts assured Chamberlain that the Soviet army lacked the capacity for an offensive war.

The Runciman Mission

In June 1938 Britain proposed that a neutral mediator be sent to Czechoslovakia to try to resolve the crisis. The Czechs agreed and in August a mission led by Lord Runciman, a veteran Liberal politician, travelled to Czechoslovakia to meet the various parties. Unfortunately neither the Sudeten Germans nor the Czechs were prepared to compromise and Runciman's mission achieved little.

The threat of war

In early September British intelligence reported that Germany was planning a war against Czechoslovakia in early autumn. In Britain there was an awareness that a crisis was brewing. The country was divided. Some, like Churchill, thought that Britain should support Czechoslovakia. Many, like Chamberlain, favoured the idea of self-determination for the Sudeten Germans and thought that war must be averted at almost any cost. The Prime Minister, aware that almost all the Dominions were hostile to the idea of fighting for Czechoslovakia, recognised the danger of taking a divided country and Empire into war.

Hitler kept up the pressure. At the **Nuremberg rally** in September, he criticised the Czech government, demanded self-determination for the Sudeten Germans and assured them they would be neither defenceless nor abandoned. Hitler's speech aroused great passion in the Sudetenland and the Czech government declared **martial law**. Several Germans were killed and thousands more fled to Germany with tales of brutal repression. War between Germany and Czechoslovakia seemed imminent.

Key terms

Great purges
In the late 1930s Stalin imprisoned or executed millions of people who were suspected of disloyalty. Many of the USSR's chief generals were killed.

Nuremberg rally
Hitler held major annual Nazi Party meetings at Nuremberg.

Martial law
The suspension of ordinary administration and policing and the imposition of military power.

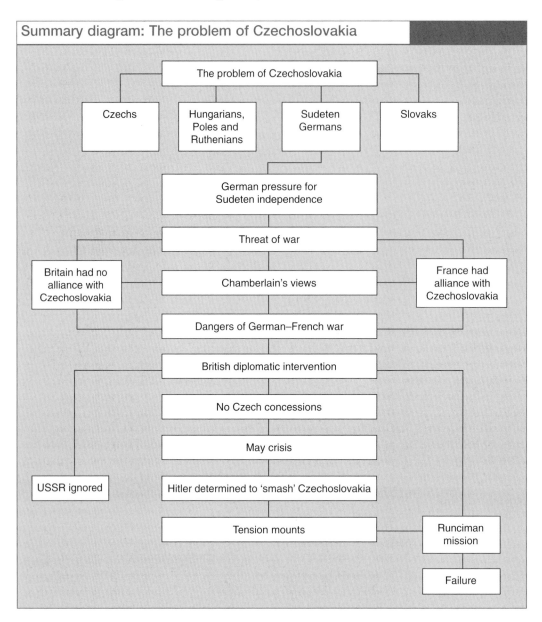

Summary diagram: The problem of Czechoslovakia

10 | The Munich Conference

Chamberlain now determined to fly to Germany to meet Hitler and ask him what his demands were. This proposal, according to Chamberlain, was 'so unconventional and daring that it rather took Halifax's breath away'. In the 1930s Prime Ministers tended to stay at home and certainly did not fly abroad. Arguably Chamberlain's plan was foolhardy: it committed Britain to imposing a negotiated settlement on the Czech government. However, it received enthusiastic approval from the Cabinet and even most Labour MPs thought it a statesman-like gesture.

Key question
Was Chamberlain right to meet Hitler to discuss the situation in Czechoslovakia?

The 'honest broker' from London urges Czechoslovakia not to allow himself to be shot by the brutal German with the machine-gun, advising him instead to put his head into the noose marked 'capitulation'. A cartoon published in *Izvestiya*, Moscow, 16 September 1938. How far is the Russian cartoon a fair representation of what was happening to Czechoslovakia in 1938?

Chamberlain wrote a brief note to Hitler, asking to meet him. Hitler agreed. He may have been flattered by Chamberlain's proposal; but he may also have been uneasy at the course of events. No one could be sure what would happen if war broke out.

The meeting at Berchtesgaden

On 15 September Chamberlain boarded an aircraft for the first time in his life and flew to meet Hitler at Berchtesgaden. The two leaders talked for three hours and reached a rough agreement. Chamberlain accepted Hitler's main demand that all the areas in Czechoslovakia in which Germans comprised over 50 per cent of the population should join Germany. In return Hitler agreed not to attack Czechoslovakia until Chamberlain had consulted with the French and Czechs. Hitler, assuming that the Czechs would refuse to cede the Sudetenland and that Britain would then wash its hands of them, was delighted.

Chamberlain flew back to Britain and set about convincing his Cabinet, the French and finally the Czechs that Hitler's demands, if met, would produce a lasting peace. The Cabinet and the

French were won over with comparative ease. The Czech government, quite naturally, was appalled at the situation. However, without French or British backing, it had little option but to accept the Sudetenland's loss. At least Chamberlain agreed to guarantee what remained of Czechoslovakia in the event of its being threatened in future by Germany.

The meeting at Bad Godesberg

On 22 September Chamberlain flew back to Germany to meet Hitler at Bad Godesberg on the Rhine, expecting that, 'I had only to discuss quietly with him the proposals that I had brought with me.' To Chamberlain's consternation, Hitler now said the previous proposals were insufficient. (Czech concessions were not what Hitler had expected or wanted.) The claims of Poland and Hungary to Czechoslovakian territory had to be met and, in addition – to protect Sudeten Germans from Czech brutality – Hitler demanded the right to occupy the Sudetenland no later than 1 October.

Faced with this ultimatum, Chamberlain returned to London. He was still in favour of accepting Hitler's demands but many of his Cabinet colleagues rejected the Godesberg proposals. Daladier also expressed doubts about the wisdom of giving in to Hitler's bullying and said that France would honour its commitments to Czechoslovakia. Not surprisingly, the Czechs stated that the new proposals were totally unacceptable. Fearing war, both Britain and France began to mobilise. Trenches, for air-raid precautions, were dug in London parks and 38 million gas masks were distributed.

In what seemed like a last bid for peace, Chamberlain sent a personal envoy, Horace Wilson, to talk to Hitler. Wilson's mission failed. However, there was still one final hope. On 27 September the British Ambassador in Italy asked Mussolini to use his influence to persuade Hitler to reconsider. Mussolini agreed, but for a few hours it was uncertain whether his request to Hitler would have any effect. On 27 September Chamberlain broadcast to the British people:

> How horrible, fantastic, incredible, it is that we should be digging trenches and trying on gas masks here because of a quarrel in a far away country between people of whom we know nothing … I would not hesitate to pay even a third visit to Germany, if I thought it would do any good.

The meeting at Munich

The next day, Chamberlain got his opportunity. He was speaking in the Commons when news came through that Hitler had accepted Mussolini's suggestion of a conference, involving Britain, France, Germany and Mussolini, to be held at Munich to work out an agreement to the Sudeten question. The Commons erupted. Speeches of congratulation came from every side: everyone wanted to shake Chamberlain's hand. Attlee, the Labour leader, and Sinclair, the Liberal leader, blessed Chamberlain's mission. The prospect of an immediate war seemed to have been

Key date

Munich Conference: 29–30 September 1938

averted and it looked as though Hitler had backed down. Only Gallagher, the single Communist MP, spoke against Chamberlain going to Munich.

On 29 September Chamberlain, Daladier, Hitler and Mussolini met at Munich to discuss the fate of Czechoslovakia. Beneš, the Czech leader, was not invited to the Conference. The talks were remarkably casual and uncoordinated, but agreement was reached on 30 September. The Munich agreement was very similar to Hitler's Godesberg proposals, although it did water down some of Germany's most extreme demands:

- The Sudeten Germans were given self-determination within Germany.
- German occupation of the Sudetenland was to be carried out in five stages, spread out over 10 days, rather than one.
- The precise borders of the new Czech state would be determined by Britain, France, Germany and Italy.

Beneš had no choice but to accept the terms or fight alone. He chose to surrender.

Before returning to London, Chamberlain persuaded Hitler to sign a joint declaration:

> We regard the agreement signed last night and the Anglo-German Naval Agreement as symbolic of the desire of our two peoples never to go to war with one another again. We are resolved that the method of consultation shall be the method adopted to deal with any other questions that may concern our two countries and we are determined to continue our efforts to remove every possible source of difference, and thus to contribute to assure the peace of Europe.

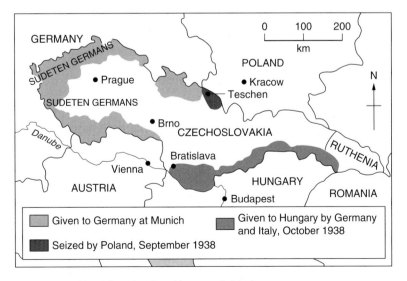

Figure 3.2: How Czechoslovakia was divided.

Blessed are the peacemakers? From left to right, Chamberlain, Daladier, Hitler, Mussolini and Ciano (the Italian Foreign Minister) at the Munich Conference.

The aftermath of Munich

Chamberlain was not convinced that Munich made peace more secure. He had few illusions about Hitler and feared that he would not be content with his recent gains. In private he regretted using the terms 'peace with honour' and 'peace for our time' in the euphoria of his return from Germany. However, he remained confident that he could handle the difficult problems that lay ahead. At least Munich gave him a breathing space. He would continue to hope and work for peace. With the Czechoslovakian problem out of the way, it might be possible to make further progress 'along the road to sanity'.

Key question
What were the immediate results of Munich?

Reaction to Munich

Some MPs were critical of the Munich agreement. Churchill described the whole conduct of British policy as a 'total and unmitigated disaster'. Labour leaders censured Chamberlain for failing to obtain better terms. Some Conservatives were uneasy that Hitler's bullying seemed to have worked. In the event, however, only Duff Cooper, First Lord of the Admiralty, resigned, and fewer than 30 Conservatives abstained rather than support the motion by which the House approved the policy whereby war had been averted and peace was being sought.

The press was far from unanimous in support of Munich. *The Daily Worker*, *Reynolds News*, the *Manchester Guardian* and the *Daily Herald* were critical. But the majority of newspapers, both national and local, supported Chamberlain's policy.

'A Great Mediator', a *Punch* cartoon from 1938. John Bull: 'I've known many Prime Ministers in my time, sir, but never one who worked so hard for security in the face of such terrible odds.' Was Chamberlain a 'great mediator'?

It is difficult to tell how the majority of Britons viewed the Munich agreement. Chamberlain certainly suffered no run of by-election disasters after September 1938. There was undoubtedly great relief that war had been averted and many gave Chamberlain credit for the preservation of peace. However, if public opinion polls can be trusted (they were still in their infancy), most Britons distrusted Hitler and feared for the future.

The situation in 1938–9

In the autumn of 1938 Chamberlain continued to work for improved relations with Germany:

Key question
Was there any hope of peace in 1938–9?

- Britain held out the prospect of a return of some German colonies.
- There were Anglo-German talks on industrial, financial and trade links.
- Britain welcomed and encouraged an improvement in relations between France and Germany.

Meanwhile, Chamberlain worked hard to improve relations with Italy. In November he proposed the implementation of the Anglo-Italian agreement of April 1938. While his critics questioned the extent to which the previously stated British conditions had been satisfied, his action had the overwhelming support of the Commons. In January 1939 Chamberlain and Halifax visited Italy and met Mussolini. Mussolini welcomed them but was not impressed. 'These are the tired sons of a long line of rich men and they will lose their empire', he said. Chamberlain, by contrast, was pleased with the reception he received from the Italian crowds and thought there was a good chance of detaching Mussolini from Hitler.

In public Chamberlain and members of his government continued to talk optimistically of Hitler's peaceful intentions. Their aim was to avoid any increase in tension. However, Hitler refused to make even the smallest sign of goodwill to Britain. Instead he made a number of anti-British speeches and the German press continued to make venomous attacks on Britain. Events in Germany on the night of 9–10 November 1938 further damaged Anglo-German relations. Following the killing by a Jew of a German diplomat in Paris, Jewish shops throughout Germany were wrecked and synagogues set on fire. 'Crystal Night' (because of the smashed glass windows), as the anti-Jewish **pogrom** became known, appalled most British people.

Pogrom
An organised attack on Jews.

Key term

Summary diagram: The Munich Conference

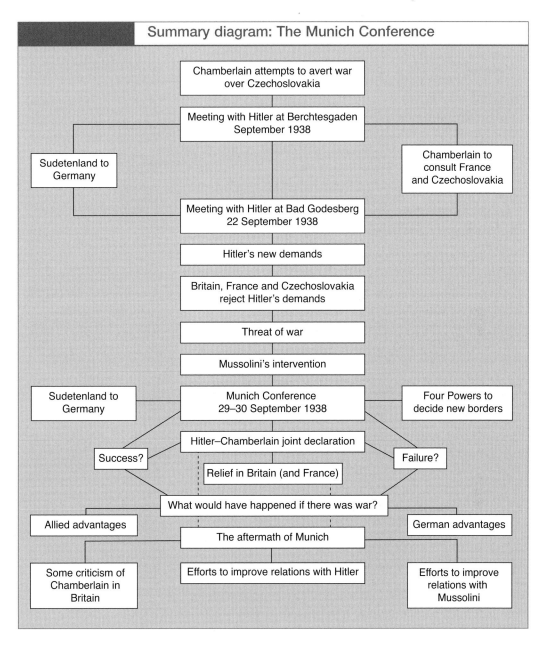

11 | Key Debate

Was the Munich Conference a 'total and unmitigated disaster'?

Failure?

The Munich agreement, and Chamberlain's role in the whole Czechoslovakian crisis, have been the subject of massive debate. The Munich Conference is usually viewed as a terrible failure for Britain. Many historians think that Chamberlain was outplayed by Hitler at almost every point. Britain had been forced to sacrifice a friend to avert war. Czechoslovakia had been stripped of territory, so much so that she was now indefensible. Arguably Britain should have done the honourable thing and gone to war against Germany.

Success?

However, Chamberlain saw Munich as a victory rather than a defeat. Hitler had backed down and not gone to war. In Chamberlain's view, German military superiority over Britain and France would never again be so great. He could claim that from a position of military weakness he had achieved most of his aims. He had avoided war, Germany's legitimate grievances had been settled, and (most of) Czechoslovakia remained as an independent state.

In 1938 most people in Britain and France also saw Munich as a triumph rather than a defeat. Both Chamberlain and Daladier were treated as heroes on their return from Germany. Chamberlain, overcome by the large crowd which greeted him at the airport, waved the piece of paper he had signed with Hitler and promised, 'Peace for our time'. President Roosevelt sent Chamberlain a telegram with the simple words: 'Good man'.

What would have happened if … ?

What the likely outcome would have been of a war over Czechoslovakia in 1938 has intrigued historians ever since Munich. Many have accepted Churchill's view that it would have been better for Britain to have fought Germany in 1938 than in 1939:

- The German army was not as strong in 1938 as Chamberlain and most British military experts imagined. It was short of tanks, fuel, ammunition and reserves.
- The *Luftwaffe* was not ready or able to launch a serious attack on Britain (see Table 3.1).
- Most German generals were worried by the prospect of war.
- The French army was the largest and best equipped in Europe.
- Czech forces were far from negligible. The Czechs had a strong defence line along the German frontier.
- The USSR might have joined the war on Czechoslovakia's side.

Table 3.1: German air strength in August–September 1938

	Actual German air strength August 1938		British estimates of German air strength September 1938	
	Total	Combat ready	Total	Combat ready
Fighters	643	453	810	717
Bombers	1157	582	1235	1019
Dive-bombers	207	159	247	227

However, it is far from certain that Britain and France would have been successful:

- Neither country was ready for war.
- In 1938 Britain was virtually defenceless against air attack. It had few fighter aircraft and very little **radar** defence.
- Czech armed forces were weak and divided; most Sudeten Germans and Slovaks preferred to fight against the Czechs than for them. Czech defences, situated in the Sudetenland, were by no means complete. The Germans anticipated over-running Czechoslovakia in little more than 10 days. French forces, deployed along the Maginot Line, could have done little to help.
- It is unlikely that the USSR would have come to Czechoslovakia's assistance. Neither Poland nor Romania was prepared to tolerate Soviet troops in their territory, so it would have been difficult for the USSR to have sent direct help.
- The British Dominions were reluctant to fight over Czechoslovakia.
- The British public was far from united in its determination to fight.

It can thus be claimed (although this was not Chamberlain's intention) that Munich brought valuable time for Britain to bolster its defences. Interestingly, Hitler did not view Munich as a great success. Although he had gained the Sudetenland in return for nothing save a promise of future good conduct, he had been denied a military triumph. He was confident that he could have defeated Czechoslovakia quickly and regretted his decision to reach agreement at Munich.

Key term

Radar
The use of high-powered radio pulses for locating objects (for example, enemy planes).

Some key books in the debate

R.J. Caputi, *Neville Chamberlain and Appeasement* (Susquehanna University Press, 2000).
D. Faber, *The 1938 Appeasement Crisis* (Simon & Schuster, 2008).
F. McDonough, *Hitler, Chamberlain and Appeasement* (Cambridge University Press, 2002).
R.A.C. Parker, *Chamberlain and Appeasement: British Policy and the Coming of the Second World War* (Macmillan, 1993).

Study Guide: AS Questions

In the style of AQA

Question 1

(a) Explain why the Lytton Commission was set up in December 1931.

(b) 'Between 1931 and 1937 British foreign policy was continually weak.' Explain why you agree or disagree with this view.

Exam tips

The cross-references are intended to take you straight to the material that will help you to answer the questions.

(a) The answer should focus on a variety of reasons for the establishment of the Lytton Commission. Obviously you will need to refer to the Japanese invasion of Manchuria (page 53) but do not become distracted into describing this. The weakness of the League militarily will need consideration (page 54) as will the hesitancy of the Western powers to act (page 54). You will want to mention that the Commission was actually proposed by the Japanese and that its intention was to seek a peaceful solution to the situation in Manchuria. This can be supported by comments on the British desire to avoid war. Try to provide some general and more specific reasons and to identify what you consider to be the most important reason. Your answer should conclude with a well-supported judgement on the reasons.

(b) The key words here are 'continually weak'. You are being asked to assess British foreign policy and it might be helpful to provide some definition of what constitutes strong/weak policy at the outset. You will need to refer to British policy over Japan (page 54), Germany (pages 56–9) and Italy (pages 56–63) and British non-involvement in the Spanish Civil War (pages 65–6). You are likely to emphasise Britain's constant desire for compromise and reliance on collective security, but whether this was a strength or weakness will depend on your definition. Evidence against the quotation might include Britain's:

- need to maintain friendly relations with Japan (pages 54–5)
- curbing the German challenge through the naval agreement (page 58)
- taking direct action over the Italian invasion of Abyssinia (pages 60–2).

Ensure you have decided how you are going to argue before you begin and that you follow a clear line of argument throughout your essay which progresses logically to a well-substantiated conclusion.

Question 2

(a) Explain why Chamberlain followed a policy of appeasement in 1938.

(b) 'The Munich agreement was a triumph for Chamberlain.' Explain why you agree or disagree with this view.

Exam tips

The cross-references are intended to take you straight to the material that will help you to answer the questions.

(a) You will need to focus on the reasons for Chamberlain's appeasement policy in the face of the German annexation of Austria and the taking of the Sudetenland from Czechoslovakia. Among the factors you might consider are:

- Chamberlain's belief that war achieved nothing and that change (which he believed necessary) could therefore be achieved peacefully (pages 68–9)
- his business background and belief in face-to-face discussion (page 69)
- his failure to understand Hitler's true intent (page 72)
- suspicions of the Foreign Office (page 70)
- the possibility that he was playing for time since Britain had still to rearm (page 87).

Other general factors might include:

- the need to support Hitler, who was resisting the spread of communism (page 56)
- Britain's own economic problems, which were considered a higher priority (pages 66–7)
- the fear that the USA would not support Britain if she stood up to Hitler (pages 70–1).

Remember you should concentrate on reasons, and the links between them, not how Chamberlain went about his policy.

(b) You will need to explain the Munich agreement (pages 78–81) but the main focus of your answer should be on whether it was a triumph or a failure for Chamberlain. In support of the quotation you might argue that Chamberlain received a hero's welcome in Britain and that many people in Britain were relieved that war no longer seemed likely. Chamberlain appeared to have settled Germany's legitimate grievances and maintained contacts and diplomacy. There is certainly evidence to support the view that at the time it seemed a triumph – even if Chamberlain had only bought time for rearmament. However, balanced against this must be set Germany's subsequent takeover of the rest of Czechoslovakia, Hitler's designs on Poland and the coming of war. It could be argued that the Munich agreement simply made Hitler more confident and that Chamberlain had been duped. Furthermore, some opinion in Britain had already turned against appeasement before Munich and Chamberlain has been accused of being short-sighted. You will need to come to your own decision and argue accordingly throughout your answer in order to provide a convincing conclusion.

Study Guide: A2 Question

In the style of Edexcel

'Inconsistent and ill-judged.' How far do you agree with this verdict on British foreign policy in the years 1930–6?

Exam tips

The cross-references are intended to take you straight to the material that will help you to answer the question.

The question requires you to reach two judgements: how far foreign policy was 'consistent' and how far, in the light of its consequences, the policy adopted was mistaken. You should deal with Britain's policy towards the League of Nations and to three main challengers to the status quo in the period: Japan, Italy and Germany.

You could argue for consistency in the policy of commitment to disarmament and to the appeasing of Germany. However, in the light of Abyssinian crisis (pages 60–3), how consistent was Britain's policy in relation to the League?

In dealing with 'ill-judged' be careful to appreciate the extent to which this is matter of debate – even in the case of the Abyssinian crisis, the outcome of which dealt a blow to collective security and to Britain's policy of disarmament. What is your overall judgement? You could choose to argue that foreign policy in the period 1935–6 was ill-judged but that the conclusion is more finely balanced for the earlier period (1930–4).

In the style of OCR B
Read the following extract about British armaments in the 1930s and then answer the questions that follow.

The question has been debated whether Hitler or the Allies gained the more in strength in the year that followed Munich. Many persons in Britain who knew our nakedness felt a sense of relief as each month our air force developed and the Hurricane and Spitfire types approached issue. The number of formed squadrons grew and the ack-ack guns multiplied. Also the general pressure of industrial preparation for war continued to quicken. But these improvements, invaluable though they seemed, were petty compared with the mighty advance in German armaments. As has been explained, munitions production on a nation-wide plan is a four years' task. The first year yields nothing, the second very little, the third a lot, and the fourth a flood. Hitler's Germany in this period was already in the third or fourth year of intense preparation under conditions of grip and drive which were almost the same as those of war. Britain, on the other hand, had only been moving on a non-emergency basis, with a weaker impulse and on a far smaller scale. In 1938–9 British military expenditure of all kinds reached £304 millions, and German was at least £1500 millions. It is probable that in this last year before the outbreak Germany manufactured at least double, and possibly treble, the munitions of Britain and France put together, and also that her great plants for tank production reached full capacity. They were therefore getting weapons at a far higher rate than we.

The subjugation of Czechoslovakia robbed the Allies of the Czech Army of twenty-one regular divisions, fifteen or sixteen second-line divisions already mobilised, and also their mountain fortress line, which in the days of Munich had required the deployment of thirty German divisions, or the main strength of the mobile and fully-trained German Army. According to Generals Halder and Jodl, there were but thirteen German divisions, of which only five were composed of first-line troops, left in the West at the time of the Munich arrangement. We certainly suffered a loss through the fall of Czechoslovakia equivalent to some thirty-five divisions. Besides this the Skoda works, the second most important arsenal in Central Europe, the production of which between August 1938 and September 1939 was in itself nearly equal to the actual output of British arms factories in that period, was made to change sides adversely. While all Germany was working under intense and almost war pressure, French labour had achieved as early as 1936 the long-desired forty-hours week.

Even more disastrous was the alteration in the relative strength of the French and German Armies. With every month that passed, from 1938 onwards, the German Army not only increased in numbers and formations and in the accumulation of reserves, but in quality and maturity. The advance in training and general proficiency kept pace with the ever-augmenting equipment. No similar improvements or expansion was open to the French Army. It was being overtaken along every path. In 1935 France, unaided by her previous allies, could have invaded and reoccupied Germany almost without serious fighting. In 1936 there could still be no doubt of her overwhelmingly superior strength. We now know, from the German revelations, that this continued in 1938, and it was the knowledge of their weakness which led the German High Command to do their utmost to restrain Hitler from every one of the successful strokes by which his fame was enhanced.

(a) What can you learn from this extract about the interpretations, approaches and methods of this historian? Refer to the extract and to your knowledge to support your answer.

(b) Some historians believe (like Churchill) that the Munich agreement favoured German rearmament. However, other historians are equally convinced that Britain and France benefited from avoiding war in September 1938. Explain how this debate has contributed to our understanding of appeasement. In your view, which side has provided the most convincing argument?

Exam tips

Part (a)

Knowledge and understanding

Your answer should display knowledge and understanding of the general international situation in the 1930s (particularly the situation in 1937–8) and should focus particularly on the Munich Conference and its results.

Knowledge and understanding of historians' approaches to assessing the success or failure of Munich – from a British perspective – should also be demonstrated and used to support your answer, e.g. to what extent did Munich benefit Germany or the Allies?

Understanding of interpretations

The key point of this interpretation is that it was written by Winston Churchill, who completed his history of the Second World War in 1948. Churchill held strong views about appeasement and about the Munich Conference during the 1930s and his views had not changed much when he came to write the volume on the causes of the war – *The Gathering Storm*. He believed that the Allies should have gone to war with Germany in 1938. What evidence does he use in the extract to support his argument?

Understanding of approaches/methods

People who are key participants in major events (like Churchill) often write their version of those events at a later period. Their versions often carry some weight. However, they (quite naturally) often try to justify their own actions and opinions and this can colour their version of events. Churchill was convinced that the Munich agreement was a mistake at the time and remained convinced thereafter. Show from the text how Churchill's approach led to what he wrote, in particular his basic conclusion that Munich was a terrible mistake (i.e. consider how far his approach influenced the conclusion that he reached).

Part (b)

Knowledge and understanding

You will need to display your knowledge and understanding of the military strengths and weaknesses of both sides in 1938 and the extent to which both sides benefited from the (one year) delay in war.

   You will also need to point out that the Munich Conference had other results, apart from further rearmament. Consideration of contemporary attitudes is important. Would Allied public opinion have supported war in 1938? Was Poland a (potentially) better ally in 1939 than Czechoslovakia would have been in 1938? What might the USSR have done in 1938?

Understanding of approaches/methods

It is worth pointing out that Munich was hotly debated at the time and has continued to be a major source of debate ever since. It is unlikely that there will ever be anything approaching consensus about the results of the Conference. Historians can only speculate about what would have happened *if* the Allies had gone to war with Hitler in 1938. Historians are rarely happy with '*ifs*'. Let's face it: no one really knows what would have happened '*if*'. But '*ifs*' often make for good historical debate – and that debate can suggest that one line of argument is better than another. Good answers should contrast the alternative approaches adopted in explaining appeasement: the role of structures versus the role of human agency. How have these been driven by the availability of the evidence (at the time and since)? Was appeasement traditional British foreign policy? Did appeasement drive or follow public opinion?

Evaluation of approaches/methods

What have historians learned from Churchill's approach and how has it contributed to our understanding? To what extent has it dominated the way appeasement has been written about? Have structuralist approaches enabled us to understand better the broader context in which the politicians of 1938 had to operate? What of recent emphases on the personal role of Chamberlain? You must decide which line of argument to support. Are you convinced by Churchill's argument that Munich was a mistake and the Allies would have been better fighting Hitler in 1938? Or do you support the view that the Allies benefited from the months of peace which followed Munich? What arguments/evidence draw you to one opinion rather than the other?

4 The Coming of War 1939

POINTS TO CONSIDER

This chapter should give you an understanding of the events that led Britain to declare war on Germany in September 1939. It should also enable you to assess the wisdom of appeasement and the statesmanship of Neville Chamberlain. As you read the chapter try to identify what Chamberlain could have done that was different. Should Britain have gone to war in 1939? To what extent was Chamberlain to blame for the Second World War? The chapter has been divided into the following themes:

- The uneasy peace, January–March 1939
- The end of Czechoslovakia
- The Polish guarantee
- The drift to war
- Anglo-Soviet relations
- The outbreak of war
- Interpreting British Foreign policy 1919–39

Key dates

1939	March	The end of Czechoslovakia
	March	British guarantee to Poland
	April	Britain introduced conscription
	May	The Pact of Steel between Germany and Italy
	August	The Nazi–Soviet Pact
	1 September	Germany invaded Poland
	3 September	Britain and France declared war on Germany

1 | The Uneasy Peace, January–March 1939

In early 1939 Chamberlain received disturbing (and incorrect) reports from British intelligence services predicting German moves against Poland, Czechoslovakia, the Ukraine, and even the Netherlands or Switzerland. In February the Cabinet agreed that a German attack on Holland or Switzerland would lead to a British declaration of war. Foreign Secretary Lord Halifax, who was beginning to emerge as a political force in his own right, thought clear limits should be placed on Germany's ambitions. While his views are sometimes seen as diverging from those of

Key question
Why did Hitler continue to pose a threat in early 1939?

Chamberlain, in reality his thinking was not very different. Neither man was prepared to give Hitler a totally free hand.

Britain and France

In the circumstances, Britain drew even closer to France. Both countries had common commitments to democracy and common fears about their own security. However, Anglo-French relations had been marked by years of mistrust. French politicians believed Britain might well leave them in the lurch and thought that Britain was not prepared to repeat the great 'effort of blood' made in the First World War.

Many British politicians were similarly suspicious of the French. Chamberlain thought that France 'never can keep a secret for more than half an hour – nor a government for more than nine months'. As late as November 1938 the Chiefs of Staff were opposed to conducting talks with France in too much detail for fear of being committed to a French war plan over which they had no control. In addition, there were fears that France might be losing the will to resist Germany. Some French politicians seemed prepared to accept German predominance in Eastern Europe. However, most were not. In 1938 pacifism had been the prevailing mood in France; but in 1939 the public mood swung in favour of resisting Nazi expansion. Most Frenchmen feared that if Hitler gobbled up more territory in the east, Germany might ultimately prove too strong in the west.

The French government was anxious to obtain firmer pledges of British support. In particular, it wanted Britain to commit itself to sending a large army to defend France. In February Chamberlain, accepting that in the event of war Britain would have to help France defend its territory, agreed to detailed military talks with the French. Britain also committed itself to raising an army of 32 divisions. This was a radical change in Britain's defence policy.

British rearmament

Key question
How successful were British rearmament efforts in 1938–9?

Chamberlain, unlike many of his left-wing critics, had favoured rearmament. After Munich he was more determined than ever that its pace should not slacken. The best policy, he thought, was 'to hope for the best but be prepared for the worst'. In his view the main purpose of rearmament was to deter Hitler.

Much of the increase in the number of aircraft in 1938–9 came from the maturing of plans which had been made in 1935. Rearmament had long been geared to reach its peak in 1939–40. But Britain's spending on rearmament rose considerably after October 1938. The production of aircraft increased from 240 a month in 1938 to 660 a month in September 1939. By the end of 1939 British aircraft production was expected to, and indeed did, overtake German production. This was partly because of increased emphasis on building fast fighter aircraft (Hurricanes and Spitfires) which were only a quarter of the cost of heavy bombers.

Britain's radar defences also improved. In September 1938 only the Thames estuary had radar. By September 1939, a radar chain ran from the Orkneys to the Isle of Wight. There was suddenly the real possibility that the German bomber would not always get through.

From 1936 to 1938 British intelligence had consistently exaggerated Germany's strength. However, after Munich it arrived at a more realistic assessment. Chamberlain was told that Germany faced a growing economic crisis and would not be able to risk, let alone sustain, a major war. In a long war of attrition, Britain and France's economic strength and the power of the naval blockade should ensure eventual victory.

By 1939, therefore, Chamberlain was much more confident of Britain's capacity to fight. As a result, he may have been prepared to take a firmer line than in 1938. But he still hoped for, and talked of, peace.

Table 4.1: Contemporary estimates of land forces 1938–9 (Divisions)

	January 1938	April 1939
Germany	81	120–130
Italy	73	85
France	100	100
Britain*	2	16
USSR	125	125
Czechoslovakia	34	–
Poland	40	40

* British forces available for the Continent.

Table 4.2: Contemporary estimates of air strengths 1935–9

Year	France	Germany	Britain	Italy	USSR
1935	1696	728	1020	1300	1700
1936	1010	650	1200	–	–
1937	1380	1233	1550	1350	–
1938	1454	3104	1606	1810	3280
1939	1792	3699	2075	1531	3361

Table 4.3: Contemporary estimates of naval strengths in 1939

	Capital ships	Aircraft carriers	Submarines
Germany	5	–	65
Italy	4	–	104
France	7	1	78
Britain	15	6	57
USSR	3	–	18
United States	15	5	87
Japan	9	5	60

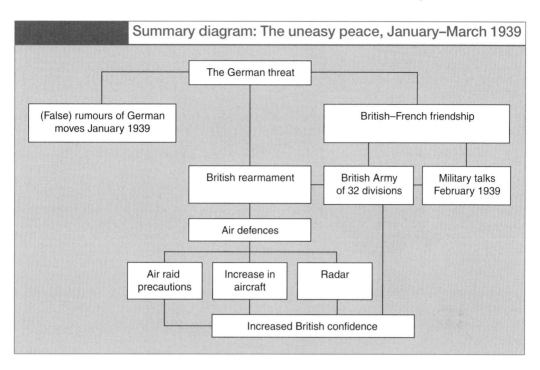

Summary diagram: The uneasy peace, January–March 1939

The German threat

(False) rumours of German moves January 1939

British–French friendship

British rearmament

British Army of 32 divisions

Military talks February 1939

Air defences

Air raid precautions

Increase in aircraft

Radar

Increased British confidence

2 | The End of Czechoslovakia

Key question
Why did the end of Czechoslovakia have such an impact on Chamberlain?

Key date

The end of Czechoslovakia: March 1939

Without its defences in the Sudetenland, Czechoslovakia was at Germany's mercy. It also faced serious internal problems. Many Slovaks had little love for what they saw as a Czech-dominated state. After Munich, Hitler encouraged the Slovaks to seek independence. Poland and Hungary also continued to lay claim to Czechoslovakian territory. By early March the situation was so bad, internally and externally, that President Hácha, who had replaced Beneš, proclaimed martial law. This desperate attempt to preserve Czechoslovakia's unity actually speeded its downfall. Hitler instructed the Slovak nationalist leaders to appeal to Germany for protection and to declare independence. At the same time Hungary issued an ultimatum demanding Ruthenia.

With his country falling apart, Hácha asked for a meeting with Hitler, hoping the German leader might do something to help Czechoslovakia. Hitler received Hácha on 15 March. He told him that the German army intended to enter the country in a few hours' time and that his only choice was war or a peaceable occupation. Hácha broke down under the threats. He signed a paper entrusting the fate of the Czech people to Hitler. On 15 March, German troops entered Czechoslovakia on the pretext that it was on the verge of civil war. Hitler established a German **protectorate** of Bohemia and Moravia. Slovakia was nominally independent, but under German protection. Hitler allowed Hungary to take Ruthenia.

Key term

Protectorate
A territory administered by another, usually much stronger state.

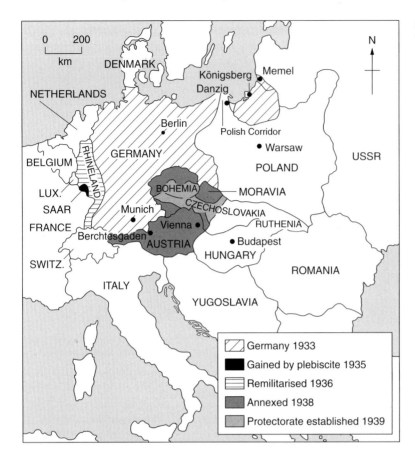

British reaction

Hitler's takeover of Czechoslovakia had important repercussions. He had clearly ignored the Munich agreement (pages 80–1), broken a signed agreement with Chamberlain and dismembered a small neighbour without warning or provocation. Moreover, this time he could not claim that he was uniting Germans within one German state. There was a sense of outrage in Britain as a whole and a marked shift of opinion in the Conservative Party and in the press. Most British people now felt that something must be done to stop Hitler before he controlled the whole of Europe.

Chamberlain's immediate pronouncement was mild. He made it clear that there was no question of going to war. Czechoslovakia had collapsed as a result of internal disruption which freed Britain from any obligation. His apparent 'soft' line angered many MPs, and he faced pressure from the press and even from within his own Cabinet to do or say something stronger. All this clearly had an effect on Chamberlain. He would certainly have had political problems if he had continued meekly to accept Hitler's latest action. However, arguably he did not simply cave in to public pressure. He was indignant himself at the turn of events and Hitler's total disregard of the Munich agreement. His anger and determination to resist further German aggression was made clear at a speech he made on 17 March:

Germany under her present regime has sprung a series of unpleasant surprises upon the world. The Rhineland, the Austrian *Anschluss*, the severance of the Sudetenland – all these things shocked and affronted public opinion throughout the world. Yet, however much we might take exception to the methods which were adopted in each of these cases, there was something to be said, whether on account of racial affinity or of just claims too long resisted, for the necessity of a change in the existing situation.

But the events which have taken place this week in complete disregard of the principles laid down by the German government itself seem to fall into a different category, and they must cause us all to be asking ourselves: 'Is this the end of an old adventure, or is it the beginning of a new? Is this the last attack upon a small state, or is it to be followed by others? Is this in fact, a step in the direction of an attempt to dominate the world by force? It is only six weeks ago that ... I pointed out that any demand to dominate the world by force was one which the democracies must resist ...

The next day Britain and France delivered sharp protests to Germany. Chamberlain told the Cabinet that his hopes of working with Hitler were over: 'No reliance could be placed on any of the assurances given by the Nazi leaders.'

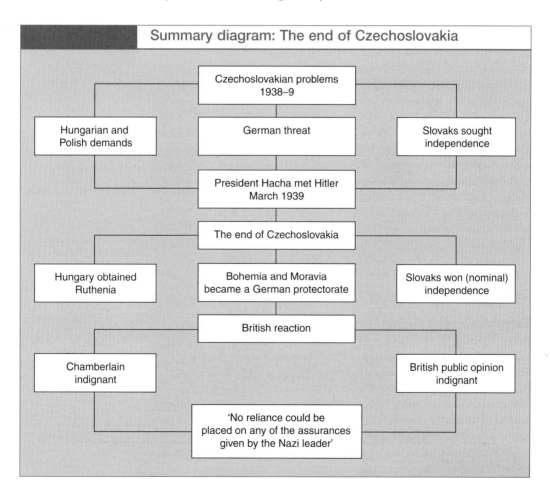

Summary diagram: The end of Czechoslovakia

Czechoslovakian problems 1938–9

Hungarian and Polish demands

German threat

Slovaks sought independence

President Hacha met Hitler March 1939

The end of Czechoslovakia

Hungary obtained Ruthenia

Bohemia and Moravia became a German protectorate

Slovaks won (nominal) independence

British reaction

Chamberlain indignant

British public opinion indignant

'No reliance could be placed on any of the assurances given by the Nazi leader'

3 | The Polish Guarantee

On 17 March there was a rumour that Germany was about to deliver an **ultimatum** to Romania. The effects of this – false – rumour were electric. On 20 March Chamberlain proposed that Britain, France, Poland and the USSR should issue a joint declaration that if there was a threat to the independence of any European state they would consult immediately on the steps to be taken. The British plan came to nothing. Poland had no wish to make any agreement with the USSR. Stalin was also reluctant to commit himself.

Memel

In March 1939 Hitler issued an ultimatum demanding that Memel, a town given to Lithuania after 1919, should be handed back to Germany. On 21 March Lithuania returned Memel. Britain and France took no action. It was inconceivable to think of going to war over Memel, a German city to which Hitler could lay reasonable claim. However, Poland now seemed to be Hitler's next target – and this was another matter.

Danzig and the Polish Corridor

There were some 800,000 Germans in Poland. The Polish Corridor divided East Prussia from the rest of Germany. Danzig was 96 per cent German, and, although nominally a Free City under the supervision of the League of Nations, had been run by the Nazis since 1934. However, Poland controlled Danzig's trade and foreign relations. This was an unsatisfactory arrangement, liable to create friction even with goodwill on all sides. No German government, whatever its political complexion, was likely to accept the Danzig solution as permanent, and Hitler's government was no exception. Polish governments were equally determined that things should remain as they were. The loss of Danzig to Germany might well compromise the rest of the gains Poland had made from Germany in 1919.

Nevertheless, German relations with Poland had been remarkably friendly since the signing of the German–Polish non-aggression treaty in 1934 (page 58). On a number of occasions Germany had suggested to the Poles that the agreement might be turned into an alliance against the USSR, but the Poles did not take up these suggestions.

German threats 1938–9

After Munich, Hitler assumed that Poland would be drawn into the German orbit. In October 1938 German Foreign Minister Ribbentrop asked the Poles to give up Danzig. In return Poland would receive guarantees of its borders, German friendship and the prospect of territory in the Ukraine. In January 1939 Hitler met Colonel Beck, the Polish Foreign Minister, and added a demand for a German-controlled road or rail link across the Polish Corridor. To Hitler's surprise, the Poles, fearful of becoming a German **satellite**, refused to consider these suggestions.

Key question
Why was Poland a problem in 1938–9?

Key date

British guarantee to Poland: March 1939

Key terms

Ultimatum
A final offer or demand.

Satellite
A country that is subordinate to another.

German demands now became more insistent. In secret Hitler admitted that he was not simply after Danzig. The whole question of living space in the east was at stake. He was quite prepared to compel Poland, by force if necessary, to come within the German sphere of influence. However, at this stage he hoped for a diplomatic rather than a military triumph.

Tension mounted. Poland declared that any German attempt to alter Danzig's status would lead to war. By the end of March there were rumours that a German attack on Poland was imminent. Britain and France feared that Poland might be overrun unless they came to her support.

Key question
Was Chamberlain wise to offer the Polish guarantee?

Key terms

Anti-Semitic
Anti-Jewish.

Blank cheques
In diplomatic terms, it means complete freedom to act as one thinks best.

The guarantee

On 31 March Britain took the unprecedented step of offering a guarantee to Poland: if it were the victim of an unprovoked attack, Britain would come to its aid. France offered a similar guarantee. The Polish government accepted both offers.

The Polish guarantee was condemned by a few at the time and by many since. Of all the East European states, Poland, a right-wing military dictatorship and very **anti-Semitic**, was probably the one that Britain liked least. In fact, until 1939 Poland had few friends, except for Germany:

- Poland had distanced itself from the League of Nations.
- It had accepted Japanese and Italian expansion.
- It had won territory from Czechoslovakia in 1938–9.
- Beck was considered totally untrustworthy.

Hitler's demands – Danzig and access across the Polish Corridor – were far more reasonable than his demands of Czechoslovakia in 1938. Many historians regard the guarantees as '**blank cheques**' given to a country notorious for its reckless diplomacy. Moreover, in the last resort, the 'cheques' were worthless because there was little that Britain or France could do to support Poland. In the event of war France intended to defend the Maginot Line, not attack Germany. Britain had no large army and no plans to bomb German cities: to do so would simply invite German retaliation.

Support for the Polish guarantee

In defence of Chamberlain's change of policy, there was a feeling in political circles in Britain that something had to be seen to be done. The Polish guarantee was designed as a clear warning to Hitler. If he continued to push for German expansion, he would face the prospect of a two-front war. Poland was seen as a useful ally, possibly stronger than the USSR, whom it had defeated in war in 1920–1, and certainly more reliable.

Moreover, Chamberlain did not see the guarantee as a total commitment to Poland. There was a let-out clause. Britain had guaranteed Polish independence, not its territorial integrity. The future of Danzig was still thought to be negotiable. In Chamberlain's mind it was still a question of discovering the right mix of diplomacy and strength to persuade Hitler to negotiate honestly and constructively. The guarantee was intended to display British resolve and to deter Hitler from further aggression.

Unfortunately the guarantee angered, rather than deterred Hitler. He abandoned any thought of accommodation with Poland. At the end of March he ordered his Chief of Staff to prepare for war with Poland by the end of August.

Summary diagram: The Polish guarantee

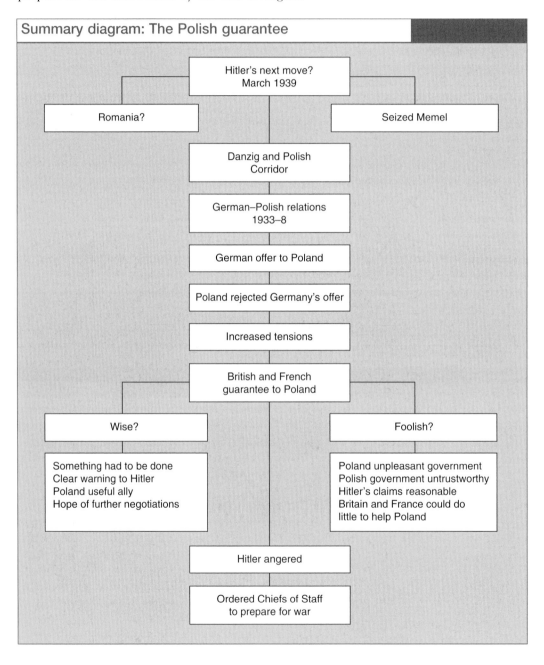

4 | The Drift to War

Mussolini's actions

Key question
Why did Italy become a threat in 1939?

Mussolini was almost as disturbed as Chamberlain by the German occupation of Czechoslovakia. Hitler had left him ignorant of his intentions and this was a blow to the Italian dictator's pride. Determined not to be outdone, Mussolini embarked on his own foreign policy initiative. In April 1939 Italian forces occupied Albania, an Italian satellite in all but name since 1936. He also announced that the Balkans and the eastern Mediterranean should be regarded as being within the Italian sphere of influence.

This was a definite breach of the 1938 Anglo-Italian agreement. However, Britain had no wish to drive Mussolini into complete co-operation with Hitler. Chamberlain hoped that the Italian leader might exert a restraining influence on his German counterpart. Nevertheless Mussolini's aggressive words and

Key dates

Britain introduced conscription: April 1939

The Pact of Steel between Germany and Italy: May 1939

'An Old Story Retold.' Hitler: 'It's all right; you know the proverb – "Barking dogs don't bite"?' Mussolini: 'Oh yes, *I* know it, and *you* know it; but does the dog know it?' A cartoon from *Punch*, 5 April 1939. What point is the cartoonist trying to make?

actions, coming only three weeks after the takeover of Czechoslovakia, seemed to:

- indicate a greater degree of co-operation between Germany and Italy than was actually the case
- pose a further threat to East European stability.

Britain and France now issued guarantees to Greece and Romania in the same terms as those given to Poland. In little more than two weeks Britain and France had undertaken obligations stretching from the Baltic to the Mediterranean.

Hitler was pleased by Mussolini's action. Italy's Balkan ambitions might well preoccupy Britain and France while he settled the Polish question. It was a further bonus when Mussolini, to Hitler's surprise, proposed a close military alliance, which was signed in May in Berlin. The 'Pact of Steel' required each power to help the other in the event of war. This indicated that there was little hope of detaching Mussolini from Hitler as part of the strategy for containing Germany.

The mood in Britain

Most people in Britain now favoured standing firm against the dictators. There were demands for faster rearmament, alliance with the USSR, a broadening of the National Government and the inclusion in it of Winston Churchill, who was seen as a consistently strong opponent of Hitler. Chamberlain was aware of the pressure from his own party, and from the country at large. At the end of March his government announced the doubling of the **territorial army**. In April conscription was introduced for the first time in peacetime.

Territorial army
Britain's voluntary military force.

Key term

Hitler's actions

Hitler used the announcement of the introduction of conscription in Britain to repudiate the Anglo-German Naval Agreement of 1935 (page 58). He emphasised his desire for friendship with Britain, but he insisted that, just as he did not interfere in British policy in Palestine and elsewhere, so Britain had no right to interfere with German policy in its sphere of influence.

Key question
Why did Anglo-German relations deteriorate in the spring and summer of 1939?

In May Hitler told his generals he intended to attack Poland 'at the first available opportunity' but that he was still hopeful of detaching Britain and France from Poland and thus averting a major war. Meanwhile German diplomats worked hard and with some success to secure support from (or improve relations with) a host of countries including Sweden, Denmark, Latvia, Estonia, Hungary, Yugoslavia, Romania, Bulgaria and Finland.

As the summer wore on there was increasing tension over Danzig. The Germans claimed that the British guarantee resulted in Poland refusing reasonable terms. They also accused Poland of launching a reign of terror against the German minority in Poland. These stories, although exaggerated, had a foundation of truth.

The Polish government continued to make it clear that it had no intention of giving in to Hitler. Most Poles believed that if they stood firm they could call Hitler's bluff. They had no wish to go the way of Austria and Czechoslovakia.

Chamberlain's position

Everything now depended on Hitler. There was little Chamberlain could do beyond stressing Britain's determination to stand by its new commitments. However, he had not given up all hope of peace. He still thought there was a chance that Hitler would come to see that nothing would be gained by force which might not be gained by negotiation. Even so, Britain and France spent much of the summer co-ordinating their military preparations. It was evident to most people, including Chamberlain, that Britain might well be drawn into war over Poland.

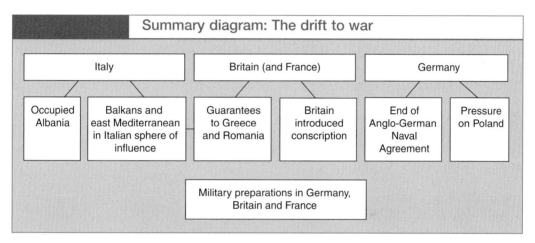

Summary diagram: The drift to war

Italy		Britain (and France)		Germany	
Occupied Albania	Balkans and east Mediterranean in Italian sphere of influence	Guarantees to Greece and Romania	Britain introduced conscription	End of Anglo-German Naval Agreement	Pressure on Poland

Military preparations in Germany, Britain and France

Key question
Why did Britain fail to reach agreement with the USSR?

5 | Anglo-Soviet Relations

A big question still remained: how could Britain and France actually help Poland if Germany attacked it? Only the USSR could offer Poland immediate military help. Most French and many British politicians, especially those on the left, thought the only sensible course of action was to forge an alliance with the USSR.

Anglo-Soviet relations 1931–8

For most of the 1920s and 1930s British governments, dominated by the Conservatives, had shown no wish to reach an agreement, or even establish much contact, with the USSR. Both as a state and as the centre of an international revolutionary movement, the USSR was seen as a threat to traditional British values and interests. Indeed many Conservatives considered communism a more serious threat than fascism, and regarded Nazi Germany as a useful bulwark against the threat of Soviet expansion.

In 1935, faced with the threat of Hitler, the USSR:

- abandoned its opposition to the League of Nations and became a supporter of the principle of collective security
- signed defence pacts with France and Czechoslovakia and suggested high-level talks between Soviet and British diplomats.

However, the USSR failed to weld a powerful alliance capable of deterring Nazi aggression. After 1935 neither France nor the USSR made any real efforts to strengthen the defence pact. The USSR had its own internal problems, while France had no wish to anger Britain, Italy and Poland, all of whom disapproved of the Franco-Soviet agreement.

The British government continued to oppose any alliance with the USSR. Many Conservatives were angered by the fact that Stalin gave support to the Republicans in the Spanish Civil War (see page 65), and some preferred a compromise deal with Germany to co-operation with the USSR. Both Baldwin and Chamberlain suspected that the real aim of Soviet policy was to embroil Britain and France in a war against Germany and Italy, a war from which the USSR was likely to reap the most benefit.

Little effort was made to secure Soviet co-operation in 1938. The USSR's appeal for an international conference immediately after the *Anschluss* was dismissed as premature by the British Foreign Office. Soviet approaches to Britain and France during the Czechoslovakian crisis were ignored. Stalin was not invited to attend the Munich Conference.

Chamberlain's policy in 1939

In 1939 Chamberlain still had no desire to ally with the USSR. He distrusted Stalin and feared and hated the Soviet state and system. In March he declared:

Key question
Why was Chamberlain not keen to ally with the USSR?

> I must confess to the most profound distrust of Russia. I have no belief in her ability to maintain an effective offensive, even if she wanted to. And I distrust her motives, which seem to me to have little connection with our ideas of liberty and to be concerned only with getting everyone else by the ears.

In Chamberlain's view, there were many good reasons for not allying with the USSR. He believed that a policy of 'encirclement' of Germany, as in 1914, could be counterproductive. It might lead to, rather than prevent, war. British intelligence reported that, after Stalin's purges, Soviet forces were of little military value. Eighty per cent of all Soviet senior army officers had been killed or imprisoned. It was also likely that a Soviet agreement might alienate those East European countries that Britain was trying to win over. These states had no wish to reach agreement with the USSR, particularly if that agreement involved Soviet troops occupying their soil. They feared, with some justification, that once Soviet troops were there, it would be difficult to remove them. There was the added risk that an Anglo-Russian alliance might drive Spain and Japan into the arms of Hitler.

British public opinion

In 1939 Stalin had a far worse record of terror and mass murder than Hitler. However, Stalin's terror was concealed, ignored or even justified by many on the left who ideologically preferred communism to fascism. Even those who viewed fascism and communism with equal distaste were more worried by Hitler's Germany than Stalin's Russia.

Therefore, Chamberlain found himself at odds with public opinion in Britain. Most people supported some kind of deal with the USSR. This is evident from a number of opinion polls carried out at the time (see Table 4.4).

Table 4.4: British opinion polls 1938–9

If there was a war between Germany and Russia, which side would you rather see win? (December 1938)

- Germany 15%
- Russia 85%
- No opinion 10%

If you had to choose between Fascism and Communism which side would you choose? (January 1939)

- Fascism 26%
- Communism 74%
- No answer 16%

Would you like to see Great Britain and Soviet Russia being more friendly to each other? (March 1939)

- Yes 84%
- No 7%
- No opinion 9%

Are you in favour of a military alliance between Great Britain, France and Russia? (June 1939)

- Yes 84%
- No 9%
- No opinion 7%

Chamberlain was under pressure from France, from the press, from Parliament and even from within his Cabinet, to establish closer relations with the USSR. Lloyd George, in a speech in May 1939, reflected the views of many:

> The Polish army is a brave one, but in no way comparable to Germany's. If we are going in without the help of Russia, we are walking into a trap. It is the only country whose armies can get there. If Russia is not being brought into the matter because the Poles feel that they do not want them there, it is for us to declare the conditions, and unless the Poles are prepared to accept the only conditions with which we can successfully help them, the responsibility must be theirs … Without Russia, these three guarantees of help to Poland, Rumania and Greece, are the most reckless commitments that any country has ever entered into. It is madness.

Anglo-Soviet negotiations 1939

In late April 1939 Chamberlain finally agreed to negotiations with the USSR. He did so without much conviction. He still saw Hitler and Stalin as much-of-a-muchness and disliked being forced to choose between them. His main aims seem to have been to placate opposition at home and to use the possibility of an Anglo-Soviet alliance as a further warning to Hitler.

Stalin's own thinking in 1939 remains a matter of guesswork. On the surface his position was serious. Hitler was a sworn enemy of Bolshevism and Japan was a threat to the USSR in Asia. Therefore, Stalin faced a two-front war. He also feared that Hitler's eastwards expansion was being encouraged by Britain and France. This had never been Chamberlain's policy, although, in the interests of his country, perhaps it should have been. Indeed from March 1939 Chamberlain, far from deliberately encouraging Hitler to move eastwards, as many on the left then and later charged him with, was actually committed to stopping him.

Chamberlain's policy gave Stalin some room for manoeuvre. He could afford to press for favourable terms from Britain and France, and also to throw out feelers to Germany about a possible deal. He made it clear in a speech in March 1939 that dealing with a fascist regime was no more repugnant than dealing with liberal-democratic states. He was in a position to keep his options open and see who would make the best offer.

The Anglo-Soviet discussions, starting in late April and continuing throughout the summer, were complex and slow. British negotiators refused Soviet proposals, submitted counterproposals, which were unacceptable to the Soviets, and then generally ended up accepting the USSR's first proposals. Halifax was invited to Moscow but he declined the invitation. Chamberlain did virtually nothing. He placed little value on the outcome of the negotiations and admitted in private that he would not mind much if they broke down.

The British–French military mission

A British and French military mission, which travelled by boat and train, rather than plane, finally arrived in Moscow in early August. The British team was led by Admiral Reginald Aylmer Ranfurly Pluckett-Ernle-Erle-Drax, a man whose name was more impressive than his importance. While the French had instructions to secure the signing of a military convention in the minimum of time, British representatives had been instructed to go 'very slowly'.

The talks got nowhere. The Western powers, not eager to trust the Soviet general staff with secret military plans, tried to restrict the discussions to general principles rather than precise plans. The talks deadlocked when the Soviets asked whether Poland would accept the entry of Soviet troops before the event of a German attack. The Poles, deeply suspicious of Soviet intentions, would not budge on this issue. 'We have no military agreement with the Russians', said Beck. 'We do not wish to have one.' Chamberlain sympathised with Poland, and did not see why the presence of Soviet troops in Poland should be necessary or desirable.

Key question
Why did Hitler and Stalin sign the Nazi–Soviet Pact?

Key date

The Nazi–Soviet Pact: August 1939

The Nazi–Soviet Pact

The Soviet government maintained that it was the attitude of the Western powers to the question of the entry of Soviet troops into Poland which convinced them that Britain and France were not in earnest in their negotiations. However, it is equally possible that the military discussions were a shameless deception, that the Soviets simply made a series of demands that they knew Britain and France could not accept, and that Stalin, courted by Germany, had no wish for an alliance with the West.

From 1933 the USSR had occasionally made approaches to Germany suggesting the need for improved relations. The Nazis had rebuffed each of these initiatives. The idea of a Nazi–Soviet agreement made no sense at all in ideological terms. However, in 1939 Hitler realised that a deal with Stalin would very much strengthen his position, at least in the short term. In January

RENDEZVOUS

'The scum of the earth, I believe?', 'The bloody assassin of the workers, I presume?' A cartoon by David Low published in the *Evening Standard*, 20 September 1939. What is the message of the cartoon? What is the significance of the figure on the floor?

1939, therefore, German diplomats began to make overtures to the USSR.

The Soviet response was favourable and German–Soviet talks began. In mid-August, with his planned invasion of Poland less than a week away, Hitler sent a personal message to Stalin asking if Ribbentrop, the German Foreign Minister, could visit Moscow. Stalin reacted favourably. Accordingly, Ribbentrop flew to Moscow and on 23 August signed the Nazi–Soviet non-aggression pact. Secret clauses of the pact divided Poland and Eastern Europe into spheres of German and Soviet influence.

News of the Nazi–Soviet Pact came as a bombshell in London. Most experts had dismissed as unthinkable the idea that the great ideological enemies could reach agreement.

Was Chamberlain to blame for the Nazi–Soviet Pact?

Much criticism has been levelled at Chamberlain for his failure to secure a Soviet alliance. Certainly he had little enthusiasm for the Grand Alliance of Poland, the USSR, France and Britain envisaged by Churchill. However, such an alliance was probably beyond even the most skilled British statesman. Poland was not interested in a Soviet alliance and it appears that the Soviets had no wish for an alliance with the Western powers. Stalin had no love of Britain or France. The only thing the West had to offer him was the prospect of immediate war, a war in which the USSR would do most of the fighting. Hitler, by contrast, offered peace and territory. No British government could have matched the German offer: Soviet supremacy over the Baltic States and eastern Poland. From Stalin's point of view the Nazi–Soviet Pact seemed to best protect Soviet interests, at least in the short term.

The Nazi–Soviet Pact was a decisive event. When Hitler heard news of its signing over dinner he banged the table in delight and shouted, 'I have them!' He realised that Poland could not now be defended and thought that Britain and France would realise the same. The way was open for the German attack on Poland, planned to start at 4.30a.m. on 26 August.

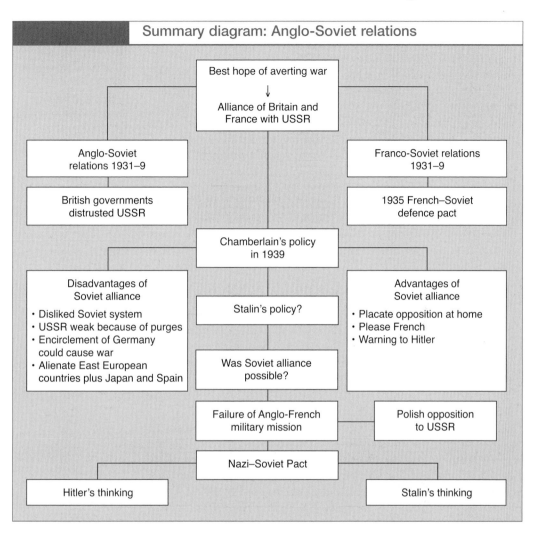

Summary diagram: Anglo-Soviet relations

Best hope of averting war
↓
Alliance of Britain and France with USSR

Anglo-Soviet relations 1931–9

Franco-Soviet relations 1931–9

British governments distrusted USSR

1935 French–Soviet defence pact

Chamberlain's policy in 1939

Disadvantages of Soviet alliance
• Disliked Soviet system
• USSR weak because of purges
• Encirclement of Germany could cause war
• Alienate East European countries plus Japan and Spain

Stalin's policy?

Advantages of Soviet alliance
• Placate opposition at home
• Please French
• Warning to Hitler

Was Soviet alliance possible?

Failure of Anglo-French military mission

Polish opposition to USSR

Nazi–Soviet Pact

Hitler's thinking

Stalin's thinking

6 | The Outbreak of War

Key question
Was war inevitable after the Nazi–Soviet Pact?

War on two fronts
From Germany's point of view, this meant a war in the east (against Poland) and a war in the west (against France and Britain).

Hitler was prepared to gamble on, but still did not expect or want a **war on two fronts**. He thought the British and French leaders were 'little worms' who would find a way to wriggle out of their commitments to Poland. However, Chamberlain had no intention of abandoning Poland. The Nazi–Soviet Pact did not unduly worry him. He believed that Britain, France and Poland were strong enough to deter Hitler. Nor could he have made his intentions much clearer. On 22 August he sent a personal letter to Hitler stating explicitly that Britain would fight if Germany attacked Poland. On 25 August Britain and Poland signed a treaty of alliance. French politicians also made it clear that France would stand firm.

Attempts to prevent war

Hitler, surprised by the Anglo-French determination, was also shaken by Mussolini's announcement that Italy intended to remain neutral, despite the Pact of Steel. The German leader thus decided to postpone his invasion for five or six days, hoping in the meantime to detach the Western powers from Poland. He made an extraordinary proposal to Britain. If Britain gave Germany a free hand in Danzig and the Corridor, he would guarantee the British Empire and try to reach agreement on disarmament. Chamberlain's government saw this overture more as a ploy to divide Britain from France and Poland than as a serious basis for negotiation. By now Hitler had regained his nerve. He ordered the attack on Poland to begin on 1 September.

There were flurries of last-minute diplomatic activity. On 29 August Hitler demanded that a Polish **plenipotentiary** be sent to Berlin on 30 August to receive the German terms relating to Danzig and the Polish Corridor. Perhaps this proposal was expected to be taken seriously; but perhaps it was intended to drive a wedge between Britain and Poland by demonstrating German reasonableness. Lord Halifax believed that the terms were not unreasonable but that the German timescale – 24 hours – certainly was. The Polish government decided not to comply with the German demands.

Key dates

Germany invaded Poland: 1 September 1939

Britain and France declared war on Germany: 3 September 1939

Key term

Plenipotentiary
A special ambassador or envoy with full powers to negotiate.

The invasion of Poland

On 31 August Mussolini proposed that a conference should meet to try to resolve the Polish crisis. This sounded ominously like a second Munich. However, this time Mussolini's proposal came too late. That same evening Germany claimed that one of its wireless stations near the Polish border had been attacked by Poles. This claim, which was totally fabricated, was used as the excuse for war. At 4.45a.m. on 1 September German troops invaded Poland and German planes bombed Warsaw.

Chamberlain's response

Chamberlain was ready to honour Britain's commitment to Poland but hoped there might be a last-minute reprieve. Mussolini persisted with his conference proposal and Bonnet, the French Foreign Minister, was enthusiastic. However, Britain insisted that a condition for such a conference was withdrawal of German troops from Poland. If Germany did not suspend hostilities, Britain warned Germany that it would fight. But on 2 September – a day and a half after the German attack – Britain still had not declared war or even sent an ultimatum to Germany. The reason for this delay was Chamberlain's wish to keep in step with the French who were anxious to complete their general mobilisation process before declaring war. However, it seemed to many British politicians as though the Prime Minister was trying to evade his commitments.

On 2 September Chamberlain told the Commons that he was prepared to forget everything that had happened if Germany

agreed to withdraw its forces from Poland. He made no mention
of an ultimatum to Germany. This did not satisfy his critics. Both
Labour and Conservative MPs made clear their opinion that war
must be declared at once. At a Cabinet meeting later that evening
Chamberlain accepted the inevitable. At 9.00a.m. on 3 September
Britain finally delivered an ultimatum to Germany. Germany
made no reply and at 11.00a.m. Britain declared war. France
followed suit and declared war at 5.00p.m. Britain's declaration of
war automatically brought in India and the colonies. The
Dominions were free to decide for themselves, but within one
week Australia, New Zealand, South Africa and Canada had all
declared war on Germany.

British support for the war

Chamberlain had been forced into a war that he and the British
public had always wanted to avoid. However, in September 1939
most people in Britain seem to have accepted the necessity for
war. At the end of September a Gallup Poll asked Britons whether
they were in favour of 'fighting until Hitlerism was done away
with'. The wording of the question might have been ambiguous,
but there seems little doubt about the resolve of the British
public: 89 per cent of those asked said they supported waging war
against 'Hitlerism'.

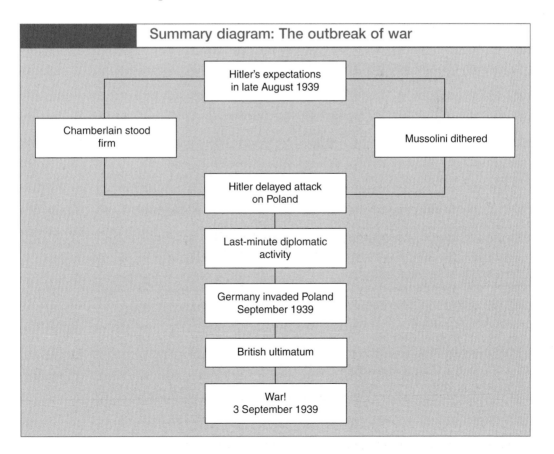

Summary diagram: The outbreak of war

Hitler's expectations in late August 1939

Chamberlain stood firm

Mussolini dithered

Hitler delayed attack on Poland

Last-minute diplomatic activity

Germany invaded Poland September 1939

British ultimatum

War! 3 September 1939

7 | Key Debate

To what extent was Chamberlain a 'guilty man'?

The case against Chamberlain

For many years after 1939 Chamberlain was criticised as one of the main 'guilty men' who had failed to stand up to Hitler. The views of Churchill carried great weight and shaped much historical thinking. Churchill thought the Second World War 'unnecessary' and subtitled his book, *The Gathering Storm*, 'How the English-speaking peoples through their unwisdom, carelessness and good nature allowed the wicked to rearm'. In consequence, Chamberlain has often been depicted as one of the great 'losers' of modern British history – a rather pathetic old man whose policies helped to cause the Second World War. The criticisms of Chamberlain are many, varied and conflicting.

The main criticism of Chamberlain is that his efforts to appease Hitler made little sense. Hitler made no secret of his aim to dominate Europe and the world. He was a ruthless tyrant who was prepared to use war to achieve his ends. In consequence the only correct policy was to stand firm against him. Appeasement simply whetted his appetite and encouraged him to make fresh demands. With each surrender Germany grew stronger and more dangerous.

Some historians blame Chamberlain not for his policy of appeasement, but for his failure to stand by it to the end. They see his policy falling between two stools, with the result that Britain stumbled into a disastrous war against Germany, a war which Britain should have avoided at all costs. Chamberlain is particularly criticised for allying with Poland. Arguably Britain had no moral obligation or self-evident interest to fight a major war over Poland. In 1939 the Germans had a reasonable case. Annexation of Poland would not necessarily have strengthened Germany. It would simply have brought it face to face with the USSR.

It has also been argued that Chamberlain should have allowed – even encouraged – Hitler to expand eastwards, and thus ultimately to fight the USSR. It is true that Britain and France might have been in danger if Germany had defeated the USSR; Hitler could have followed a Soviet victory by an attack on France. But would Hitler have beaten the USSR? And if he had done so, would this have strengthened or weakened Germany? It is possible to claim that Britain had little to lose and much to gain from a German–Soviet war.

More recently historian R.A.C. Parker has suggested that Chamberlain did have alternative choices other than to appease or go to war. Parker argues that Chamberlain might have 'tried to build a barrier to Hitler's expansion', through seeking closer ties with France and other European countries, sooner than March 1939.

In the end the main indictment against Chamberlain is that he failed. In September 1939 Britain was forced into war – a war in which it had little to gain and everything to lose. Chamberlain himself admitted that everything he had hoped for and believed in had 'crashed in ruins'.

The case for Chamberlain

Over the past three decades historians have tended to view Chamberlain more sympathetically. Most of the charges against him can be answered and much can be said in his defence.

Appeasement was a logical policy to follow both before and after 1937. The policy of avoiding confrontation by negotiation and concession was a deep-rooted British tradition (and remains a fundamental purpose of diplomacy today). Chamberlain saw appeasement not as surrender but as a positive effort to achieve a settlement of all the difficult issues which had plagued Europe since 1919. Like many people in Britain, he felt that Germany had some legitimate grievances. Justice did not become injustice because it was demanded by a dictator.

Moreover, he realised that the only alternative to appeasement was war – a war for which Britain was woefully unprepared and which it might not win. Britain had little to gain from even a successful war. As many as 750,000 British lives had been lost in the First World War. Another conflict might well result in an even greater loss of life. It would also be ruinously expensive and seriously damage Britain's economic position.

Chamberlain had few illusions about Hitler. He feared his ambition and unpredictability. However, he realised that he was not in a position to get rid of the German leader and thus had little alternative but to work with him. He hoped that active diplomacy could reduce the threat of war.

Unfortunately Chamberlain's policies failed. However, the situation in September 1939 might have been worse. Britain and France were firmly allied and stronger than in 1938. They had more tanks and troops than Germany and would soon have more planes. Their economic strength was much greater. They also had what seemed like a useful ally in Poland, who they hoped might keep Germany occupied until at least the spring of 1940. In 1939, Hitler was isolated. Both Italy and Japan were not prepared (as yet) to risk war with Britain. The British people and the Dominions were united in favour of war in a way that seemed inconceivable in 1938. Most people felt the time had come to resist German expansion. Every effort had been made to satisfy German grievances, but Hitler had proved that he could not be trusted. Enough was enough. To do nothing was simply to put off the evil hour. The French government and most French people reached the same conclusion.

Most recent historians see Chamberlain as a helpless rather than a 'guilty' man. He thought of himself as a typical Englishman, upright and honourable, a man of brains and common sense. Perhaps his estimate of himself was not so far wrong. Appeasement seems more sensible now than it did a generation ago: it was certainly not a policy of shameful cowardice. Chamberlain believed that appeasement's chances of success were good enough to warrant giving it every opportunity. The fact that it failed does not mean that it was not worth attempting.

In reality, the ambitions of Hitler, and not the mistakes of Chamberlain, were responsible for the outbreak of war. Hitler's willingness to take risks for ever higher stakes resulted in Europe stumbling from crisis to crisis in 1938–9. This built up an almost irresistible pressure for war by 1939. If Britain and France were not prepared to accept German domination of Eastern Europe, then he was ready to fight them. There was nothing accidental about his attack on Poland. He hoped the Western powers would not join in, but he was prepared to take that risk.

Some key books in the debate

J. Charmley, *Chamberlain and the Lost Peace* (Hodder & Stoughton, 1984).

F. McDonough, *Neville Chamberlain, Appeasement and the British Road to War* (Manchester University Press, 1998).

R.A.C. Parker, *Chamberlain and Appeasement: British Policy and the Coming of the Second World War* (Macmillan, 1993).

W.R. Rock, *British Appeasement in the 1930s* (Edward Arnold, 1977).

Summary diagram: Neville Chamberlain

The case against Chamberlain	The case for Chamberlain
1. He tried to appease an unappeasable Hitler. Appeasement simply encouraged Hitler to make new demands	1. Appeasement was logical. Germany had legitimate grievances. The only alternative was war (for which Britain was unprepared)
2. Weak and indecisive	2. Strong, successful politician
3. Little diplomatic experience: easily duped	3. Well-informed on foreign matters. Did not trust Hitler or Mussolini
4. Autocratic, pig-headed. Surrounded by 'yes' men and refused to listen to critics, e.g. Churchill and the Labour Party	4. Prepared to change his policies and listen to views different to his own. His critics were not worth listening to: Churchill was a war-monger; the Labour Party (irrationally) favoured war and disarmament
5. Conducted foreign policy on his own, ignoring advice of the Foreign Office, his Cabinet and Parliament	5. Chamberlain's foreign policy was in line with the views of the Foreign Office, his Cabinet and Parliament
6. Munich – a disaster: sacrificed Czechoslovakia; Britain and its allies were better prepared for war in 1938 than 1939	6. Munich – a triumph: averted war; Britain and her allies were better prepared in 1939 than 1938
7. Failed to ensure Britain rearmed	7. Did more than anyone to ensure Britain was ready for war
8. Failed to build a 'Grand Alliance' with the USSR and the USA	8. A 'Grand Alliance' was impossible. The USSR could not be trusted and the USA had no interest in an alliance
9. His policy fell between two stools: • he should not have abandoned appeasement and allied with Poland in 1939 • he should have encouraged Hitler to go eastwards – against Russia	9. He had to stand firm in 1939: • the aim of the Polish alliance was to deter Hitler, not bring about war • if Germany defeated Poland (and Russia) it would dominate Europe and threaten Britain

8 | Interpreting British Foreign Policy 1919–39

Key question
To what extent were British statesmen to blame for the outbreak of the Second World War?

Most historians have been critical of the conduct of British foreign policy in the inter-war period. This is not too surprising. In 1919 Britain emerged victoriously from the First World War. Yet only 20 years later, it found itself engaged in a Second World War. By the time this war ended in 1945 Britain was no longer the great superpower it had appeared to be in 1919. It seems obvious that British governments must be held responsible.

Historians have tended to criticise successive governments for some or all of the following reasons:

- for failing to face up to the evil personified by Hitler
- for not rearming sufficiently
- for failing to ally with the USA or the USSR
- for allowing Germany to become a threat to world peace.

The prime ministers of the 1930s – Ramsay MacDonald, Stanley Baldwin and Neville Chamberlain – have been particularly blamed.

However, it is possible to question the extent to which inter-war statesmen in general, and MacDonald, Baldwin and Chamberlain in particular, should be blamed for adopting misguided policies. Several issues are of crucial importance in considering collective or individual culpability, not least:

- To what extent did Britain have the power to be able to influence world events?
- What alternatives were open to Britain, especially in the 1930s?
- Should Britain have gone to war in 1939?

How great was Great Britain?

In 1939 few doubted that Britain was still a great power. Although Hitler was prepared to risk war against Britain, he hoped until the very end to avert such a conflict. Britain controlled a massive Empire, had the world's strongest navy, and was the world's greatest trading nation. However, Britain was not as 'great' as some politicians at the time imagined. Britain's power needs to be seen in relation to that of other countries:

- By the 1930s the USSR, Germany and France all had far larger and stronger armies than Britain.
- The USA and Japan had powerful navies.
- The USA was stronger economically than Britain.
- Germany produced more coal, iron and steel.
- Stalin's **Five-Year Plans** led to a great increase in Soviet industrial production.
- The USA, the USSR and Germany had much larger populations.

Five-Year Plans
In the late 1920s Stalin embarked on ambitious efforts to make the USSR a major industrial power. Every industry had a five-year target.

Key term

Key question
To what extent did the Empire contribute to Britain's strength?

The British Empire

The British Empire gave Britain the appearance of being a great world power, covering nearly one-quarter of the earth's land surface at its peak in 1932. However, the Empire was not as strong as many Britons imagined:

- By 1931 the most developed parts of the Empire – the 'white' Dominions – were effectively independent. This meant that Britain could no longer take their support for granted. Many Afrikaner South Africans and French Canadians had no love for Britain. The same was even more true of the southern Irish.
- British control of India was superficial. It very much depended on the Indians themselves, and they were growing restive. By 1939 the granting of dominion status to India seemed highly likely, if not inevitable.
- Much of the rest of the Empire was underdeveloped. British colonial policy in the inter-war years was essentially one of benevolent neglect.

Key term

Paper tiger
Something that is far less strong than it might appear to be.

Therefore, the British Empire was something of a '**paper tiger**'. Indeed, some historians view the over-extended Empire as a strategic liability, rather than a strength. It cost a great deal to administer and defend. It may be, as well, that focus on imperial problems meant that Britain paid less attention to problems in Europe.

British economic power

It is possible to overstate Britain's economic decline. Preferential trade with the Empire helped to sustain British industry through the harsh economic climate of the 1930s. Nevertheless, other countries were overtaking British industrial production. In the 1930s Britain started to have a persistent balance of payments deficit, reflecting its weakening competitive position. Throughout the period the country found it difficult to get rid of the intractable problem of unemployment that reached its peak at three million in the early 1930s. Britain's economic difficulties reduced its capacity to increase its armaments.

Key question
What were Britain's main defence problems?

British defence problems

For hundreds of years Britain had been able to rely on naval power for security. Battleships, however, were no longer sufficient. During the First World War German submarines, by sinking merchant ships carrying foodstuffs and other raw materials, had threatened to starve Britain into surrender.

More serious still were aircraft developments. Enemy bombers could now leap-frog the English Channel. The pre-eminent position of London, home for one-fifth of the British population, the centre of government, finance and trade, made it a more significant target than anywhere else in Europe. In 1937 the Chiefs of Staff estimated that there might be 20,000 casualties in London in the first 24 hours of war, rising to 150,000 within one week. In the event these estimates were way off target: civilian casualties in Britain during the whole of the Second World War from aerial bombing amounted to about 147,000. But Chamberlain was not to know that his military experts had exaggerated the effects of German bombing.

In the 1920s Britain had enjoyed some freedom of manoeuvre to promote its world interests without serious threat to its position:

- Germany was still recovering from defeat.
- Both the USA and the USSR, for very different reasons, withdrew from international diplomacy.

However, in the 1930s Britain was threatened by the growing strength and ambitions of Germany, Italy and Japan. It lacked the military resources to meet – unassisted – the challenge of these potential rivals.

What alternative policies might Britain have adopted?

As early as 1922, Conservative leader Bonar Law had declared: 'We cannot act alone as the policeman of the world.' Yet government critics in the 1930s, both on the left and right, demanded that Britain should take on aggressors wherever they appeared.

The left thought Britain should do this through the League of Nations, believing that the League would preserve peace without a special effort on anyone's part. Many on the left called for action against Germany, Italy and Japan and yet supported British disarmament, imagining that moral force and the threat of sanctions would be sufficient to stop Hitler, Mussolini and/or the Japanese militarists.

The right appreciated the importance of force. However, politicians such as Churchill tended to overestimate Britain's strength. Churchill believed that Britain could and should have stopped Hitler and the other aggressors sooner. It is often forgotten that, in all probability, this would not have avoided war. Churchill's war – or wars – would simply have been fought sooner rather than later and this may not have been to Britain's advantage. At least by fighting when it did, Britain – ultimately – was on the winning side.

British governments throughout the inter-war years were more realistic than their critics. They were aware of the fragility of British power and the degree to which it rested on appearances rather than on substance. In the 1930s the Chiefs of Staff stressed repeatedly that Britain was incapable of defying Germany, Italy and Japan simultaneously. Aware of Britain's vulnerability, British statesmen did their best to avoid conflict.

Perhaps British governments should have spent more on armaments. However, as Treasury officials argued, this would have weakened an already strained economy. Only if Britain was economically strong had it much hope of winning a war against Germany. Public opinion, which preferred government spending on social welfare to defence, was also a limiting factor.

Should Britain have gone to war in 1939?

Throughout the inter-war period most governments had attempted to avoid continental entanglements that might force Britain into war. In particular, most statesmen accepted that Britain had no great interests in Central or Eastern Europe. Danzig and the Polish Corridor, in Austen Chamberlain's view, were something 'for which no British government ever will or ever can risk the bones of a British grenadier'.

Neville Chamberlain, Austen's half-brother, held very similar views. Somewhat ironically it was events in Central and Eastern Europe in 1938–9 that convinced Neville Chamberlain, and most Britons, that Hitler must be stopped. In September 1939 Britain went to war as a result of a quarrel between Germany and Poland over Danzig and the Polish Corridor. Since 1945 most historians have claimed that Britain was right to go to war. The main debate has been whether Britain should have gone to war sooner than 1939.

However, Chamberlain's decisions to guarantee Poland's security in March 1939 and then to declare war on Germany in September can certainly be criticised. By guaranteeing Poland, Britain had been shocked into doing what Chamberlain had firmly refused to do over Czechoslovakia, namely to leave Britain's decision for peace and war effectively in Hitler's hands. In 1939 Britain went to war, in A.J.P. Taylor's view, for 'that part of the peace settlement which they [British statesmen] had long regarded as least defensible'. Poland – corrupt, élitist and racist – was not a state that any nation could be proud of having to fight to save. Taylor's views are worth serious consideration:

- What had Britain to gain by going to war in 1939?
- How could Britain help Poland?
- Did British assurances of support encourage Poland to take an unreasonable and intransigent attitude to Germany?
- Was Hitler really an immediate threat to Britain?
- Might it not have been to Britain's advantage to encourage Hitler to keep pressing eastwards so that he would come up against the USSR?

Were British politicians 'guilty men'?

According to Churchill when writing about his ancestor, the Duke of Marlborough, Britain invariably threw away the fruits of victory after a successful war. It is possible to levy this charge at British statesmen (collectively and individually) after the First World War, and Churchill, in particular, did so. Nevertheless, it is important to realise the difficult problems British governments and statesmen faced. Most statesmen – Churchill was an exception – realised that another world war, even a successful one, was the most likely way of throwing away the fruits of victory of the First World War.

The much-maligned inter-war policy-makers did their best to avoid war. In the end circumstances – and Hitler – conspired against them and their best was not good enough. However, it is worth remembering that historians today, even with the benefit of hindsight, disagree about the wisest course of action. Statesmen at the time had to respond to crises quickly and with little time for calm reflection. Nor did they have access to the range and quality of information available to later historians. In the circumstances British statesmen inevitably made mistakes. But given the problems they faced, it may be that they deserve some sympathy.

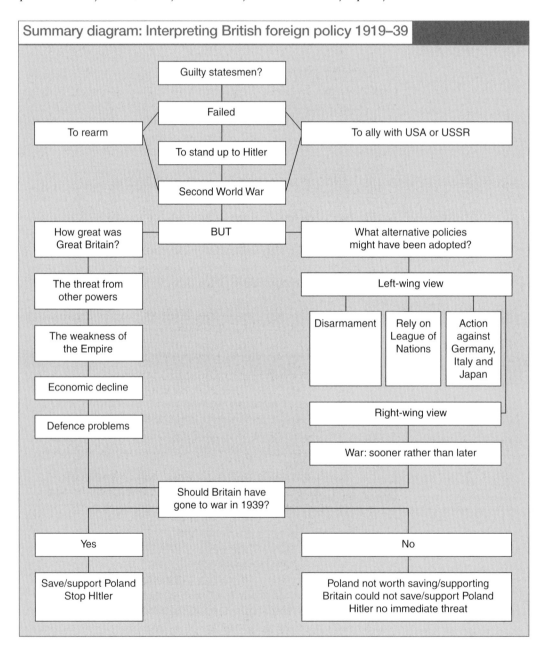

Summary diagram: Interpreting British foreign policy 1919–39

Study Guide: AS Questions

In the style of AQA

(a) Explain why Britain provided Poland with a guarantee of support in March 1939.

(b) 'It was Chamberlain's actions that drove Stalin to make the Nazi–Soviet Pact.' Explain why you agree or disagree with this view.

Exam tips

The cross-references are intended to take you straight to the material that will help you to answer the questions.

(a) This question requires you to think of a range of reasons for the guarantee that was given to Poland. Among these you might include:

- the German threats to Poland and demands for Danzig and the Polish Corridor (pages 100–1)
- the weak position of Poland's allies (page 95)
- the French (page 95)
- Britain's history of appeasement, particularly over Czechoslovakia, and the need to show resolution and to provide Hitler with a clear warning (pages 95–6).

You should try to identify which of the factors you mention was the most important and provide some judgement in your conclusion.

(b) The focus of this question is on why Stalin made the Nazi–Soviet Pact and you will need to consider both evidence which suggest that Chamberlain drove him to it and evidence which disagrees and points to other factors being equally or more important. In support of the quotation you will need to refer to the failure of the British to reach an agreement with the USSR between 1931 and 1938 (pages 105–6), and could consider factors such as:

- ideological suspicion and horror at Stalin's record of terror (page 106)
- the lack of British faith in the Soviet military (page 106)
- the desire not to encircle and provoke Germany (who might turn to Spain or Japan) (page 106)
- the fear of alienating the Eastern European countries (page 106).

Other factors which may have influenced Stalin's decision might include Stalin's own suspicions of Britain (and France) (page 108) and the fact that a German alliance could bring tangible benefits: peace and territory (page 110). You will need to decide how you will argue, but try to ensure that you show both sides in your essay and develop a line of argument throughout the answer so as to end with a well-supported conclusion.

Study Guide: A2 Questions

In the style of Edexcel

Study Sources 1, 2 and 3. How far do you agree with the view that the Munich agreement reflected Chamberlain's lack of a realistic alternative? Explain your answer, using Sources 1, 2 and 3 and your own knowledge of this controversy.

Source 1

From: A.J.P. Taylor, The Origins of the Second World War, *published in 1969*.

The British position [on the fate of Czechoslovakia] was complicated. Morality counted for a great deal. The British statesman used practical arguments: the danger from air attack; the backwardness of their rearmament; the impossibility, even if adequately armed, of helping Czechoslovakia. But these arguments were used to reinforce morality, not to silence it. The British policy over Czechoslovakia originated in the belief that Germany had a moral right to the Sudeten German territory, on the grounds of national principle.

Source 2

From: Anthony Adamthwaite, The Making of the Second World War, *published in 1977*.

Although the hysterical relief which greeted Munich testified to the strength of support for appeasement, this does not mean that no other policy was possible at the time. Enough attention has not been paid to the question whether given other men in power in Britain and France, with other conceptions guiding them, the climate of opinion might not have been different. Winston Churchill's 'grand alliance' against Germany offered an alternative to appeasement. The Cabinet Foreign Policy Committee discussed the idea in the week after the *Anschluss*. No one spoke up for it and it was never thoroughly explored because it ran completely counter to the goal of détente.

Source 3

From: F. McDonough, Neville Chamberlain, Appeasement and the British Road to War, *published in 1998*.

It is important to examine what Chamberlain expected to follow from Munich. It seems that he believed that Hitler was anxious for British friendship. It is equally apparent that Chamberlain had not lost faith in conciliation and diplomacy as the best weapons to prevent war. On 3 October, Chamberlain believed 'contacts with the Dictator Powers had opened up the possibility that we might be able to reach some agreement with them which would stop the armaments race'. On 31 October Chamberlain told the Cabinet: 'Our foreign policy was one of appeasement' with the central aim of 'establishing relations with the Dictator Powers which will lead to a settlement in Europe'.

Exam tips

The cross-references are intended to take you straight to the material that will help you to answer the questions.

You are asked to use the sources and your own knowledge. The sources raise issues for you. You can use these as the core of your plan. They contain points for and against the stated claim. Your answers will be stronger if you cross-refer between the sources rather than treating them separately.

Make sure you have identified all the issues raised by the sources, and then add in your own knowledge – both to make more of the issues in the sources (add depth to the coverage) and to add new points (extend the range covered). In the advice given below, links are made to the relevant pages where information can be found.

The sources raise key aspects for discussion which you can expand upon and assess from your own knowledge.

Points which can be explored to counter the view stated in the question are:

- Chamberlain's belief in appeasement (Sources 3 and 1 and pages 68–90).
- His acceptance of the grounds of national principle underpinning Hitler's demands (Source 1 and page 75).
- The possibility of a grand alliance against Hitler (Source 2 and page 70).

Points which support the view are:

- The British public's reluctance to go to war (Source 2 and page 87).
- The impossibility of helping Czechoslovakia (Source 1 and page 75).
- The rearmament position (Source 1 and pages 86–7).

You should also consider other relevant issues not raised by the sources – with what justification could Chamberlain view Munich as a triumph rather than a settlement borne of necessity and lack of alternative (pages 86–7)?

In the style of OCR B
Question 1

Read the following extract about appeasement and then answer the questions that follow.

Chamberlain's judgement of Hitler's personality (not on the whole it would seem differing from that of Halifax and his Cabinet colleagues) favoured the 'brain-storm' theory that he was a brutal, fanatical man, basically shrewd, but liable to be pushed into violence by his own gusts of passion rather than by long-term plans of gain or aggression. It accordingly seemed necessary to take care not to 'drive him over the edge' and to try to separate him from the wilder and more fanatical followers who worked on his feelings. Nevile Henderson shared this view. Chamberlain had looked for signs of madness at Berchtesgaden in 1938. A week after the outbreak of war on 10 September 1939, he noted his opinion that Hitler had been wavering up to a late date, half inclined to accept a 'peaceful and reasonable solution of the Polish question', but that 'at the last moment some brainstorm took possession of him – maybe Ribbentrop stirred him up'. There was some support for this view at the time among historians, who had been interpreting German policy in 1914 on rather similar lines, and it was remarked in the first edition of this work that 'whatever the ultimate aims and vaguer dreams of Hitler there seems no evidence to support the view that he had any precise objective after March 1939 except the destruction of Poland'.

Today there is ample evidence from German sources of a severely practical programme of rearmament, carefully planned to produce victory when Germany's relative superiority was greatest (in 1939 or 1940), and not when full re-equipment was complete (some time between 1943 and 1945, when her opponents' rearmament would be complete too). The basic political assumptions seem to have taken their final shape by 1937. By this stage Hitler had abandoned hope of an agreement with Britain and France, was reasonably sure of Italian co-operation, was convinced that the *Reich*'s need for food supplies and raw material sources called for territorial expansion 'in the East', and was apprehensive about Russia's growing power, which he had affected to despise in *Mein Kampf*. … His ultimate aim was concrete, grandiose, and not original: it was the creation of a great European land empire, comparable in size and resources with the United States, incorporating the fertile agricultural land of Poland and the Soviet Ukraine. The enslavement or extermination of a great many Slavs was implicit in the programme; the hegemony of Europe a natural consequence.

Chamberlain had never doubted that a rearmed Nazi Germany would throw its weight about, and from 1934 onward his steady support of rearmament up to the limits of security shows his belief that only the certainty of effective resistance would check German heavy-handedness by showing Hitler that it would be unprofitable. He also banked on the anti-war sentiment of the German masses. If he failed to penetrate the deeper intentions of Hitler he was not so gullible as not to suspect that they might exist. He knew that England's huge responsibilities throughout the world vastly exceeded her resources. He had no gifts for warlike oratory, and if he had he would not have used them: his aim was to bring all Europe to a reasonable state of peace.

(a) What can you learn from this extract about the interpretations, approaches and methods of this historian? Refer to the extract and to your knowledge to support your answer.

(b) Some historians are critical of Chamberlain's appeasement policies. Others are sympathetic. Explain how their debates have contributed to our understandings of appeasement. Which side of the debate, from your point of view, is most convincing and why?

Exam tips

Part (a)

Knowledge and understanding

Knowledge and understanding of Hitler's ideas and beliefs, his foreign policy during the 1930s, reactions to this policy by Britain and the general international situation in the 1930s should be demonstrated and used to support the answer.

Knowledge and understanding of the relevant approaches to studying appeasement should be demonstrated and used to support the answer, e.g. the fact that some historians are critical of appeasement while others are sympathetic.

Understanding of interpretations

To what extent is the author of the extract generally sympathetic to Chamberlain? What were Hitler's aims in foreign policy after 1933? Are all historians in agreement with the view given here about Hitler's aims?

Understanding of approaches/methods

How has the author's approach/method influenced his interpretation (detailed references to the text will be needed)? The author's approach is intentionalist, placing the emphasis on human agency in two ways: he assumes that Hitler had a long-term plan and that Chamberlain controlled British foreign policy. How have more recent approaches changed our understanding of appeasement? Did Hitler have a long-term plan? Was it the same as this historian assumes? Explain the limitations of an intentionalist view, e.g. to what extent was Chamberlain in control of British foreign policy?

Part (b)

Knowledge and understanding

You must display knowledge and understanding of the different approaches to appeasement. You must also display knowledge of the international situation in the 1930s, particularly from 1937 to

1939. How strong was Britain's international position? How strong were Britain's armed forces? What were Hitler's aims? Did British governments have a realistic alternative?

Understanding of approaches/methods
Why do some historians focus on the role of the individual rather than the role of circumstance? How do such approaches differ? How have they influenced the way that appeasement is presented by historians? What are the main arguments of those who are critical of Chamberlain and appeasement? What are the main arguments of those who are supportive of Chamberlain's policies? Which side of the argument does the extract support – and what evidence does it emphasise? Stress that the historiographical debates on appeasement are a 'good thing' rather than a 'bad'. The fact that there is an ongoing debate maintains interest in the topic and results in new interpretations.

Evaluation of approaches/methods
What new questions have been asked and what new perspectives gained from an intentionalist approach? What has been learned from an intentionalist approach that could not be learned from other approaches? In your view, which side of the argument is more convincing? Was appeasement a weak and foolish policy which simply encouraged Hitler and which was always doomed to failure? Or was it a rational policy, given Britain's international position in the late 1930s?

Question 2

Read the following extracts about appeasement and then answer the questions that follow:

Czecho-Slovakia had been diminished and weakened by the Munich settlement. On 15 March 1939 it fell to pieces. Slovakia became an independent state. Sub-Carpathian Ukraine was seized by Hungary. Hácha, who had succeeded Beneš as Czechoslovak president after Munich, placed the destinies of his country in Hitler's hands. Bohemia or 'Czechia' became a German protectorate. German administrators, including the *Gestapo*, moved in and established the same Nazi dictatorship as in Germany …

The English people … had been told by Chamberlain, by other ministers, by Hitler himself, that Munich was a final settlement. The Sudeten territories were Hitler's 'last territorial demand in Europe'. He wished only to include all Germans in the greater Germany, and Czecho-Slovakia, relieved of her embarrassing German minority, would henceforth enjoy a modest independence … Now Hitler had dismembered his small neighbour without warning or provocation and had carried off the most valuable, industrial part for himself. Here was clear proof of planned aggression. Hitler's word could never be trusted again. He was on the march to world domination, like the Kaiser before him. Nothing would stop him except a firm front of resistance. Such was the almost universal reaction of English opinion. The great majority of Conservatives had backed Chamberlain. They had loyally voiced the arguments of appeasement, had brushed passionately aside the charges of cowardice and betrayal. Now it seemed that Churchill, Duff Cooper, the Liberal and Labour oppositions, had been right. Great Britain and her powerful National government had been made fools of, or ministers had fooled their followers. There were deeper factors at work. Appeasement never sat comfortably on Tory shoulders. It was in spirit and origin a Left-wing cause, and its leaders had a Nonconformist background. True Conservatives reverted easily to a belief in British might.

The government moved more slowly. Halifax was relieved at escaping from 'the somewhat embarrassing commitment of a guarantee in which we and the French had been involved'. In the House of Commons on 15 March, Chamberlain speculated that the end of Czechoslovakia 'may or may not have been inevitable' and Simon explained that it was impossible to fulfil a guarantee to a state which had ceased to exist. The underground rumblings soon broke to the surface. Perhaps the government whips reported discontent on the backbenches. Perhaps Halifax heard the call of conscience in the watches of the night. Probably there was nothing so clear-cut, only a succession of doubts and resentments which shook Chamberlain's previous confidence. On 17 March he addressed the Birmingham Conservative association. He was among his own people – jewellers, locksmiths, makers of pots and pans. His prepared speech was an elaborate defence of Munich: no one 'could possibly have saved Czechoslovakia from invasion and destruction'. At the last moment he threw in a reference to what had happened two days before. The audience applauded his protest, and with each roar Chamberlain's improvisations grew stronger. 'Any attempt to dominate the world by force was one which the Democracies must resist'. Appeasement and Munich were eclipsed. The apologies which Simon was still making in the House of Commons seemed a world away. Chamberlain had turned British foreign policy upside down.

(a) What can you learn from this extract about the interpretations, approaches and methods of this historian? Refer to the extract and to your knowledge to support your answer.

(b) Some historians regard the decision to stand firm against Hitler after March 1939 as rational. Others think the decision was totally irrational. Explain how these debates have contributed to our understanding of the end of appeasement. Given the debates, is it possible to reach any consensus about the wisdom of British foreign policy from 15 March to 4 September 1939?

Exam tips

Part (a)

Knowledge and understanding

Knowledge and understanding of Chamberlain's efforts to appease Hitler in 1937 and (particularly) 1938, not least at the Munich Conference, should be demonstrated and used to support the answer.

Knowledge and understanding of the relevant approaches to studying appeasement – and its end – should be demonstrated and used to support the answer, e.g. the differences between placing the emphasis on individuals (like Chamberlain) and placing it on other factors (for example, public opinion).

Understanding of interpretations

You need to say something about the views displayed in this extract. Does the author criticise anyone in particular? Why does he suggest that Chamberlain changed his mind on 17 March? Is the author at odds with accepted opinion? The explanation should be supported throughout by clear references to the text.

Understanding of approaches/methods

To what extent does the author of the extract see Chamberlain in control of his own destiny? To what extent does he suggest that Chamberlain was swayed by public opinion?

Why – and to what extent – have debates about the end of appeasement changed over the last half century? Compare the author's approach to other approaches to appeasement. Your explanation should be supported throughout by clear references to the extract.

Part (b)

Knowledge and understanding

You will need to display your knowledge of what happened next: the Polish guarantee, the drift to war, the Nazi–Soviet Pact, the German invasion of Poland and the British and French declaration of war. You should also explain what the available evidence shows us.

Understanding of approaches/methods

Why are some historians critical of Chamberlain's abandonment of appeasement? Why are many supportive? To what extent was Chamberlain in control of the situation post-March 1939? Did he control public opinion or did public opinion control him? Did he have much control over the House of Commons? Did he have much influence over Hitler or Stalin?

Evaluation of approaches/methods

Explain the impact of the available evidence on our understanding of policy decisions during this period. Has the debate about the rationality of British foreign policy post-March 1939 been decided? If not, is it possible to reach some kind of consensus? The easy answers are probably no, no and no but you will need to say why this is the case. It is also worth stressing that serious historiographical disagreements are no bad thing. They are very much the lifeblood of history and do broaden our understanding of events, decisions, results, etc., because, even if debate does not reveal newly discovered evidence, it shows us how to ask different questions of existing evidence. Has this debate confirmed or challenged the view presented at the time? Have these views been influenced by hindsight or modern values? What has been learned from this approach? Has it changed the way that appeasement is written about?

You will also need to provide a brief summary of your own opinion and your main reasons for holding it. For example, given the evidence, Chamberlain was right to abandon appeasement after March 1939. Hitler's takeover of Czechoslovakia made it apparent that he could not be trusted. Most Britons were now determined to stop any further advance by Hitler which could only increase Germany's future strength. Or, given the evidence, Chamberlain was foolish to abandon appeasement after March 1939. There was no way that Britain could defend Poland and it made sense to encourage Hitler to go east against – ultimately – Stalin. Few Britons actually wanted war. Thus Chamberlain could have persuaded most of his countrymen to accept a realistic policy which would have given Britain time to prepare its defences – just in case!

5 The Second World War 1939–45

POINTS TO CONSIDER

In this chapter you will be studying Britain's role in the Second World War. The so-called 'world' war was essentially a European conflict in the years 1939–41. Most European states were drawn into the struggle (only Spain, Portugal, Sweden, Switzerland, Turkey and Eire remained neutral). It was not really a genuine world war until December 1941 when Japan's attack on Pearl Harbor brought the USA into the war. The second phase of the war, from 1941 to 1945, ended with Europe in ruins, its economy crippled, and with the armies of Britain, the USA and the USSR meeting in the heart of the continent. This chapter aims to explore why the war became a world war and why it ended with Allied victory. It particularly seeks to assess the role of Winston Churchill. This will be done by focusing on the following themes:

- From Chamberlain to Churchill 1939–40
- Britain alone 1940–1
- The Grand Alliance 1941–2
- The turn of the tide 1942–3
- Victory 1944–5
- Churchill as war leader

Key dates

1939	September	Germany defeated Poland
1940	April	German forces overran Denmark and Norway
	May	Chamberlain resigned: Churchill became Prime Minister
	June	Fall of France
	Aug–Sept	Battle of Britain
1941	March	US Lend–Lease to Britain
	June	Germany invaded the USSR
	December	Pearl Harbor: Japan at war with the USA and Britain
	December	Hitler declared war on the USA
1942	February	Fall of Singapore
	November	Battle of El Alamein
1943	January	German surrender at Stalingrad
	January	Casablanca Conference

	July	Allied occupation of Sicily
	September	Allied invasion of Italy
	November	Teheran Conference
1944	June	Allied invasion of France
1945	February	Yalta Conference
	April	Deaths of Roosevelt, Mussolini and Hitler
	May	German surrender
	July	Potsdam Conference
	August	Atom bombs dropped on Hiroshima and Nagasaki
	August	Japan surrendered

1 | From Chamberlain to Churchill 1939–40

Key date

Germany defeated Poland: September 1939

In September 1939 Neville Chamberlain, who for two years had attempted to keep peace, found himself leading a nation at war. He wrote in his diary 'I hate and loathe this war. I was never meant to be a War Minister'. But his sense of duty, and a natural reluctance to step down from the premiership, kept him in office. As proof of his determination to wage war to the best of his ability, Chamberlain reformed his government, bringing in Churchill as First Lord of the Admiralty.

Key question

Which side seemed favourite to win in September 1939?

Readiness for war

None of the three main combatants – Britain, France or Germany – was fully prepared for war in 1939. Britain and France had some important advantages (see Table 5.1):

- The Royal Navy was more than a match for the German fleet.
- The combined army of Britain and France had more men than the German army.
- The French army held the Maginot Line (see page 39) – a strong defence system.
- Poland seemed a useful ally.
- German rearmament was by no means complete in 1939. It had few submarines (or U-boats) and its army was short of motor transport and tanks.

However, Germany had several key advantages:

- Its air force was stronger in 1939–40.
- Senior German officers were willing to experiment with new weapons and new tactics.
- French commanders failed to appreciate the power of tanks and aircraft.

The collapse of Poland

While Britain prepared for war, Germany struck. Using tanks and aircraft to considerable effect, German forces cut through Poland at great speed. To make matters worse, in mid-September the

Table 5.1: The balance of power in 1939

	Great Britain	France	USSR	USA	Poland	Germany	Italy
Population (thousands)	47,692	41,600	167,300	129,825	34,662	68,424	43,779
National income ($m)	23,550	10,296	31,410	67,600	3,189	33,347	6,895
Reserves (millions)	0.4	4.6	12.0*	–[†]	1.5	2.2	4.8
Peacetime armies (millions)	0.22	0.8	1.7*	0.19	0.29	0.8	0.8
Aircraft (first line)	2,075	600	5,000*	800	390	4,500*	1,500[‡]
Destroyers	184	28	28	181	4	17	60
Submarines	58	70	150	99	5	56	100

* Approximate. [†] Not available. [‡] For 1940.

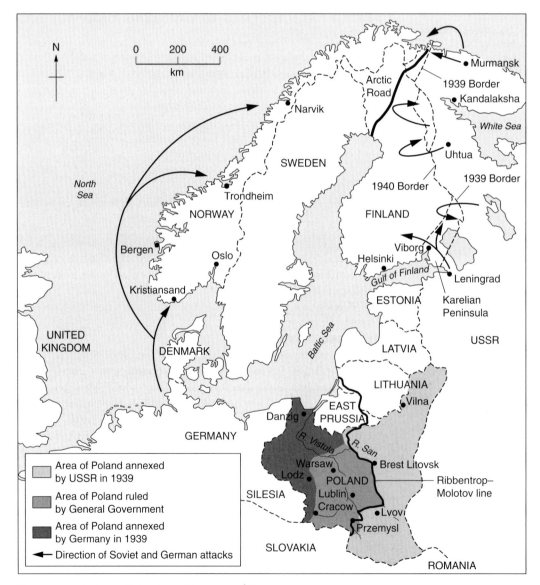

Figure 5.1: Poland, Finland and Norway 1939–40.

USSR invaded Poland from the east. Polish resistance collapsed and Germany and the USSR divided Poland along the so-called Ribbentrop–Molotov line (see Figure 5.1). A Polish government-in-exile was set up in London to try to continue the struggle, but effectively Poland, and the prospect of an Eastern Front, had disappeared. The Germans were now able to transfer most of their forces to the west.

France and Britain had done little to help Poland. The French, aware of the terrible casualty lists of the First World War, had no intention of launching a major offensive against German frontier fortifications, even though only one-third of the German army was in the west in September 1939. Years would elapse before Britain was in a position to send large numbers of troops to the Continent. Chamberlain remained confident that an economic blockade would bring Germany to its knees.

The phoney war

Key question
Could Britain and France have done more in the so-called phoney war?

In October Hitler offered vague but possibly genuine peace proposals. There were good reasons for the Western democracies to make peace: war against Germany was certain to be costly in terms of blood and money. But few British politicians were prepared to trust Hitler. There was thus no peace and for several months not much war to speak of either. This was the period of 'phoney war'. All the opposing armies were content to wait behind their defensive lines. The RAF confined its activities to dropping propaganda leaflets on German cities. No country wished to be the first to launch aerial assaults on civilians. In Britain far more people died from road accidents caused by blackout restrictions (see page 185) than from bombing. Only at sea was there a reminder that this was a real war. Fortunately Germany did not yet have sufficient U-boats to pose a serious threat to Allied shipping. Neither Italy nor Japan tried to exploit the situation at this stage so the worst fears of British defence planners were not realised.

The Russo-Finnish War

Key question
Should Britain and France have sent help to Finland?

Key term
Baltic States
Lithuania, Latvia and Estonia.

The main country to exploit the situation was the USSR. In October the **Baltic States** were forced to accept Soviet garrisons. Stalin then turned on Finland, but the Finns resisted his demands for territory. In November 1939 the USSR invaded Finland. To everyone's surprise, the tenacious Finns held up the vastly superior Soviet forces. Many politicians (especially Churchill) thought Britain and France should send help to Finland and fight the USSR as well as Germany. A plan to send 100,000 troops to Finland, via Norway and Sweden, enabling the Allies to cut off Swedish iron ore supplies to Germany, was devised. 'The only charitable conclusion is to assume that the British and French governments had taken leave of their senses', wrote A.J.P. Taylor. But in March 1940, just as the Allied force was about to move, the Russo-Finnish war came to an abrupt end. Finland ceded territory but not as much as Stalin had initially demanded.

Norway

Although the Allies could no longer help Finland, the idea of blocking Swedish iron ore to Germany was not abandoned. The winter supply route went via Narvik in Norway and then down the Norwegian coast to Germany. In April 1940 the Allies decided to block this route by laying mines in Norwegian territorial waters. The day after the Allies began mining, Germany occupied Denmark and seized the main towns in Norway. Denmark simply surrendered. Norway tried to resist and Allied troops were sent to its defence. But the campaign was badly planned and executed and by the end of April Allied forces were driven from most of Norway.

The fall of Chamberlain

On 7–8 May the Norwegian campaign was debated in the Commons. Many MPs were angry at the way it had been conducted. Strangely their target was not Churchill, who had been largely responsible for the operation, but Chamberlain. Many MPs felt that he failed to project vigour and vision. Some 40 Conservative MPs voted against the government and a further 60 abstained. The government had a majority of 81 but this was far less than its usual majority of over 200. Chamberlain was clearly losing the confidence of the Commons and probably of the nation as well. Discussions took place about how the government might be strengthened. Labour leaders said they were prepared to serve in a coalition government but not under Chamberlain. Chamberlain decided he must resign. There were really only two possible successors:

- Lord Halifax (the Foreign Secretary)
- Winston Churchill.

Churchill becomes Prime Minister

While most of the nation favoured Churchill, he was not as popular in the Cabinet or in Parliament. His record over the previous three decades had often been suspect and Chamberlain, King George VI and many Conservative MPs would have preferred Halifax. Realising it would be difficult to run the war from the House of Lords, Halifax was not eager to lead. Churchill had no such inhibitions. Convinced he was the right man for the job, he became Prime Minister on 10 May. His new government included Chamberlain and also Labour and Liberal leaders. In a speech to the Commons on 10 May Churchill admitted:

> I have nothing to offer but blood, toil, tears and sweat … You ask, What is our policy? I will say: it is to wage war, by sea, land and air, with all our might and with all the strength that God can give us: to wage war against a monstrous tyranny, never surpassed in the dark, lamentable catalogue of human crime … You ask, what is our aim? I can answer in one word: Victory – victory at all costs, victory in spite of all terror, victory, however long and hard the road may be.

Key question
How did Churchill become Prime Minister?

Key dates

German forces overran Denmark and Norway: April 1940

Chamberlain resigned: Churchill became Prime Minister: May 1940

Profile: Winston Churchill 1874–1965

1874	– Born in Blenheim Palace, the son of Lord Randolph Churchill and his American wife Jenny
1898	– Fought in the Sudan
1899	– Became a war correspondent in the Boer War: captured by the Boers and escaped
1900	– Became Conservative MP for Oldham
1904	– Joined the Liberal Party
1910–11	– Home Secretary
1911–15	– First Lord of the Admiralty
1915	– Resigned after being blamed for the Gallipoli campaign
1915–16	– Commanded a battalion in France
1917–19	– Minister of Munitions
1918–21	– Secretary for War
1921–2	– Secretary for Colonies
1922–64	– Conservative MP for Woodford
1924–9	– Chancellor of the Exchequer
1939–40	– First Lord of the Admiralty
1940–5	– Prime Minister
1945–51	– Leader of the Opposition
1951–5	– Prime Minister
1955	– Resigned as Prime Minister
1965	– Died

While Churchill is often seen as the twentieth century's greatest Englishman, critics point out that he presided over the demise of Britain as a great world power. The following, written by US playwright Roger Sherwood, a speechwriter for President Roosevelt, give some idea of Churchill's style:

> Churchill always seemed to be at his Command Post on the precarious beach-head and the guns were continually blazing in his conversation; wherever he was, there was the battlefront. Churchill was getting full steam up about 10 o'clock in the evening; often after his harassed staff had struggled to bed about 2.00 or 3.00a.m. they would be routed out. Churchill's consumption of alcohol continued at quite regular intervals through most of his waking hours without visible effect …
>
> Churchill could talk for an hour or more and hold any audience spellbound. Here was one who certainly knew his stuff, who could recite fact and figure and chapter and verse, and in superb English prose.

The following speech, made on 4 June 1940, is one of Churchill's most famous:

> We shall not flag or fail. We shall go on to the end, we shall fight in France, we shall fight on the seas and oceans, we shall fight with growing confidence and growing strength in the air, we shall defend our island, whatever the cost may be, we shall fight on the beaches, we shall fight on the landing grounds, we shall fight in the fields and in the streets, we shall fight in the hills, we shall never surrender.

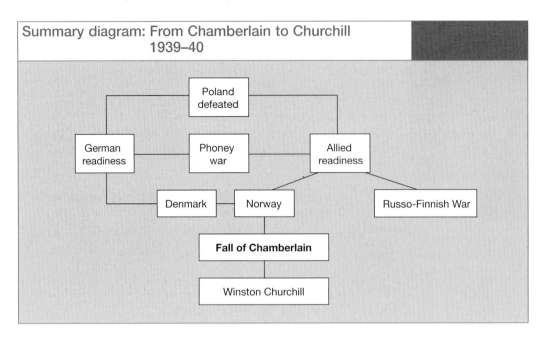

2 | Britain Alone 1940–1

Key question
How serious was
Britain's position in
the summer of 1940?

The first weeks of Churchill's government coincided with a series
of disasters.

The fall of France

On 10 May German forces invaded and quickly occupied the
Netherlands and Belgium. Other German units broke through
the French line near Sedan and drove a great wedge between the
Allied armies in France. Within 10 days German tanks had
reached the English Channel. Most of the British forces were
deployed to the north of the German thrust and evacuation
seemed the only alternative to annihilation. At the end of
May and the start of June, around 350,000 British and Allied
troops were evacuated from Dunkirk in a motley collection of
vessels.

Fall of France: June
1940

Battle of Britain:
August–September
1940

Key dates

Dunkirk is sometimes viewed as a success. Certainly, the
number of men who managed to return to Britain far exceeded
the most optimistic forecasts at the start of the operation. But as
Churchill admitted, 'Wars are not won by evacuations.' The
evacuated troops had left behind all their heavy weapons and
transport and were in a chaotic and demoralised state.

France's position was now desperate. On 10 June Italy joined
the war on Germany's side. Churchill did his best to encourage
France to resist but he had little to offer except words. The
French government, after anguished debate, surrendered.
Marshal Pétain became French leader and on 22 June accepted
the German armistice terms:

- North-west France was put under German military occupation.
- The remainder kept its own government, now sited at Vichy.

Figure 5.2: The German conquest of Western Europe.

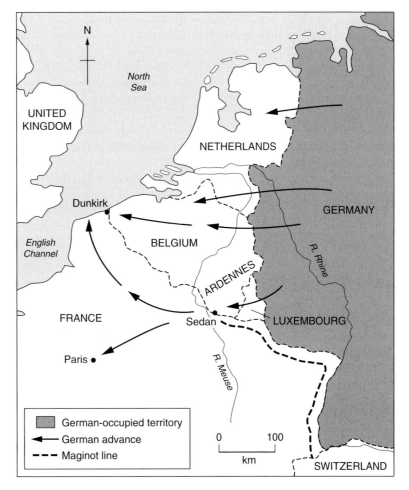

Figure 5.2: The German conquest of Western Europe.

General Charles de Gaulle escaped to Britain but his 'Free French' organisation had few supporters at this stage.

While the British tend to blame French political and military leaders for the fall of France, the French still argue that Britain should have fought rather than fled from Dunkirk. This debate was academic in the summer of 1940. What mattered was that Britain now stood alone against a Nazi-dominated Europe. Britain's position seemed hopeless. Nobody, not even the optimistic Churchill, could contemplate British forces landing on the Continent and defeating the Germans. Nor was there any prospect of bombing or blockading Germany into surrender. Instead there was a real possibility that German forces would now conquer Britain.

The Battle of Britain

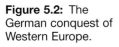

Key question
Should Britain have made peace with Hitler in July 1940?

In July Hitler launched another 'peace offensive'. He was prepared to guarantee the British Empire in return for Britain accepting German conquests in Europe. It is likely that either Chamberlain or Halifax might well have accepted the lenient terms. But a defiant Churchill resolved to fight on, declaring he would never 'parley' with Hitler. There is little doubt that he reflected the views of most Britons.

Hitler now declared his intention to invade Britain. At the end of July he gave orders for a massed air offensive to be followed by a cross-Channel assault in September, 'if we have the impression that the English are smashed'. Already contemplating a war against the USSR, Hitler may not have had much confidence in **Operation Sealion**. Nevertheless, if the *Luftwaffe* had destroyed Britain's air power, a German invasion would certainly have been improvised. The **Battle of Britain**, therefore, was vital to Britain's survival. At the outset the *Luftwaffe* had some 4550 planes compared to the RAF's 3000. In early September the RAF was perilously close to defeat. But the Germans blundered by turning away from bombing radar stations and airbases to bombing London. This gave the RAF time to recover and on 15 September, they destroyed over 50 German aircraft. Simply by remaining as a viable force the RAF won the Battle of Britain. Any plans Hitler might have had to invade Britain were postponed.

The *Luftwaffe* now turned its attention to night bombardment of cities, especially London. Although some 45,000 people died in the **blitz**, the Germans did not have enough bombers to shatter the British economy or civilian morale. All they succeeded in doing was generating a durable anger among most Britons.

The search for allies

In the autumn of 1940 Chamberlain died and Halifax went as Ambassador to Washington. Anthony Eden now became Foreign Secretary, a post he was to retain until 1945. The main task of Churchill, Eden and all British diplomats in 1940–1 was to find allies. Churchill remained optimistic, convinced that the logic of events would eventually cause the USA and the USSR to become engaged on Britain's side; and that this 'Grand Alliance' would prove irresistible.

From the start President Roosevelt had sympathised with the British cause. In 1939 he and Churchill had begun a private correspondence which became a vital channel for Anglo-American relations throughout the war. In late 1939 Roosevelt had persuaded Congress to amend the **Neutrality Act** to allow the Allies to purchase arms on a '**cash and carry**' basis. After the fall of France, Roosevelt was even more prepared to give Britain assistance. The USA now provided Britain with 50 destroyers in return for the right to establish bases in British possessions in the West Indies. Roosevelt talked about the USA becoming the 'arsenal of democracy' and in March 1941 signed the Lend–Lease Bill which made enormous quantities of US resources available to Britain. Although opinion polls in the USA revealed massive sympathy for the British cause, most Americans still had no wish to get involved in the war.

The USSR gave Britain no sympathy at all. Sir Stafford Cripps, sent as ambassador to Moscow to try to improve Anglo-Russian relations, was kept at arm's length by Stalin. Britain had nothing to offer the USSR as adequate compensation for a break with Germany. Cripps wrote gloomily in August 1940 that if the

Key terms

Operation Sealion
The German code name for the invasion of Britain.

Battle of Britain
The aerial conflict fought over Britain between the RAF and the *Luftwaffe* from July to September 1940.

Blitz
A shortened form of the German word *blitzkrieg* (or lightning war). The term was used to describe the bombing of British cities by the *Luftwaffe* in 1940–1.

Key question
Why was an alliance with the USA so vital for Britain?

US Lend–Lease to Britain: March 1941

Key date

Key terms

Neutrality Acts
A series of Acts passed by the US Congress between 1935 and 1939 prohibiting the US government giving loans to belligerent nations and placing embargoes on shipments of arms.

Cash and carry
Britain was now able to acquire US weapons, provided it paid for them and they were transported in British ships.

Figure 5.3: Europe and North Africa 1939–45.

Soviets had to choose between the two sides 'there is no doubt whatever they would choose Germany'. However, German–Soviet relations did give Britain some hope. The USSR's annexation of the Baltic States and ambitions in the Balkans angered Hitler. The Nazi–Soviet Pact of August 1939 (see page 109) had simply been a marriage of convenience. Hitler loathed communism and dreamed of winning *lebensraum* in the east.

The Tripartite Pact

In September 1940 Germany, Italy and Japan drew up the Tripartite Pact. Fortunately this was a vague expression of friendship rather than a fully fledged alliance and Japan did not yet join the war against Britain. Mussolini was Hitler's chief ally in 1940–1. Italian forces threatened Britain's position in Egypt and the Middle East. Churchill believed that control of the Suez Canal was essential, so much so that he was even prepared to send troops to Egypt when Britain itself faced the threat of invasion. An Italian invasion of Egypt in September 1940 was defeated and Britain followed this up by occupying Italian Somaliland, Ethiopia and much of Libya (see Figure 5.3). An Italian invasion of Greece in October 1940 also failed.

The situation in early 1941

The Italian disasters in North Africa and Greece were a blow to **Axis** prestige. There was the possibility that:

- the French in North Africa might support Britain
- Britain might establish a permanent foothold in Greece.

Hitler, therefore, sent General Rommel and the Afrika Korps to Libya to bolster the Italians. He also put pressure on Greece to submit to humiliating terms. The Greeks were determined to resist. In March 1941 there was a *coup d'état* in Yugoslavia. The new government was anti-German. In April the Germans quickly overran both Yugoslavia and Greece, driving out a British Expeditionary Force in the process. They went on to capture Crete. Meanwhile, Rommel inflicted a series of defeats on British forces in North Africa.

The only way Britain could strike at Germany was bombing. But British bombing raids had little pattern, purpose or success. Casualties among bomber aircrews were almost as great as German civilian casualties. German U-boats were far more effective than British bombers. Germany had rapidly increased its U-boat fleet and by 1941 was winning the **Battle of the Atlantic**.

Axis
The term Axis Powers was used to describe Germany, Italy and Japan.

Coup d'état
The overthrow of a government by force or subversive action.

Battle of the Atlantic
The name given by Churchill in 1941 to the struggle to protect the merchant ships bringing supplies to Britain. The chief threat came from German U-boats.

Key terms

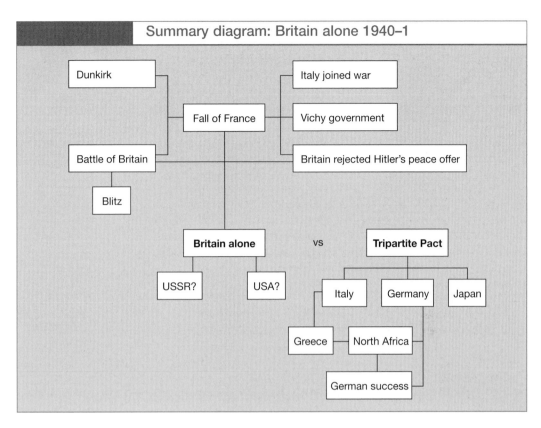

Summary diagram: Britain alone 1940–1

3 | The Grand Alliance 1941–2

Key question
How could Britain help the USSR in 1941–2?

Key date

Germany invaded the USSR: June 1941

On 22 June 1941 Hitler launched Operation Barbarossa: the invasion of the USSR. Churchill immediately declared that, 'the cause of any Russian fighting for his hearth and home is the cause of free men and free people in every quarter of the globe… we shall give whatever help we can to Russia'. Within weeks Britain and the USSR concluded an agreement for mutual assistance.

The Soviet situation in late 1941

Many British experts anticipated an early Soviet collapse as German forces advanced eastwards. But although the Red Army suffered heavy casualties, it continued to fight, and as Churchill observed, what mattered was not so much where the Russian front happened to lie, but that the front was still in existence. From Britain's point of view the good news was that it now had an ally who was able to absorb the greatest weight of the German military machine.

In July 1941 Stalin asked Britain to launch an attack in the west to divert German forces from Russia. Churchill pressed for an attack in Norway or Normandy. But his Chiefs of Staff convinced him that even a small-scale diversionary attack was out of the question. The only way in which Britain could help the USSR was in the matter of supply. Unfortunately there was no easy way of

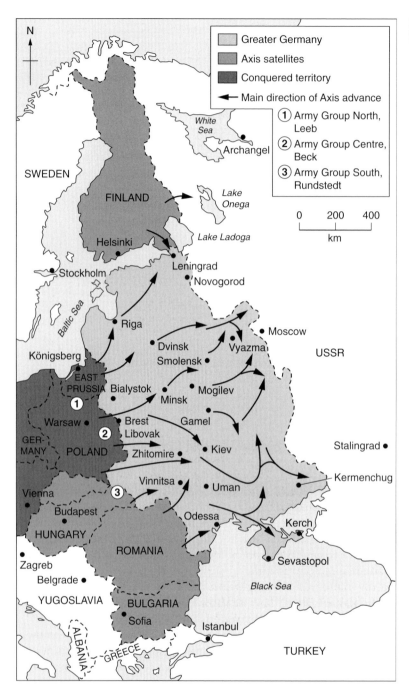

Figure 5.4: Operation Barbarossa.

sending materials to the USSR and there was the added problem that Britain itself was short of military equipment. Roosevelt, however, agreed to extend Lend–Lease to the USSR.

The American situation in late 1941

By mid-1941 it was clear that Roosevelt was far from a neutral bystander. In August, he and Churchill agreed to a joint statement of principles – the Atlantic Charter. This made it clear that the Allies were 'fighting' (or not in the USA's case) for a wide

Key question
Why was the USA hardly neutral by the summer of 1941?

range of 'freedoms', not for any territorial goals. The vagueness of some of the phraseology helped to conceal important differences between the USA and Britain on several matters, not least the future of the British Empire. Nor did the USA yet declare war on Germany. Roosevelt, however, was edging the USA nearer to war:

Key dates

Pearl Harbor: Japan at war with the USA and Britain: December 1941

Hitler declared war on the USA: December 1941

- In July 1941 US forces occupied Iceland.
- The USA undertook responsibility for the escort of convoys from the USA to the mid-Atlantic. This brought US ships into conflict with German U-boats.

But it was events in the Pacific, not the Atlantic, which finally brought the USA into the war.

Pearl Harbor

From 1939 Britain had relied on the USA to deter Japan from exploiting the situation in the Far East. American–Japanese relations had deteriorated steadily throughout 1940–1. In 1941, rather than attack the USSR, Japan turned its attention southwards, taking over **French Indo-China**. The USA responded by freezing all Japanese assets and then imposing an oil embargo on Japan. Japan had now to decide whether to withdraw from China and Indo-China (as the USA demanded) or seize more territory from which it could obtain the raw materials (especially oil) it needed to go on fighting. Such an expansionist policy was bound to lead to war with the USA and Britain. In October a new government took office in Japan determined to bring matters to a head. Intense diplomatic efforts continued through November but Japan and the USA failed to reach agreement.

Key terms

French Indo-China Pre-1954 Vietnam, Laos and Cambodia were ruled by France. The whole area was known as Indo-China.

Europe first strategy The strategic notion that the Allies should focus on defeating Germany (and Italy) before Japan.

On 7 December 1941 the Japanese attacked Pearl Harbor in Hawaii, destroying a large part of the US Pacific fleet. Immediately afterwards Japan declared war on Britain and the USA. Both Britain and the USA had expected a Japanese attack but they did not know precisely where or when, and neither had made adequate preparations. From Britain's point of view this hardly mattered. The important thing was that the USA was now in the war. Churchill later said that 'he went to bed and slept the sleep of the saved and thankful'. On 11 December Germany and Italy, honouring the commitments of the Tripartite Pact, declared war on the USA. This, according to A.J.P. Taylor, was either an act of 'gratuitous loyalty or [of] folly'. If Hitler had not declared war, the USA might well have concentrated its energies on the war against Japan rather than on the war in Europe.

'Europe first'

Churchill rushed across the Atlantic to meet Roosevelt. Both leaders confirmed that overall priority should be given to a **Europe first strategy**. Strategy and operational control were to be co-ordinated through a Combined Chiefs of Staff. Roosevelt invented a grand name – the United Nations – for the Allied powers, and in January 1942 all joined in a declaration that they would wage war together and not make a separate peace.

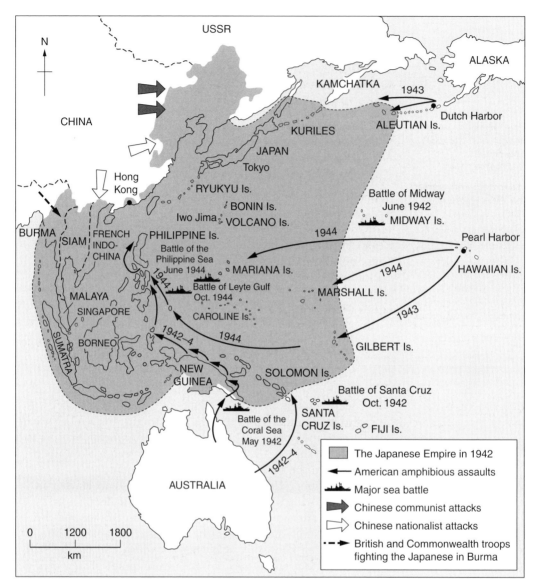

Figure 5.5: The war in the Pacific.

Anglo-Russian relations in early 1942

While Churchill was in Washington, British Foreign Secretary
Eden visited Moscow. This visit was not so friendly. Stalin seemed
more concerned with the USSR's post-war position than with the
war itself. He proposed a secret treaty whereby Britain would
accept the USSR's acquisitions of 1939–40 and, in return, the
USSR would support aspirations which Britain might have for
bases in Western Europe. Eden was in no position to sign such a
document, even if he had wished to do so. It would contravene
not merely Britain's guarantee to Poland but also the Atlantic
Charter. It was clear that Stalin had little time for the idealistic
vision of the Charter. He was determined to maintain the USSR's
1941 frontiers. Churchill's reaction to Stalin's proposal was sharp.

Key question
Why were Allied
relations with Stalin
so difficult?

The Baltic States, he declared 'were acquired by acts of aggression in shameful collusion with Hitler'. The transfer of their peoples against their will would be 'contrary to all the principles for which we are fighting this war and would dishonour our cause'. A long-term alliance, signed between Britain and the USSR in May 1942, made no mention of frontiers.

In May 1942 Molotov, the Soviet Foreign Minister, pressed the Allies to launch a direct attack on German-occupied Europe. US leaders favoured the idea but the British were far more cautious. Military chiefs pointed out that the Allies lacked sufficient men, aircraft and landing craft. In August Churchill visited Moscow to explain that there could be no **Second Front** in 1942. Although Stalin looked 'very glum' at this news, he seemed to have been impressed by Churchill's talk of strategic bombing and the proposed Allied landings in North Africa. Despite their mutual suspicions, the two men established a working relationship.

The importance of the Grand Alliance

The **Grand Alliance** between Britain, the USA and the USSR meant that there was every likelihood of ultimate victory. However, from Britain's point of view there were serious potential problems:

- Churchill already deeply mistrusted Stalin.
- For all their common ties, the USA and Britain had different approaches to world affairs. Roosevelt regarded the British Empire with suspicion, an obstacle to US commerce and an affront to the concept of self-determination.
- As the USA harnessed its vast resources for war, it was clear that Britain was likely to be the poor relation.

Axis success in early 1942

Britain and the USA suffered appalling defeats at the hands of the Japanese in the Far East. The loss of Singapore in February 1942 was described by Churchill as 'the worst disaster and largest capitulation in British history'. By the summer of 1942 Japanese forces were threatening Australia and India. German forces continued to be successful in North Africa and Russia. The Battle of the Atlantic was going badly. By 1942 the Germans had nearly 400 U-boats and every month merchant shipping losses rose. Mass British bomber attacks, including the first 1000-plane raid on Cologne in March 1942, did not live up to the expectations of Air Chief Marshal 'Bomber' Harris.

Key terms

Second Front
The term used to describe an Allied invasion of northern France.

Grand Alliance
Churchill's term for the wartime alliance between Britain (and its Empire), the USA and the USSR. (Roosevelt called it the United Nations.)

Key question
Was it possible that the Axis powers could win the Second World War after 1941?

Key date
Fall of Singapore: February 1942

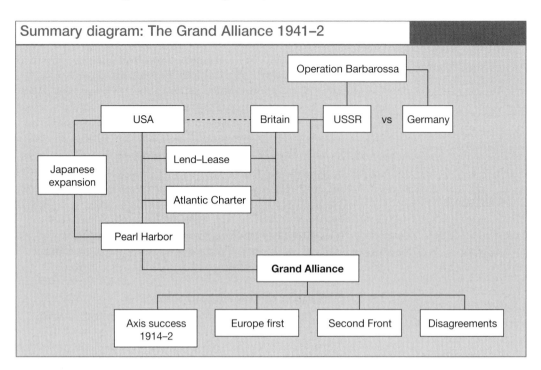

Summary diagram: The Grand Alliance 1941–2

4 | The Turn of the Tide 1942–3

During 1942–3 the Allied military situation improved.

The Pacific
In the summer of 1942 Japanese expansion was checked decisively by US naval victories at the Coral Sea and Midway.

The Battle of the Atlantic
By the summer of 1943 Atlantic shipping losses were substantially reduced and a large number of U-boats were sunk. The Atlantic became a relatively safe seaway. This meant that a huge US build-up of men and supplies in Britain could proceed largely unhindered.

Bombing of Germany
In 1943 Allied air raids finally began to inflict damage on German cities. The USA adopted a policy of daylight raids aimed at particular targets. Britain continued to attack German cities by night. Just how much damage was inflicted is debatable.

North Africa
In November 1942 General Montgomery defeated Rommel at the battle of El Alamein in Egypt. This gave Churchill the fillip of a major British victory. Rommel was forced to retreat across Libya and Axis hopes of capturing the Suez Canal ended. Meanwhile, an Anglo-American force, under the command of US General Eisenhower, landed in French Morocco. Vichy French resistance to the invasion quickly crumbled.

Key question
Why did the war turn in the Allies' favour in 1942–3?

Key dates
Battle of El Alamein: November 1942

German surrender at Stalingrad: January 1943

Figure 5.6: The Mediterranean 1942–3.

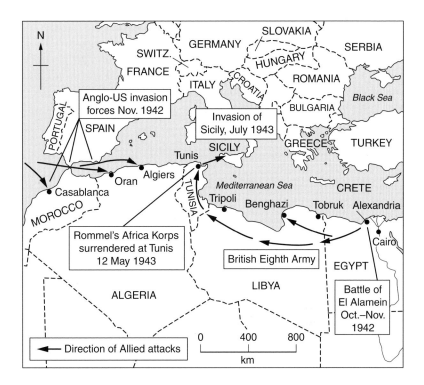

Stalingrad and Kursk

In 1942 German forces advanced again in the USSR, reaching Stalingrad by the autumn. Fierce fighting took place over the winter. Finally in January 1943 the German troops surrendered. Stalingrad is often seen as the decisive battle of the war. Certainly it proved that the Soviets could defeat the Germans. Stalingrad was followed by other Soviet victories, notably the battle of Kursk, and German forces in the USSR began a slow retreat.

The Second Front

Key question
Should the Allies have opened up a Second Front in France in 1943?

The Soviets, doing most of the hard fighting and tying down most of the German forces, continued to press the Allies to open up a Second Front. The Americans, confident of their greater resources, supported the idea of an immediate attack on France, believing the Allies should not waste time and effort on subsidiary theatres of war. But Churchill, convinced that the idea of a seaborne attack on France was militarily unsound, resisted the Second Front pressure.

In 1942–3 Churchill still played a dominant role in determining Allied strategy. Although US strength was growing rapidly, British forces in Europe still outnumbered the Americans, and weight of numbers tended to determine weight of influence. Churchill continued to favour military action in the Mediterranean, not so much because he thought this would benefit the British Empire (as many Americans suspected) but more because he thought it would help to win the war. Given that so many Allied troops were already in North Africa, the logical next step was an attack on Sicily followed by a campaign in Italy. This offered the opportunity of attacking the Axis on the 'cheap' without the risk of enormous losses which Churchill feared might occur if there was an early confrontation with German forces on the French mainland.

Casablanca

In January 1943 Roosevelt and Churchill met at Casablanca in Morocco. They discussed war aims and agreed that the Axis powers must unconditionally surrender. This decision has been criticised by some historians, who argue that it resulted in Germany and Japan fighting to the bitter end when the war was clearly over. But in reality it probably made little difference. German and Japanese leaders and many of their people were determined to fight to the last man and the Allies were already committed to total victory. More importantly, at Casablanca Churchill persuaded a reluctant Roosevelt to agree to an Allied landing in Sicily.

> **Key question**
> Was the policy of unconditional surrender a mistake?

The invasion of Italy

In July 1943 the Allies invaded and occupied Sicily. This led to the overthrow of Mussolini. The new Italian government began secret negotiations for an armistice. It now made sense, even to those US military chiefs who supported an immediate invasion of France, to invade the Italian mainland. A meeting between Churchill and Roosevelt at Quebec in August confirmed that the Americans would indeed support an Italian campaign, provided Britain gave priority to an invasion of France in 1944.

The Allied invasion of Italy began in September 1943 and the Italian government immediately announced that it had changed sides. The Germans rushed forces into Italy, restored Mussolini, but henceforward treated the country as occupied territory. The Allied advance up the Italian peninsula developed into a slogging match. Aneurin Bevan's description of the Allies 'climbing up the backbone' seemed more apt than Churchill's idea of the 'soft underbelly'. But the Allies did slowly push northwards, entering Rome in June 1944.

> **Key question**
> Was the Allied invasion of Italy a mistake?

> **Key dates**
>
> Casablanca Conference: January 1943
>
> Allied occupation of Sicily: July 1943
>
> Allied invasion of Italy: September 1943

The problem of Poland

Meanwhile the Soviets advanced westwards. This meant that it became difficult to postpone decisions on the future of Poland. In 1943 the USSR proposed that the eastern frontier of Poland should follow roughly the 'Curzon Line'. This line, drawn up by the Allies in 1919 as a potential but never an actual frontier, was similar to the dividing line between German and Soviet occupation of Poland in September 1939. Poland would be compensated for its losses in the east by gaining territory at Germany's expense in the west. The Polish government-in-exile in London had no intention of giving away territory and its relations with the USSR rapidly deteriorated.

> **Key question**
> Why was Poland so much of a problem for the Allies?

The discovery, by the Germans, of a mass grave of 8000–10,000 Polish officers in Katyn forest made matters worse. These officers, the Germans (correctly) declared, had been murdered by Soviet authorities in 1940. The Soviets announced (wrongly) that the Germans themselves were responsible for the atrocity. The Polish government-in-exile proposed that the International Red Cross should investigate the matter. Stalin responded by breaking diplomatic relations with the London Poles. Churchill faced something of a dilemma. He thought that the German revelations were 'probably true' but realised that Hitler hoped to use the Katyn discovery to drive a wedge between the Western allies and the USSR. Britain, therefore, largely ignored the Katyn massacre.

The Teheran Conference

Despite arguments over Poland, relations between the Soviets and the Western allies remained generally good. All the Big Three seemed determined to leave aside political differences in order to win the war. Roosevelt hoped that Stalin, suitably handled, would work for a world of peace and democracy. The Teheran Conference, held in the Iranian capital in November 1943, was the first attended by Roosevelt, Churchill and Stalin. It was in many ways the high water mark of Allied unity. For Churchill, however, Teheran was something of a disaster. Roosevelt showed

Key question
Why was the Teheran Conference a disaster for Churchill?

Key date

Teheran Conference: November 1943

The Big Three at Teheran: Stalin, Roosevelt and Churchill. Roosevelt is in the centre. Is this just an accident?

that he was prepared to deal directly with Stalin and it was clear that British influence was fading. Churchill later remarked: 'There I sat with the great Russian bear on one side of me, with paws outstretched, and on the other side the great American buffalo, and between the two sat the poor little English donkey who was the only one … who knew the right way home.'

The main outcome of the Teheran Conference was that Churchill and Roosevelt agreed to invade France in May 1944 while Stalin agreed to attack Japan after the end of the German war. There was also some discussion of Poland's future. Churchill was prepared to accept Stalin's frontier proposals for Poland but his efforts to bully the London Poles into acceptance met with little success.

Operation Overlord

Meanwhile the military build-up in Britain in preparation for Operation Overlord, the invasion of France, continued. By the summer of 1944 there were some 500,000 American servicemen in Britain. The Germans knew that an attack on 'Fortress Europe' was coming. What they did not know was when and where. General Eisenhower, the Allied Supreme Commander, did all he could to keep them guessing.

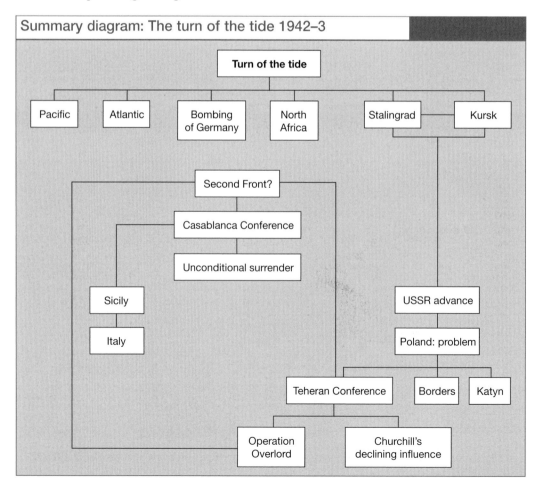

Summary diagram: The turn of the tide 1942–3

Key question
How did the Allies
defeat Germany in
1944–5?

5 | Victory 1944–5

By 1944–5 the Allied powers of Britain, the USA and the USSR
were out-fighting and out-producing the Axis powers of Germany
and Japan (see Table 5.2).

The liberation of France

On 6 June 1944 – D-Day – Anglo-American forces landed on the
Normandy beaches in France and established a permanent
bridgehead (see Figure 5.7). It took weeks of hard fighting before
the Allies were able to force their way inland. But in mid-August
German resistance, first in Normandy and then throughout
France, collapsed. Paris was liberated and Allied troops advanced
into Belgium and the Netherlands.

Key date

Allied invasion of
France: June 1944

Allied bombing

By 1944–5 Allied aircraft enjoyed almost complete control of
the air. German cities were now bombed unmercifully.
Bombing raids on Dresden in February 1945 killed at least
30,000 people.

Table 5.2: Weapons production of the major powers 1939–45

	1939	1940	1941	1942	1943	1944	1945
Aircraft							
Britain	7,940	15,049	20,094	23,672	26,263	26,461	12,070
USA	5,856	12,804	26,277	47,826	85,998	96,318	49,761
USSR	10,382	10,565	15,735	25,436	34,900	40,300	20,900
Germany	8,295	10,247	11,776	15,409	24,807	39,807	7,540
Japan	4,467	4,758	5,088	8,861	16,693	28,180	11,066
Major vessels							
Britain	57	148	236	239	224	188	64
USA	–	–	544	1,854	2,654	2,247	1,513
USSR	–	33	62	19	13	23	11
Germany (U-boats only)	15	40	196	224	270	189	0
Japan	21	30	49	68	122	248	51
Tanks*							
Britain	969	1,399	4,841	8,611	7,476	5,000	2,100
USA	–	c.400	4,052	24,997	29,497	17,565	11,968
USSR	2,950	2,794	6,590	24,446	24,089	28,963	15,400
Germany	c.1,300	2,200	5,200	9,200	17,300	22,100	4,400
Japan	c.200	1,023	1,024	1,191	790	401	142
Artillery pieces†							
Britain	1,400	1,900	5,300	6,600	12,200	12,400	–
USA	–	c.1,800	29,615	72,658	67,544	33,558	19,699
USSR	17,348	15,300	42,300	127,000	130,300	122,400	31,000
Germany	c.2,000	5,000	7,000	12,000	27,000	41,000	–

Dashes indicate reliable figures unavailable.
* Includes self-propelled guns for Germany and the USSR.
† Medium and heavy calibre only for Germany, USA and Britain; all artillery pieces for the USSR.
  Soviet heavy artillery production in 1942 was 49,100, in 1943 48,400 and in 1944 56,100.

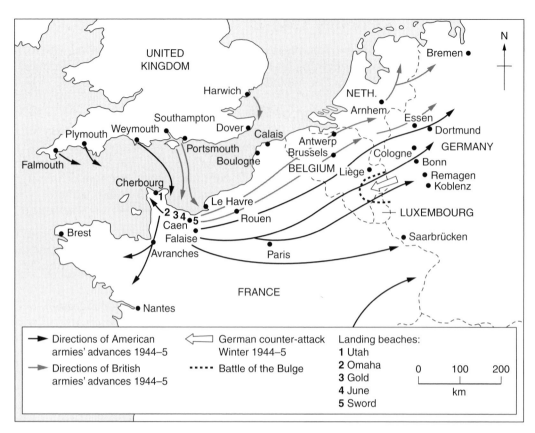

Figure 5.7: The Second Front 1944–5.

Soviet advance

The Soviets continued their advance in the east. The major problem as far as Britain was concerned was who would control various parts of Eastern Europe after the war. Poland remained an area of concern. The Polish government-in-exile was unwilling to work with the Soviet-backed Polish 'Committee of National Liberation'. Events in Warsaw in August and September 1944 aggravated the situation. Expecting Soviet assistance, the Polish capital rose up against the occupying Germans. But the Soviets gave no help and the rising was brutally crushed.

Churchill and the USSR

Churchill was increasingly worried about Soviet aims and apparent US aimlessness, especially with regard to Eastern Europe. An Anglo-American Conference at Quebec in September 1944 achieved little and as 1944 was a presidential election year, Roosevelt refused to be drawn on questions of relations with the USSR until after the election. In October 1944 Churchill and Eden went to Moscow. Churchill and Stalin failed to reach agreement over Poland but had more success in discussing the rest of Eastern Europe. On his return to Britain, Churchill declared that, 'Our relations with the Soviet Union were never

Key question
Was Churchill right to be suspicious of Stalin in 1944–5?

more close, intimate and cordial than they are at the present time.'

Stalin's good faith was soon demonstrated in action. Attempts by communists to seize power in Greece were thwarted by British troops. Stalin made no effort to help the Greek communists and a pro-British government was set up. But Churchill still feared Stalin's ambitions. This fear intensified his desire to see a resurrected France which might stand with Britain against the USSR. This would be essential given the likelihood that US troops would withdraw from Europe at the end of the war.

The Yalta Conference

Key question
Did Roosevelt make too many concessions to Stalin at Yalta?

Key date
Yalta Conference: February 1945

Key term
United Nations
An association of states formed in 1945 to promote peace and international security and co-operation, taking over many of the functions of the dissolved League of Nations.

In February 1945 Churchill, Roosevelt and Stalin met at Yalta in the Crimea. Agreement on several matters, such as the principle of the future occupation of Germany and its division into three occupation zones, had been reached before the meeting. But the Big Three were able to resolve a number of issues:

- Churchill won acceptance from the other two for the proposal that a military zone for France should be carved out of the area proposed for Britain.
- There was agreement that there should be free elections in the countries of liberated Europe.
- Stalin agreed to join both the **United Nations** and the war against Japan within three months of the war against Germany ending.
- Agreement was reached on Poland's frontiers. The eastern frontier was fixed on the lines which Stalin had proposed long before. Poland's western frontier was to be the Oder–Neisse river line which meant that a good deal of Germany would come under Polish rule.
- Stalin accepted that there would be 'free and unfettered' elections in Poland.

After the war Churchill claimed that a frail and dying Roosevelt was misled into making too many concessions to the USSR. Certainly Churchill had wanted to take a tougher line on a number of issues and had received no support from Roosevelt. However, it is hard to see how Britain or the USA could have taken up a different position at Yalta or got better terms. Soviet forces already controlled much of Eastern Europe. Roosevelt's main concerns were to end the fighting against Germany and Japan as quickly as possible, and to remain on good terms with Stalin after the war. At least Stalin had committed himself to the United Nations (Roosevelt's great hope for the future) and to war against Japan. The Yalta Conference ended in a blaze of apparent friendship and goodwill and Churchill returned to London saying he had 'every confidence in Stalin'.

The Polish situation in 1945

Churchill was soon shaken by reports from Poland. Polish communists seemed more concerned with arresting and executing enemies than with civil liberties. In March Churchill wrote to

Roosevelt urging him to take a tougher line on the USSR and expressing fears that they 'had underwritten a fraudulent prospectus' at Yalta. In March Eden wrote in his diary, 'I take the gloomiest view of Russian behaviour everywhere ... our foreign policy seems a sad wreck.'

Poland was an embarrassment. Britain had gone to war for the sake of Poland in 1939. But by 1945 there was little Britain could do to honour its pledges to the country. At Yalta, Britain had appeased Stalin over Poland as Chamberlain had appeased Hitler over Czechoslovakia. Churchill recognised this. He also recognised that the Soviets were on the spot and there was no way that Britain could move them from the spot.

Key dates

Deaths of Roosevelt, Mussolini and Hitler: April 1945

German surrender: May 1945

German surrender

In March 1945 Allied forces finally crossed the Rhine and cut deep into Germany (see Figure 5.8). General Montgomery and Churchill wished to press on and capture Berlin ahead of the Soviets but Eisenhower refused. By this stage in the war the Americans were increasingly calling the tune. By 1944 US armament production was six times greater than Britain's and the US had three times more men in Europe than Britain.

Key question

How important was Britain's military contribution to Allied success in 1945?

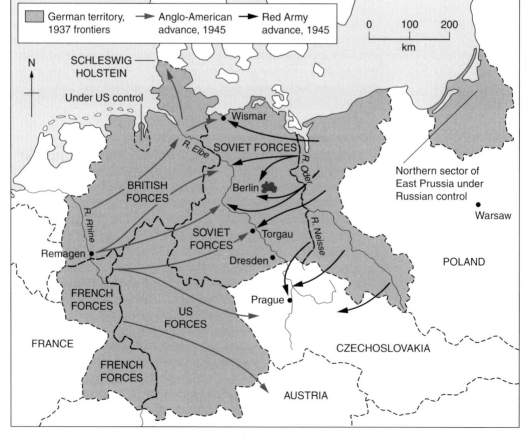

Figure 5.8: The destruction of the Third Reich.

Eisenhower had no wish to suffer more casualties than was necessary. Plans for dividing Germany into occupied zones had already been worked out and the Allies would have had to hand over to the Soviets most of the captured German territory if Montgomery had pressed on to Berlin. Moreover, the Americans had not fought the war so that Montgomery – whom they hated – could ride triumphantly on their shoulders into the German capital.

Roosevelt died in April 1945. The new President, Harry Truman, was an unknown quantity, and it would take time to establish the close relationship which Churchill had built up with Roosevelt. Mussolini and Hitler also died before the end of April. On 8 May Germany surrendered. The European conflict, which had cost over 40 million lives, was over. The war against Japan had still to be won.

The Soviet threat

Churchill was in no mood for rejoicing. He wrote to Truman warning him of the USSR's powerful military presence in Europe. He was anxious that US forces should remain in Europe. However, Truman's administration was not so convinced that Stalin was a threat to future world peace. Churchill was also at odds with British opinion. Many Britons, aware of the Soviet's valiant resistance, regarded Stalin as a kindly 'Uncle Joe' and viewed the USSR as a kind of workers' paradise.

The 1945 general election

In Britain the Labour Party decided that the moment had come to withdraw from the wartime coalition (see page 168). A general election was called for July. Voting took place on 5 July but problems involved in collecting votes from the forces overseas delayed the declaration of the results for three weeks. This meant that both Churchill and Attlee, the Labour leader, attended the start of the Potsdam Conference in July. The thinking was that if Attlee were to become Prime Minister he could easily pick up the threads of policy. In the event Labour won the election and Attlee formed a new government (see pages 200–1).

The Potsdam Conference

Key date

Potsdam Conference: July 1945

The change of government in Britain had little effect on the Potsdam Conference. Truman and Stalin were now the key players. While some progress was made with regard to issues arising from the occupation of Germany, there was deadlock over almost every other subject. During the conference Truman told Stalin that the USA had developed a new weapon, the atom bomb, which he hoped would shorten the war against Japan.

Japanese surrender

It had seemed likely that Japan might continue fighting for many more months. Although the Allies were pushing the Japanese back, they continued to meet ferocious resistance. Truman, fearing the Allies might sustain more casualties than in the war against Germany, determined, with the approval of both Churchill and Attlee, to use the new weapon. On 6 August the atom bomb was dropped on Hiroshima, killing tens of thousands of people. Although there has been much criticism of the USA using the bomb since, a decision not to drop it would have been hard to justify in August 1945. Two days later the USSR declared war on Japan. The next day a second atom bomb was dropped on Nagasaki. Japan now agreed to surrender.

Key question
Should the USA have used the atom bomb against Japan?

Key dates

Atom bombs dropped on Hiroshima and Nagasaki: August 1945

Japan surrendered: August 1945

Hiroshima, one month after the atomic bombing in September 1945.

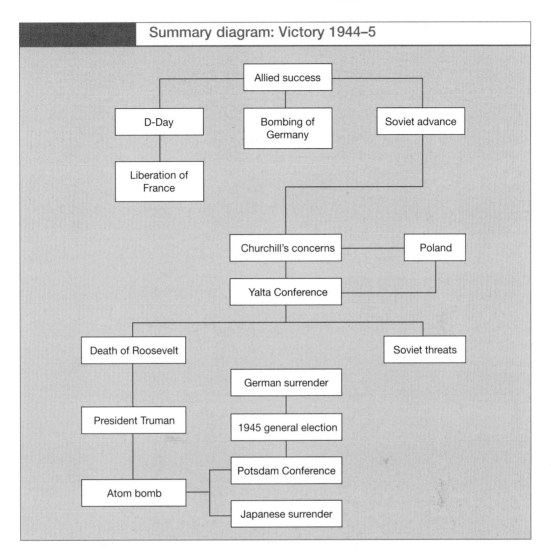

Summary diagram: Victory 1944–5

6 | Key Debate

How great a war leader was Winston Churchill?

Churchill has long been regarded as one of Britain's greatest Prime Ministers. Recently, however, historians, such as John Charmley, have questioned his greatness, pointing out that the Churchill of myth was not always the Churchill of history. Nevertheless, most historians remain convinced that Churchill was an inspired and inspiring war leader: the right man in the right job at the right time.

Background and character

Churchill's whole life had prepared him for leadership in the Second World War. He had held most of the important government offices and was a formidable negotiator and first-rate administrator. He knew more about war than any other twentieth century Prime Minister. (He had been a serving army officer, had directed the Admiralty in two world wars, and had written books about war.) He had tremendous confidence in himself. In his memoirs he recalled his emotions on becoming Prime Minister: 'I was conscious of a profound sense of relief. At last I had the authority to give direction over the whole scene. I felt as if I were walking with destiny.' Most of those who knew Churchill, and most historians who have studied him, stress his prodigious energy, his active mind and his courage. However, there were character defects. He was totally self-centred, quickly became irritable and was erratic. He was rarely able to resist an unconventional idea, sometimes to Britain's benefit, sometimes not. 'Many were moved by Churchill's words,' says historian Peter Clarke, 'not least himself'.

Churchill's leadership style

From the start Churchill struck a consistent pose of resolve. Eccentric in dress, speech and gesture, he caught and kept the confidence of the public. While many have stressed the importance of his oratory, Churchill made a more modest assessment: 'It was the nation and the race dwelling all round the globe that had the lion's heart. I had the luck to be called on to give the roar.' The '**Dunkirk spirit**' of 1940 was certainly not something that was conjured up by Churchill. Most Britons in 1940 were determined to fight to the end, whoever had been Prime Minister. Nevertheless Churchill's 'roar' was important. His speeches in the Commons and his radio broadcasts invariably succeeded in hitting the right note. In the darkest days of the war, his declarations that Britain would never surrender helped to sustain morale.

But Churchill was much more than a voice. As Chairman of the War Cabinet and Minister of Defence, he was the supreme director of Britain's war effort. He appointed and dismissed generals, admirals and air marshals. He conducted in person most of the important negotiations with Britain's international partners. He dominated his staff. Most people were in awe of his eloquent tongue and quick wit, and it was not easy to stand against him. He could not and did not do everything. His influence over his colleagues in the War Cabinet was not absolute. There were instances of his being overruled. His influence was restricted by his frequent absences through illness or forays abroad. Nevertheless, the buck stopped with Churchill, and he was quite happy to take the responsibility. Indeed he was in his element. A.J.P. Taylor said, 'He never drew breath. In this turmoil of activity he made some great mistakes and many small ones. The wonder is that he did not make more. No other man could have done what he did, and with a zest which rarely flagged.'

Dunkirk spirit
The determination of the British people (after Dunkirk) to resist Nazi aggression whatever the cost.

Key term

Churchill and military strategy

Churchill was criticised at the time, and has been criticised since, for his strategic conduct of the war: for overestimating what could be achieved by naval and air power, and for underestimating the difficulties in the way of the fulfilment of his plans. His moods frequently determined his whims and his whims determined his strategy. He has been blamed for a host of disasters, for example, Greece (see page 142), Crete (see page 142), and Singapore in 1941–2 (see page 147). Arguably, the Allies should have launched a Second Front in France in 1943 rather than in 1944. He can also be condemned for supporting the indiscriminate bombing of Germany – often seen as both immoral and ineffectual. Many have criticised him for meddling too much. President Roosevelt said of him, 'he has a hundred [ideas] a day and about four of them are good'. Erratic, impulsive, intuitive, Churchill made a number of strategic errors, and it was fortunate that some of his wilder schemes were thwarted by his military advisers (not least Sir Alan Brooke, his brilliant Chief of the Imperial Staff).

It is also possible to overrate Churchill's successes. These were sometimes due to the fact that Britain was able to intercept and decipher many of the high-level Axis radio messages. Britain's code-breakers based at Bletchley Park in Buckinghamshire (often known as Ultra) provided increasingly good information as the war progressed. The fact that Ultra was kept secret until 1973 gave the impression that some of Churchill's decisions were more inspired than was really the case.

However, Churchill has his defenders. His constant probings, suggestions and demands imparted a sense of urgency to all who came under his scrutiny. He usually supported the policy of his military experts, rarely overruling the advice he was given. The disasters which did occur were the outcome of decisions which the Chiefs of Staff had approved. To his credit Churchill forged a military team that ultimately had considerable success. His reluctance to launch a Second Front in 1943 can certainly be supported. Neither Britain nor the USA was prepared for a seaborne assault on France. Failure would have been costly in lives and could have set back the war effort by several years. Strategic bombing, which had damaging effects on German war production, can also be defended.

Some historians think that if Churchill, rather than Roosevelt or Eisenhower, had been in control in 1944–5, the Allies would have captured Berlin, much of east Germany and the Balkans ahead of the Soviets. What Churchill later described as the '**Iron Curtain**' would then have been much farther east. However, in 1944–5 Churchill did not always press very hard for some of the anti-Soviet policies which he later claimed he supported. His main concern was to defeat the existing enemies rather than prepare to deal with hypothetical future worries.

Key term

Iron Curtain
The imaginary frontier between Soviet-dominated Europe and the West.

Churchill the diplomat

Churchill did not conduct foreign policy in 'splendid isolation'. Although he provided the broad lines of policy, it was Foreign Secretary Eden who followed these up. The two men worked reasonably well together, even if Churchill's way of working was sometimes as trying to Eden as it was to the Chiefs of Staff.

Churchill believed his main task was to weld the Grand Alliance together and to ensure that the strategy pursued was the one most likely to bring about the downfall of the enemy. In seeing himself as the lynchpin of the Alliance he massively exaggerated his influence. Stalin and Roosevelt were prepared to go their own ways and even to join together on occasions against him. At Yalta Churchill played an insignificant role. He was merely a titular member of the Big Three – 'a bantam in a heavyweight league', thinks Peter Clarke. However, Churchill deserves praise for his hard work in keeping an unnatural alliance – British imperialism, US capitalism and Soviet communism – together. The eldest of the Big Three, he was also the most peripatetic, meeting Stalin five times and Roosevelt 10 times, often travelling by air at a time when such journeys were dangerous and uncomfortable.

The fact that he had an American mother gave him a head start in forming close ties with the USA. He helped persuade Americans and their President that they should assist Britain in the dark days of 1940–1. Once the USA had entered the war he established cordial relations with Roosevelt and with other leading US political and military figures. But relations were not always easy. US policy was geared to promoting British **decolonisation**. There were endless tensions over China, India, Palestine and Egypt. Churchill was also critical of US policies with regard to Stalin.

Churchill recognised that it was essential to work with Stalin but never trusted the Soviet leader. He was right to be suspicious. He later claimed that if the Americans had only listened to him, the Western powers would not have conceded control of Eastern Europe to Russia. In fairness to Roosevelt, however, it is difficult to see how the USA could have prevented this happening.

Churchill's legacy

Despite popular myth, the Second World War was hardly a glorious success for Britain. If the war was fought to save Poland, it failed. If it was fought to keep **totalitarianism** out of Europe, it failed. If it was fought to ensure the preservation of the British Empire, it barely succeeded and indeed undermined the basis of the Empire. By 1945 Britain had effectively ceded its world power to the USA and half of Europe to the USSR. It is thus possible to claim that Britain's finest hour was its gravest error. To what extent was Churchill to blame for this situation?

Perhaps the main charge levied against Churchill is that he concentrated excessively on defeating Hitler and failed sufficiently to consider Britain's role in the post-war world. Consequently, in order to stop Hitler, he bankrupted Britain, put

Key terms

Decolonisation
The process of bringing about the end of colonial rule.

Totalitarianism
A form of government that controls everything under one authority and allows no opposition.

the Empire on the road to liquidation, mortgaged the country's future to the USA, and helped raise the Soviet spectre in Europe – a menace even greater than the one destroyed. Historian John Charmley has argued that it may have been in Britain's best interest to have made peace with Hitler in 1940. British power, Charmley claims, might then have been left intact while the USSR and Germany slugged it out in Eastern Europe to the eventual benefit of Britain.

In Churchill's defence, once Britain went to war with Germany in 1939 there was probably little alternative but to go all out to defeat Hitler. A negotiated peace was out of the question as far as most Britons were concerned. The only way to defeat Hitler was to ally with the USA and the USSR. ('There is only one thing worse than fighting with allies', said Churchill, 'and that is fighting without them.') By 1945 both the USA and the USSR were far more powerful than Britain. But at least Britain emerged victorious. If henceforward it was to be a US satellite, this was far better than being a German protectorate.

Some key books in the debate

P. Addison, *Churchill: The Unexpected Hero* (Oxford University Press, 2005).

J. Charmley, *Churchill: The End Of Glory* (Hodder & Stoughton, 1992).

W.S. Churchill, *Memoirs of the Second World War* (An abridgement of the six Volumes) (Manner Books, 1991).

P. Clarke, *The Last Thousand Days of the British Empire* (Allen Lane, 2007).

M. Gilbert, *Churchill: A Life* (Holt, 1992).

R. Lamb, *Churchill as War Leader* (Bloomsbury, 1993).

R. Overy, *Why the Allies Won* (Cape, 1995).

A.J.P. Taylor, *English History 1914–1945* (Oxford University Press, 1965).

Study Guide: A2 Question

In the style of Edexcel

'Britain's resistance to Germany in the years 1939–41 was characterised by lack of resources and incompetence.' How far do you agree with this opinion?

Exam tips

The cross-references are intended to take you straight to the material that will help you to answer the question.

In assessing this view of Britain's war effort in the period before the entry of the USA into the war, you should explore how far the land, air and sea campaigns deserve this judgement.

There is scope for debate here: you can set obvious fiascos like the campaign in Norway (page 136) against the competence and preparation shown during the Battle of Britain (pages 139–40). The defence system for the Battle of Britain does not deserve the judgement 'incompetent'. The integrated structure resulted in an effective operation involving the sector stations, control apparatus and observers. In terms of resources there were powerful forces operating to the British advantage: new radar early warning system (page 87), and the new Hurricane and Spitfire aircraft (page 95). The superior level of British fighter production denied victory to the *Luftwaffe*. However, you can show that Britain was forced to evacuate from Dunkirk (page 138), British bombing raids had little pattern purpose or success (page 142) and that by 1941 Germany was winning the Battle of the Atlantic (page 142). Lack of army and naval resources can be shown in the lack of effective anti-tank guns and modern seaborne aircraft.

6 Britain and the Second World War: The Home Front

POINTS TO CONSIDER

The Second World War was regarded at the time as the 'people's war'. To an unprecedented degree the burden of war fell on the nation as a whole, testing the resolve of civilians as well as the armed forces. On the home front, the impact of the war was momentous. As in the First World War, the state stepped in to regulate social and economic life. In the Second World War, however, state intervention seemed to operate with more justice and more likelihood of the momentum being continued into the post-war world. This chapter will examine the impact of the war on Britain by focusing on the following themes:

- The phoney war
- The Churchill coalition
- The economic impact of the war
- The social impact of the war
- Morale, propaganda and civil liberties
- Britain post-1945

Key dates

1939	August	Emergency Powers Act
	September	Start of Second World War
1940	May	Fall of Chamberlain. Churchill became Prime Minister
	May	Emergency Powers Act
	September	Blitz until May 1941
1941		National Service Act
1942		Beveridge Report
1944		Education Act
1945	May	End of war in Europe
	July	Labour victory in general election
1946		National Insurance Act
1948		Establishment of the National Health Service

1 | The Phoney War

In September 1939 Chamberlain tried to form a **coalition government** with Labour. His offer was refused. Labour leaders, who had little respect for Chamberlain, felt that there was little to be gained by participating in a Chamberlain-led government. Instead, they declared that they would take a stance of 'constructive' opposition. There seemed no likelihood of Chamberlain's replacement. His government had a majority of over 200 in the Commons and he minimised the prospect of a Conservative revolt by including two of his most high-profile critics inside the government:

- Churchill became First Lord of the Admiralty.
- Eden became Dominions Secretary.

The fear of air attack

The government had made some provision to reduce the threat of air attack pre-1939:

- Serious work on civil defence had begun in 1935. By 1939 civil defence services had 1.5 million recruits – mostly unpaid volunteers.
- In 1938 Sir John Anderson, a prominent civil servant, had been put in charge of civil defence. He ordered the building of 2.5 million corrugated-steel air raid shelters which could be erected in the gardens of people's houses.
- The population was equipped with masks to survive an expected gas attack.
- Elaborate plans had been drawn up for the evacuation of children from places thought to be at risk from bombing. In September 1939 over one million children were evacuated from the big cities to reception areas in the country. When the expected attack did not materialise, most evacuees returned home.

Mobilising for war

Chamberlain's government introduced a series of measures intended to mobilise the national resources for war:

- The Emergency Powers Act (August 1939) gave the government huge powers.
- A Schedule of Reserved Occupations controlled the distribution of manpower between the armed forces and key industries.
- Targets were set for the expansion of war-related industries.
- Defence spending rose from £254 million in 1938 to £3228 million in 1940.

Unfortunately, the transition from a peacetime to a wartime economy was slow and often accompanied by muddle and confusion. A million workers remained unemployed in 1940 yet many key industries were working well below full capacity.

Key question
How effective a war leader was Chamberlain?

Key dates

Emergency Powers Act: August 1939

Start of Second World War: September 1939

Key term

Coalition government
Government by a combination of allied political parties. A coalition government is sometimes called a national government.

Key question
Why did Churchill
become Prime
Minister?

Key date

Fall of Chamberlain.
Churchill became
Prime Minister: May
1940

Chamberlain's fall

By early 1940, there was increasing criticism of Chamberlain's government:

- Labour leaders made detailed attacks on inefficient ministries, focusing on the government's failure to exert more direction of the economy.
- Chamberlain lacked inspirational qualities as a war leader.

The failure of the Norwegian campaign led to Chamberlain's downfall (see page 136). Following a debate on the conduct of the war in the Commons on 7–8 May 1940, Chamberlain's majority shrank to 81. Forty Conservatives voted against him and another 60 abstained. He determined to resign as Prime Minister.

Winston Churchill, who had long experience of Parliament and high office, was a serious contender for the leadership. As First Lord of the Admiralty, his dynamism, oratorical powers and flair for public relations had eclipsed the efforts of all other ministers. However, he had alienated the Conservative leadership on a range of political matters in the 1930s and was regarded as something of a maverick. King George VI and many senior civil servants would have preferred Lord Halifax. The latter, aware that he lacked popular support, had no wish to become Prime Minister. Churchill had no such qualms. On 10 May 1940 he was asked to form a new administration.

Churchill speaking into a microphone in 1940 ready to offer 'blood, toil, tears and sweat'.

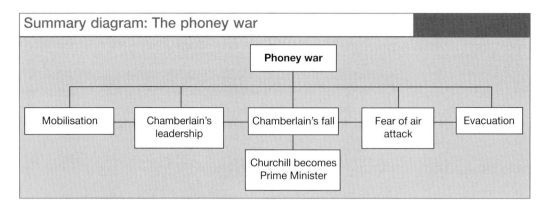

Summary diagram: The phoney war

2 | The Churchill Coalition

Churchill's position was not particularly strong in May 1940. Most Tory MPs had stayed loyal to Chamberlain during the 7–8 May debate and he remained leader of the party. When Churchill first entered the Commons as Prime Minister he was greeted by silence on the Conservative benches. It was some time before he won over the doubters in his own party.

Churchill's administration
Churchill realised the importance of getting the whole country behind him. To achieve this he needed Labour. Labour leaders were prepared to serve under him. There was an element of opportunism in their decision. They hoped that once in government they would be able to promote their own party interests. Fortunately, political interest was not incompatible with the pursuit of the national interest.

Churchill's first **War Cabinet** contained two Conservatives – Chamberlain as Lord President of the Council and Lord Halifax as Foreign Secretary, and the leader and deputy leader of the Labour Party – Clement Attlee as Lord Privy Seal and Arthur Greenwood as Minister without Portfolio. The three **service ministries** were divided between representatives of each of the main parties. Overall, though, the Conservatives had a numerical superiority in the government, reflecting the party's Commons majority. Churchill, aware of the need to retain the support of his fellow Conservatives, retained two-thirds of Chamberlain's government.

Churchill's 'finest hour'
Within six weeks of Churchill assuming the premiership, the Germans had driven the British from Dunkirk and forced France to surrender. By the end of June Britain stood alone. Employing all his oratorical talents, Churchill delivered a series of defiant speeches. This helped to forge a bond between the Prime Minister and (most) Britons and began the myth of Churchill as the saviour of the nation. In reality, Britain survived because the Royal Navy ruled the waves and the RAF prevented the *Luftwaffe* getting control of the air.

Key question
Why did Churchill want a coalition government?

War Cabinet
A small inner group of chief ministers who are mainly responsible for co-ordinating the war effort.

Service ministries
The ministries responsible for the army, navy and air force.

Key terms

Chamberlain's retirement in October (he died in November) strengthened Churchill's position. Now leader of the Conservative Party, he had more freedom to construct the government of his choice. In 1940 Sir John Anderson and Labour leaders Bevin and Morrison joined the War Cabinet. Churchill was also prepared to bring in 'outsiders':

- Newspaper proprietor Lord Beaverbrook became Minister of Aircraft Production.
- Lord Woolton, a Manchester businessman, became Minister of Food.

In selecting members of the War Cabinet, Churchill was influenced not by party feeling but by his own (sometimes eccentric) notions of competence.

Key question
Was Churchill ever in danger of being replaced?

Criticism of Churchill

Churchill's enhanced prestige and authority did not mean that his leadership was immune from criticism. By 1941 there were complaints about Churchill's irregular methods and erratic behaviour. More serious questions were asked about the organisation of the war effort, in particular the way in which production difficulties seemed to be impeding the military's effectiveness. There were suggestions that Churchill, who was Prime Minister and Minister of Defence, should be relieved of this double burden.

In the late spring of 1941, after disasters in North Africa and Greece, Churchill easily survived a vote of no confidence by 447 votes to three. More criticism followed in early 1942 after a series of defeats in the Far East (see page 147). A vote of confidence again resulted in an overwhelming endorsement of Churchill's government by 464 votes to one. The fall of Tobruk in North Africa in June 1942 brought renewed calls for a reduction of Churchill's powers. The government defeated the censure motion by 475 to 25 votes with 40 abstentions. But many who voted to support Churchill did so with misgivings. Had there been an obvious alternative, he might have been in danger. There was no such alternative and once the military tide turned in the Allies' favour in the late 1942 (see page 148), there was no longer any threat to his leadership.

Key question
Why did the Labour Party support reconstruction?

The Labour Party and reconstruction

The desperate crisis of 1940–1 engendered a national solidarity that left little role for party politics. Cabinet leaders accepted that the first priority was to defeat Hitler and for this a united effort was essential. Labour leaders like Attlee and Bevin threw their weight behind Churchill. Nevertheless, there were tensions within the coalition government and even more so among rank and file Conservative and Labour MPs, particularly about reconstruction. From the outset, Labour had claimed that the war offered an opportunity to build a new Britain, one in which the state was prepared to intervene more actively in the lives of citizens to provide greater equality, opportunity and security. As the government planned for war, so Labour argued it should also plan for peace.

For Churchill, anything not directly concerned with the winning of the war was a very low priority. He believed that **reconstruction** issues would be contentious and to address them while the war was still on would weaken national unity. But he did agree to set up a War Aims Committee in 1940 and in 1941 gave Greenwood ministerial responsibility for reconstruction questions. Greenwood's personal impact was minimal. However, in June 1941 he appointed William Beveridge to chair what was intended to be a minor committee investigating social insurance benefits. Inadvertently, this decision ensured that the coalition had to take seriously the issue of reconstruction.

Meanwhile Labour set up its own central committee on reconstruction in 1941. Subcommittees considered various subjects: land and agricultural reorganisation, transport, coal and power, social services. In February 1942 the Labour National Executive approved a document called 'The old world and the new society' which provided an ideological framework for social and economic reform.

Key terms

Reconstruction
The rebuilding and reorganisation of a society after a great upheaval.

Means testing
The method by which the government determined whether people should be given allowances and how much they should be paid.

The shift to the left

After 1940 British opinion shifted to the left. (One of the ironies of the war was that while many on the left became increasingly patriotic, many patriots became increasingly left wing.) A 'people's war', in the slogans of the time, necessitated a 'people's peace' – a better post-war Britain. There was also growing confidence in the state. The year 1940 saw the total mobilisation of the whole nation and its resources. Only through the power of the state to plan and direct could Britain hope to survive and triumph. Important sections of the media, influenced by left-wing writers and intellectuals, supported commitment to planning, equality and reform. For example, J.B. Priestley's Sunday evening *Postscripts* were heard by millions on the wireless in 1940. Popular newspapers like the *Daily Mirror* and the influential magazine *Picture Post* put over a similar message. This message was encouraged by the adulation in 1941–2 of the USSR – seemingly a successful planned society.

Labour contributed to and benefited from the change in the public mood. While Churchill concerned himself with grand strategy, the home front was dominated by Labour's big three of Attlee, Bevin and Morrison. As well as making an outstanding contribution to mobilisation, they were able to push their ideas on domestic policy through the government committees on which they served. It was largely due to Labour influence that some important wartime social legislation was passed:

- **Means testing** for the payment of benefit was ended.
- Allowances and pensions were raised.
- Bevin's Catering Wages Act aimed at improving conditions in factories.

Key question
Did Britain shift to the left after 1940?

Churchill did not necessarily oppose 'war socialism'. He simply demanded that every perceived left-wing measure be justified from the point of view of its contribution to the overall war effort.

Key question
Why was the Beveridge Report so important?

Key date

Beveridge Report: 1942

The Beveridge Report

The Beveridge Report dropped like a bombshell into an already lively reconstruction debate. Beveridge, a Liberal, had long been associated with social reform. Before the war he had built a reputation as an academic, broadcaster and newspaper columnist. With an ego and ambition to match his intellect, he was initially disappointed with his post as chair of a seemingly insignificant committee on social insurance in 1941. However, he determined to use his position to propose far-reaching social reform. His cultivation of press contacts ensured that when his report, 'Social insurance and allied services', was published in December 1942 it was met with a blaze of publicity which in turn fed public enthusiasm. The Beveridge Report, which sold 635,000 copies, was the most important document on social policy published during the war.

Beveridge proposed a rationalisation of existing insurance schemes, based on the long-established principle of contributions from worker, employer and state. In return for a weekly flat-rate contribution from the employed, the state would provide

William Beveridge, the man responsible for the Beveridge Report, addressing a group of people in 1944.

comprehensive cradle-to-grave insurance to all its citizens against unemployment, ill-health, industrial injury and old age. The main difference between Beveridge's scheme and its predecessors was the principle of universality: all those employed would contribute to the state scheme and all would be entitled to benefits. Beveridge argued his plan could only work effectively if three other conditions were realised:

* full employment was guaranteed
* family allowances were provided
* a National Health Service (NHS) was created.

Reaction to Beveridge

The Beveridge Report captured the public imagination. In 1943 one poll suggested that 88 per cent supported implementation of its proposals. The reaction in the coalition was more mixed. At the Treasury there was alarm at the prospective costs of the plan. Churchill still regarded reconstruction as tomorrow's business rather than today's. Labour ministers, not surprisingly, approved of a report which was broadly in line with Labour's own policy documents. Aware that the ideological differences at issue could not be reconciled, coalition ministers played for time. From December 1942 until February 1943 when the report was debated in Parliament, the government steered a middle line between Labour commitment and Tory caution. It welcomed the scheme in principle but refused to make any promises about spending.

In the Commons the party lines were more sharply exposed. Conservative MPs objected to Beveridge's proposals for two main reasons:

* They claimed that the post-war priority should be the revival of British export trades rather than expensive social reform.
* They argued that universal availability of benefits would weaken individual incentives and fail to target assistance to those who were in most need.

Labour MPs, by contrast, saw the postponement of reform as a betrayal of popular expectations. Previous wartime disputes in Parliament had involved issues such as **nationalisation** of coal mining and the railways. Compared with the battle over Beveridge these were mere skirmishes. In the debate between 16 and 18 February 1943, almost the whole of the parliamentary Labour Party outside the government defied ministers and supported an amendment which called for immediate action to implement Beveridge's proposals. The total of 121 votes against the coalition was the largest anti-government vote of the war. Moreover, many Labour MPs complained that their leaders were failing to exert sufficient authority within the coalition and some raised questions about the benefits of remaining partners in a Conservative-dominated government. Labour ministers responded by reminding the party of the political dangers of breaking the coalition.

Nationalisation
State control of an industry.

Key term

Most Labour MPs eventually accepted their leaders' position. Meanwhile it was clear that Labour, given its commitment to social reconstruction, would be the main beneficiary of the Beveridge Report. Beveridge commented after the parliamentary debate that the result of the post-war election was already decided: Labour would win because of the Conservative's lack of enthusiasm for his plan. While this claim says as much about Beveridge's self-importance as it does about wartime politics, opinion poll evidence lends some support to his prediction. Labour had a steady lead from early 1943 until 1945. Moreover, in four of the six by-elections in February 1943, the Tory vote fell by eight per cent. Voters seem to have transferred to 'independent' candidates who endorsed Beveridge and whose wider political stance was barely distinguishable from mainstream Labour opinion.

Implementing the Report

A growing sense that his party was suffering politically from its negative stance to Beveridge, moved Churchill to espouse reconstruction. In March 1943 he broadcast to the nation his vision of a post-war Britain that would be reconstructed under a four-year plan. Under the slogan, 'Food, Work and Homes for All', Churchill authorised schemes to be prepared for the transition period between war and peace. In November 1943 he appointed Lord Woolton to head a Ministry of Reconstruction, working through a Cabinet Reconstruction Committee. Labour members on the Committee – including Attlee, Bevin and Morrison – ensured that reconstruction did not slip down the government's list of priorities. Thus parliament considered most of the main reconstruction issues, producing **white papers** and even in some cases, for example, the 1944 Education Act and the 1945 Family Allowances Act, enacting legislation.

Wartime consensus?

Historian Paul Addison was among the first to claim that co-operation between the main parties in the wartime coalition resulted in an unusual degree of agreement – agreement which continued long after 1945. While accepting that there were some contentious areas (for example, nationalisation), Addison claimed that these were outweighed by the range of issues on which there was little to choose between the coalition partners – notably welfare reform, commitment to full employment and the operation of a **mixed economy**. According to Addison, the 1944 Education Act, the 1945 Family Allowances Act and the various white papers (on health, employment, social insurance and housing) are evidence of the coalition's commitment to shared principles of social and economic reconstruction.

However, the consensus view has been challenged by a number of scholars (for example, Harris, Pimlott and Fielding) who claim that the coalition was simply a temporary expedient, held together by the pressure of war rather than by agreement over domestic issues. As the war neared its end and minds focused on

Key date

Education Act: 1944

Key question

Was there a wartime consensus?

Key terms

White papers
Government-produced statements for the information of Parliament (and the country).

Mixed economy
An economic system where there are nationalised industries and private businesses.

reconstruction, political differences between the coalition partners became ever more apparent. While the parties might agree about which problems needed to be addressed in the aftermath of war, there was little common ground about how they should be tackled. The 1944 Education Act and the 1945 Family Allowances Act represented the limits of agreement. There was no consensus in any of the other major areas of reconstruction policy – health, employment and social insurance. The 1944–5 white papers can be seen as bland compromises which satisfied no one.

A good example of a white paper which tried but failed to disguise ideological division was that on employment. Although significant as the first official acknowledgement of the government's responsibility for maintaining high levels of employment, it contained mixed messages about how this would be achieved, fudging a host of important issues. This enabled both main parties to present the white paper as an endorsement of their separate positions. While Conservatives claimed that the document confirmed the importance of private enterprise, Labour declared that it supported the need for a commitment to state-directed economic management.

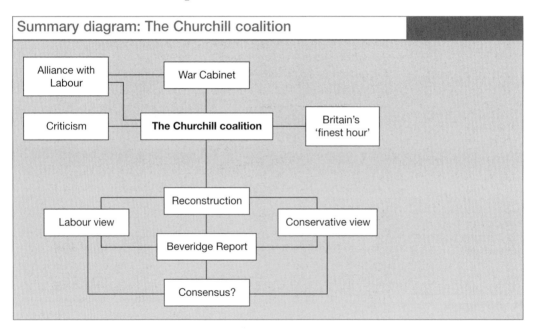

Summary diagram: The Churchill coalition

3 | The Economic Impact of the War

The British economy had been in decline for much of the inter-war period. It was overreliant on the exports of the so-called 'old' industries – textiles, coal, iron and steel and shipbuilding – which were in a bad way by 1939. These industries had failed to modernise and their productivity was low in comparison with many other countries. But not all was doom and gloom. New industries were growing rapidly. The chemical industry was as efficient as any in the world. The motor industry was thriving, promoting the advance of mass production methods, as well as

Key question
What impact did the war have on the British economy?

stimulating the expansion of other industries such as oil refining, glass and rubber. The aircraft industry, which had been small pre-1935, had grown massively thereafter, as Britain rearmed.

Mobilisation 1939–40

Key question
When did Britain fully mobilise its economy for war?

Chamberlain, his ministers and his advisers had all lived through the First World War. They knew that modern war involved the mobilisation of the nation's entire resources and thus considerable government intervention. An impressive weight of legislation was passed in 1939, giving the impression of a government moving quickly to take control of the economy. As the months passed, an extensive network of controls was established, covering almost every aspect of supply, production and trade. The machinery of government was redesigned to administer these controls. New ministries for supply, food, shipping and economic welfare were created.

But the phoney war was generally characterised by a lack of energy in terms of comprehensive planning of the nation's resources. This was largely deliberate. Chamberlain's government was ideologically opposed to extensive state intervention in the economy. Moreover, it feared that a rapid mobilisation of resources for war production would have damaging results. Confident of Britain's economic strength, Chamberlain believed that economic warfare would weaken Germany's capacity and will to fight. In his view there was no need to convert from a peace to a war economy at a pace that would cause disruption. Thus Sir John Simon's first war budget tried to limit the growth of government expenditure. An export drive was promoted in the belief that a balance of payments surplus might provide the resources needed for the war. The leisurely speed of mobilisation was evident in the fact that by May 1940 there was still over one million unemployed. Movement towards husbanding resources and reducing waste was also slow and uneven:

- While the government took over the importation of raw materials, allocations to industry allowed too many inessential goods to be made.
- Shipping space was not rigorously rationed.
- Food rationing did not start until January 1940.

Organising the war economy

The events of May–June 1940 concentrated minds on the urgency of creating a total war economy as a crucial element in what was now a struggle for survival. Churchill's government had a more active approach to the planned use of physical resources than its predecessor. Churchill was committed to victory at almost any cost while Labour members of his coalition believed in the efficacy of state control.

The new situation produced a period of improvisation. Orders and controls descended thick and fast on industry, labour and consumers as the government organised the expansion of the munitions industries and the contraction of civilian production.

Ordnance and aircraft were high priorities in 1940. Using methods described by Hugh Dalton as 'constant banditry and intrigues against all colleagues', Beaverbrook presided over a doubling of fighter production between April and September 1940. Alongside improvisation, steps were taken to ensure:

- the equipping of an army of three million men
- the building of a long-range bomber fleet
- the expansion of the Royal Navy and the merchant navy to keep Britain safe and supplied with imported raw materials and food.

The Lord President's Committee, a small group consisting mainly of Cabinet ministers and chaired by the Lord President of the Council (initially Chamberlain and then Anderson), became the real powerhouse of economic policy, co-ordinating the work of other Cabinet committees. It ensured that by 1941 there was less 'muddling through' and more planning.

Nevertheless, the conversion to a total war economy proceeded by consent rather than compulsion. While some industries and services, such as the railways, did come under direction amounting to state control, for the most part ownership (to Labour's chagrin) remained in private hands. Private firms had to work out their own ways of adapting to a situation in which the government determined prices, allocated raw materials and labour and licensed capital equipment.

Control of labour

Churchill's invitation to Ernest Bevin to take charge of the Ministry of Labour and National Service in 1940 was practical and symbolic. A leading trade unionist, there was no one more likely than he to succeed in persuading organised labour to accept the constraints on traditional labour rights that total war must bring. Bevin's main task was to distribute labour between competing needs: the armed forces, war production, and civilian industry and services. The Emergency Powers Act (May 1940) gave him the authority to require individuals to register for war work and then to direct them to work under terms and conditions laid down by the ministry. These regulations were extended over time and by 1942 all adults up to 50 years old had been registered. By 1943 10 million people were either in active service or employed in munitions industries. Some eight million employees were affected by Essential Work Orders, introduced in 1941. These kept workers in jobs which were vital to the war effort, for example, coal and shipbuilding, by restricting employees' rights to resign from a job and employers' rights to dismiss workers. While Bevin had enormous power to conscript, he understood the workers' dislike of compulsion and used his powers to direct labour sparingly. In fact, only 250,000 men and 90,000 women were directed into wartime work which they had not chosen.

Key question
Why was the mobilisation of labour so important?

Emergency Powers Act: May 1940

Key date

Shortage of skilled labour

As well as ensuring that manpower levels were adequate in each industry, the Ministry of Labour had to ensure that workers had the necessary skills. Thus, key workers had to be prevented from joining the armed forces, training programmes had to be set up for new workers, and complex jobs had to be redesigned in ways that made them suitable for unskilled workers. This process, known as dilution, usually involved dividing work into a set of less complex tasks and often made use of new machinery. While unions feared dilution might undermine the value of skilled labour, they accepted it for the sake of the war effort.

Female workers

Key question
How important were female workers?

By 1942 over four million British men – 40 per cent of those of military age – were in the armed forces. Yet amazingly there was an increase of 2.8 million workers between 1939 and 1943, of whom 2.2 million were women. Pre-1939 the prevailing view was that the proper sphere of women was the home. There was thus a need for a change of attitude among employers, male workers, husbands and women themselves. This is reflected in the prominence in official propaganda of appeals to women to take up war work. Success in getting women into the workforce was matched by success in deploying them into previously male-dominated sectors. In 1939 only 19 per cent of the insured workforce in engineering was female, 27 per cent in the chemical industry and 34 per cent in the metals industry. By 1943, the proportions had increased to 34 per cent, 52 per cent and 46 per cent, respectively. Inducements and appeals, however, did not persuade as many women as were needed. Thus, the National Service Act was introduced in December 1941. Initially aimed at unmarried women aged 20–30, the lower limit was reduced to 19 in 1942 and the upper raised to 40 in 1943. Some 200,000 women were directed into industry although far more entered the services or did war work because they expected to be directed to do so.

Key date

National Service Act: 1941

At the peak of female mobilisation in 1943, some 7.75 million women were in paid work. Only the USSR outdid Britain in exploiting the potential of female labour. Nevertheless, women might have been used more effectively. Married women were not liable under the 1941 Act and so some 10 million women remained 'unavailable' even for part-time work. Despite the need for female labour, the government, employers and trade unions obstructed demands for equal pay, which might have encouraged more women into paid work. In the engineering industry, for example, the average wage for women in 1944 was only half that for men. Women in the war industries were typically confined to low-paid, low-status work with few promotion prospects. This prejudice against women was counterproductive: skilled work was desperately needed, regardless of the gender of the person doing it.

Trade unions

Bevin recognised that the support of the unions was vital in terms of preventing industrial unrest and in increasing war production. Determined to work in co-operation with them, he ensured that they were consulted over policy. The need to maintain good relations with the unions helps to explain why Bevin was reluctant to impose statutory wage controls, preferring instead to let **free collective bargaining** continue. He believed workers were entitled to good working conditions and welfare arrangements and the right to negotiate through their union for adequate wages.

Restriction of consumer goods

From 1940 there was tight control of imports and almost all goods from abroad were either bought on government account or shipped in under licence. Imported materials were controlled at the ports and then issued to manufacturers under government licence. The government was thus able to ensure that most resources went into war materials. By 1941 the production of consumer goods had fallen to less than half the pre-war level. The concentration of production policy, begun in 1941, aimed to base consumer industries in a limited number of factories, ensuring that they then operated at full capacity. By mid-1943 concentration had been largely completed, covering 70 branches of industry. In the process many manufacturers of clothing and household goods had to conform to the Board of Trade's 'Utility' standards. This involved a simplification of design and reduction of product types in order to cut down the amount of raw materials used.

Rationing

The main restriction on consumption was rationing. Almost all foodstuffs, with the exception of bread and potatoes, were rationed by prescribed minimum quantities per week. Other items, for example clothing, were graded on a points system, enabling consumers to choose how to use their allowance and government to adjust the points weighting of items to take account of shipping losses. Rationing helped to reduce imports, thereby releasing shipping space for war materials.

Agriculture

The government instituted a drive to raise agricultural production, particularly cereals and vegetables. Farmers were given subsidies to plough up grassland and guaranteed prices for their produce. Agricultural Executive Committees oversaw the production drive, inspecting farms, giving advice or instructions, allocating machinery, fertilisers, feedstuffs and labour. They were empowered to dispossess tenants who resisted their instructions and send in their own labour to carry out the work, drawing on the **Women's Land Army**, **conscientious objectors** and prisoners of war. Pre-1939 Britain relied on imports for 70 per cent of its

Key question
Why was it important to restrict consumer goods?

Key terms

Free collective bargaining
Negotiation on pay and conditions of service between one or more trade unions on one side and an employer or association of employers on the other.

Women's Land Army
An organisation of some 80,000 women employed to work on the land.

Conscientious objectors
People who refuse to fight for reasons of conscience.

Key question
Why was agriculture so important in the war?

food. This was reduced to 60 per cent during the war, thereby saving valuable shipping space. Output rose by 81 per cent for wheat, 92 per cent for potatoes and 30 per cent for vegetables. Yield per acre was increased for nearly all crops. These remarkable gains were mainly the result of the greater use of fertilisers and machinery. In an attempt to reduce dependency on imported foodstuffs, the Ministry of Food urged everyone to reduce waste and those who could do so to grow their own vegetables or keep hens and pigs.

Finance

Key question
How did Britain pay for the war?

The war saw an enormous growth in government expenditure: from £1 billion a year in 1939 to £4 billion in 1941 and £6 billion in 1945. Somehow money had to be found to pay for the war. Aware of the need to sustain morale, the government tried to ensure that the financial burden fell equitably on the nation.

In May 1940 the famous economist J.M. Keynes joined the Treasury. He stressed the benefits of government expenditure and economic management to maintain maximum output. Instead of the Treasury assessing revenue on the basis of what the taxpayer could bear, he argued it should start at the other end: the government should first work out the national income to ascertain the war-making potential of the economy; then calculate the level of taxation and forced savings needed to allow the government to absorb a greater share of the national income. Keynes also believed that increased taxation and forced savings would absorb the **inflationary pressures** (arising from the scarcity of consumer goods). His ideas were taken up even by such traditional wartime Chancellors as Kingsley Wood and Sir John Anderson.

Key terms

Inflationary pressures
Problems arising from the rise in the price of goods and the general cost of living.

Surtax
An additional tax payable on incomes above a high level.

In addition to the high duties which consumers paid on items such as alcohol, there were increases in direct taxation. Income tax went up to 50 per cent (it had been nine per cent in 1939) and some four million new taxpayers were brought into the system. Higher earners were subject to an increased rate of **surtax**. Businesses were also heavily taxed. Purchase tax was developed into an instrument for reducing consumption. Receipts from direct taxation quadrupled and those from indirect taxation tripled.

As well as higher taxation, the government introduced compulsory saving and a range of schemes, from National Savings for small investors to Treasury bills for organisations with larger sums to invest, to encourage everyone to save.

Paying for imports

Key question
How did Britain pay for its imports?

By 1943 British exports were only half the level of 1938. Meanwhile, the cost of imports had risen by one-third. There was thus a colossal balance of trade deficit. In 1939–40 the gap was managed by running down gold and hard currency reserves and selling overseas assets. In order to raise dollars for imports from the USA, overseas British assets worth some £1000 million were sold. Another recourse was the accumulation of external debt.

Much of this was held in the form of sterling balances, that is, the credits of **sterling area** countries held in blocked accounts in London, accumulating through exports to Britain. Of Britain's £3.5 billion external liabilities in 1945, £2.7 billion was accounted for in this way.

These measures were insufficient to finance the war. US collaboration saved the day. From March 1941 the Lend–Lease Act allowed Britain to have what US goods it needed without having to find the money at once (see page 140). In total, Lend–Lease aid to Britain and it empire was £5.5 billion. In addition, Britain received $3 billion dollars worth of mutual aid from Canada, written off as a gift at the end of the war. Without Lend–Lease and Canadian help, Britain would have found it hard to carry on.

Sterling area
A group of countries (many within the Empire/ Commonwealth) with currencies tied to the British currency.

Gross domestic product
The total value of goods and services produced within a country.

Key terms

Control of inflation
The restriction of consumption by rationing helped to reduce inflationary pressures. So did government subsidies, introduced in 1941, to keep down prices. By 1945 some £250 million had been spent on food subsidies. The result was that food prices rose by only 42 per cent between 1938 and 1946, compared with an increase in personal disposable income of 68 per cent over the same period. Price control was used in other areas (especially 'utility goods') to guard against an inflationary wage–price spiral. Such measures kept the rise in the cost of living below 50 per cent between 1939 and 1945.

The national income
Britain could only sustain its war production expenditures by increasing the national income. **Gross domestic product** (GDP) grew at an average annual rate of 6.2 per cent. Of the main combatant nations, only the USA surpassed Britain's increase in real domestic product.

Key question
How successful was the performance of the war economy?

Labour mobilisation
By mid-1944 55 per cent of the labour force was either in uniform or in civilian war work, a higher proportion than that achieved in Germany or the USA, but lower than that achieved by the USSR.

War production
There was an eight-fold increase in the total output of munitions of all sorts between 1939 and 1943 and increases in all weapons of war. Aircraft production rose from 7940 in 1939 to 26,461 in 1944; tank production from 969 in 1939 to 8611 in 1942. These figures sound impressive. However, historian Mark Harrison thinks that in mobilising its domestic resources for war Britain did less well than the other main belligerents. The peak percentage on military spending (47 per cent) trailed that of the USSR from 1942 on, the USA from 1943 on, and Germany throughout the war. Moreover, war industries did not always produce good articles. For example, British tanks were slower, less

well armed and more prone to mechanical failure than those produced by the Germans, Russians and Americans.

Labour productivity

Key question
Why was British labour productivity so poor?

While the expansion of output was a great achievement, levels of productivity were not impressive. Statistics for output per worker show that although it was 15 per cent higher in 1941 than in 1939, this was in fact the best year of the war. Thereafter productivity declined to a point in 1945 when it was little better than in 1938. In some industries, notably coal and shipbuilding, productivity declined during the war. Other countries' records were much better than Britain's. German labour productivity rose by 10–12 per cent while that in the USA rose by 25 per cent between 1939 and 1944.

Historians have variously blamed inefficient management, uncooperative trade unions and government failure to invest for Britain's poor productivity record. However, there were a number of factors for which no group or institution could reasonably be held responsible:

- Despite the Schedule of Reserved Occupations, there was a shortage of skilled labour. Untrained workers could not usually match the productivity of their skilled colleagues.
- Air raid attacks damaged productivity.
- Merchant shipping losses sometimes reduced the supply of raw materials or spare parts.

Poor management

Unenterprising management often held back output. While the war lasted, profits were easily made. Government contracts removed all financial risks. There was thus no incentive to promote efficiency. In fairness to employers, major reorganisation of production methods invariably caused a stoppage in work and while in the longer term this might make a factory more efficient, short-term pressure was for volume production rather than output per worker.

Labour–employer relations

Key question
To what extent should trade unions be blamed for Britain's poor productivity?

Some contemporaries blamed the workforce, a charge that was taken up by historian Correlli Barnett, who highlighted a variety of faults: slackness, absenteeism, lack of work discipline, a willingness to conduct unofficial strikes and the reluctance of workers to abandon restrictive and/or traditional practices. The days lost through strikes in Britain was higher every year from 1941 to 1945 than in 1938–9. A large part of the problem, Barnett claimed, was the Essential Work Order (1941) which restricted the rights of employers to sack workers in key industries, thus removing an important source of discipline in the workplace.

A Joint Consultative Committee, a body with equal representation of management and unions, was created to deal with labour matters. In July 1940 the Committee agreed to create a National Arbitration Tribunal. This was to be brought into play in situations where agreement over pay or conditions of employment could not be reached. The Tribunal's ruling was binding on both sides. At the same time, strikes and lock-outs were made illegal. Nevertheless, industrial disputes did not go away. The number of working days lost through strikes increased from 1,077,000 in 1941 to a peak of 3,696,000 in 1944. Bevin was criticised by some at the time for not using his powers to force strikers to return to work.

Much of the labour conflict was concentrated in one industry: coal mining. It accounted for 46.6 per cent of the strikes and 55.7 per cent of the working days lost. Serious unrest over pay and an alarming shortfall in coal output in 1942 caused the government to set up a Ministry of Fuel and Power to regulate and supervise the coal industry. It also appointed a board of investigation with a brief to study and report on miners' pay and conditions. On the board's advice, a substantial pay award was made to miners. But unrest among miners persisted.

Poor labour relations did play a part in Britain's poor productivity record. To accord them the prime position, however, is probably unfair. Moreover, Barnett's criticism of the workforce disregards certain mitigating factors. Hours of work in Britain, for example, were usually longer than in Germany or the USA. This helps to explain why British workers were more prone to absenteeism. By focusing on labour unrest, it is easy to overlook the constructive role which the workforce played in the improvement of productivity, largely though Joint Production Committees which were used to channel ideas about efficiency and new methods from the factory floor to management.

Lack of investment

The level of capital investment was probably a more important factor in Britain's poor record of productivity than imperfect labour relations. Capital investment in Britain during the war actually declined.

Britain's economic performance: conclusion

Economic resources very much determined the outcome of the Second World War, but more the resources of the USA and the USSR than those of Britain. The war exposed the weaknesses of the British economy: antiquated plant and production techniques, lack of skilled workers, poor labour–employer relations, and conservative and complacent management and unions. However, when account is taken of the flaws and failings and the circumstances of disruption under which the resources of the nation were mobilised, what is remarkable is how well the economy performed.

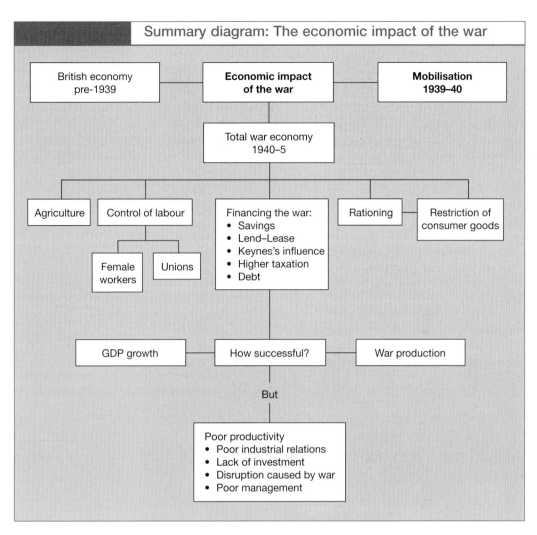

Summary diagram: The economic impact of the war

4 | The Social Impact of the War

Key question
What effect did the war have on British society?

The war was a severe test of civilian nerve. Between 1939 and 1942 more British civilians died than British soldiers. As well as the threat and reality of bombing, people had to endure separation, deprivation and restriction.

The impact of conscription

Conscription was a major disruption to family life and personal relationships. By 1945 4.2 million males and 400,000 females had served in the armed forces. Two-and-a-half million married women were deprived of their husbands' support and company. There was the constant fear that loved ones would be killed or injured. Men in the armed services were poorly paid and allowances to wives were not generous. Consequently many married women found it hard to make ends meet.

The war played havoc with people's sex lives, especially those who were recently married, and the prospect of separation prompted many couples to marry at once. Separation could lead to 'drifting': lonely wives of servicemen giving in to the temptation of extramarital affairs. Wartime life created opportunities for women to 'drift', not least the arrival (from early 1942) of hordes of well-paid US soldiers and airmen. Other opportunities came because more women were in paid work, meeting new people. 'Drifting' led to a rise in the number of unintended pregnancies. A rise in the divorce rate was another statistical feature of the war – sometimes a product of new relationships. The double standards of the time allowed for husbands in service to 'stray' if separated from their wives. However, women who 'drifted' in their husbands' absence were harshly censured.

The experience of children

The war led to the separation of children and parents. Many urban children were evacuated to rural areas to escape the threat of bombing. Evacuation, while encouraged by the government, was voluntary. To evacuate or not to evacuate was a hard decision: the break-up of the family versus the risk of violent death. In the

Key question
Did the war have a damaging effect on children?

London evacuees in 1939. What are they carrying and what appears to be their mood?

event, by 1945 four million city dwellers had spent some time in the country. While evacuation was initially an adventure for many children, most were soon homesick and some were treated appallingly by hosts who resented having evacuees dumped on them. Children raised in city slums often found it hard to fit into rural middle-class households: there were major differences in behaviour, attitudes and language. In many cases once parents heard their offspring were unhappy, they brought them home.

Even those children who were not evacuated suffered from the disruption of family life. Some had their homes destroyed by bombing. Many more effectively 'lost' their parents, given that their fathers were conscripted and their mothers working. Responsibilities were heaped on older children who had to care for younger siblings while their mothers worked.

Evacuation, the destruction of school buildings, and the shortage of books, equipment and teachers all tended to have a detrimental affect on children's education.

The blackout

Fearing a massive bombing attack, attempts were made in 1939 to prevent all artificial light after dark, making it difficult for German planes to find their way. The blackout was soon resented as a spoiler of social life. Moving about outside at night was a hazardous experience and the number of road accidents rose dramatically. Moreover, putting up the blackout was a time-consuming chore, taking up to 30 minutes a day.

The blitz

Key question
How well did Britain 'take' the blitz?

Key date

Blitz: September 1940–May 1941

Heavy bombing finally occurred in 1940–1 (see page 140). London was bombed for 76 consecutive nights from 7 September 1940 and some 10,000 people died. Many other towns shared in the devastation. Come a major attack, air raid precautions, virtually everywhere, proved to be imperfect. Public air raid shelters were too few in number and gave low protection. (In London people used the underground stations.) Little provision had been made for fire prevention, and fire services were impeded by a fragmented command. Local authorities failed to learn from the experience of other towns. Most muddled through, relying on the freely given efforts of public-spirited citizens. After a heavy raid, chaos and improvisation were the order of the day. There was a tendency to insist that everything was under control when it was not. Without the contribution of the Women's Voluntary Services (WVS) it is hard to imagine post-raid services functioning at all. The WVS, deploying a million volunteers, set up field kitchens and staffed rest centres for those who lost homes.

Popular images of the blitz emphasise that the crisis was met by shared defiance and common endeavour: communal shelters; bomb-damaged shops and businesses which refused to close; neighbours taking in homeless families; volunteer wardens, fire-fighters and rescue workers scrambling through rubble in search of survivors. These were, and still are, seen as:

- the outward expressions of a new communal culture
- testimony to the strength of British society under the challenge of war.

The blitz, however, was not just a story of brave resistance, self-sacrifice and social solidarity. Official reports indicate that the raids also drew responses of a different kind. A report on Coventry, for example, referred to 'great depression, a widespread feeling of impotence … and many open signs of hysteria'. In Bristol there was talk of the people having been let down by the government and of the possibility of a negotiated peace. Nor is there much evidence that the air raids helped to break down barriers of social isolation and class consciousness. Only a minority of the population used communal shelters: for most people the blitz was very much a personal or family experience. If the raids promoted wider social identification, they did so within specific localities rather than across the nation as a whole. The fact that working-class areas of high population density suffered most and often had the least adequate shelter provision produced a degree of class-based resentment.

Nevertheless, urban Britain did not suffer any lengthy period of social breakdown under the pressure of raids. Most townspeople adjusted to a level of danger that was endurable and, with luck, survivable. Where bombing was a persistent hazard, the adaptations to normal life it imposed were particularly trying. Along with the mental strain of the fear of death, there was the problem of shortage of sleep and the sheer unpleasantness of being forced to go to ground in air raid shelters. Thankfully most experienced the real thing only occasionally.

Rationing

Food – its price, quantity, quality and variety – was an unwelcome preoccupation at all levels of society. In the early months of war the government had tended to let the market sort itself out. This had proved socially divisive: the poor were hardest hit by the price inflation that followed the disruption of commerce. The government quickly learned from its mistake. Its rationing system ensured a basic sort of fairness (even King George VI had a ration book) and won general approval. Rationing meant that in terms of calorific and nutritional needs people did not go short. (Indeed, the general level of health was higher during the war than before it.) The dull monotony of the average wartime diet, however, was a hardship. Some foods (for example, bananas) disappeared and many others were intermittent. Queuing for food became a feature of many people's lives.

Given the shortage of all consumer goods, people had to 'make do and mend'. Wartime surveys suggest that most people accepted austerity as a tiresome but necessary precondition for winning the war. What hurt was relative deprivation. Thus the arrival of affluent US servicemen aroused mixed feelings of admiration, envy and resentment. While some women benefited

> **Key question**
> Why was rationing perceived to be successful?

from US generosity (obtaining cosmetics and nylon stockings), for many people feeling like poor relations was another irritation of war.

Travel problems

Travel was a major source of frustration. While the war increased the need for many people to travel (for example, conscripts and evacuees), it made it more difficult to do so. After 1939 railway lines were not repaired and there was little new stock. A contracting railway system had to cope with a 70 per cent increase in passenger traffic. Moreover, passenger transport had a lower priority than the needs of the military and the war economy. Crowding, queuing and delays were the inevitable result. Road transport was no better:

- There was a contraction of bus services.
- Few people had cars. Those who did were unable to use them because petrol was strictly rationed.

Rising crime rates

Wartime crime rates were comparatively low when set against statistics post-1945 but the fact remains that an increase in several categories of crime occurred during the war, contradicting the idea that a new communal culture developed:

- The aftermath of air raids provided opportunities for looting to become widespread (albeit it was often more akin to salvaging than to stealing).
- Throughout the war the **black market** flourished. Dock workers stole imported food and other goods. Retailers found loopholes in the **coupons** system to secure extra goods which then sold on the black market.
- Normally law-abiding citizens often responded to wartime privation by pilfering goods from work, drawing rations under false names and buying forged or stolen ration coupons on the black market.

Positive social aspects of the war

There were some positive aspects despite the hardship that many people were enduring:

- Full employment was restored after the hard times of the 1930s.
- For poor families the official food allowance was well above their usual expectations.
- There was a blunting of class division, resulting from the sense of a shared crisis and everyone doing their bit for the war effort.
- While many leisure pursuits (for example, professional sport) were adversely affected by the war, some flourished, not least radio listening. There were large audiences for comedy shows and popular music programmes.
- Some 25–30 million cinema tickets were sold each week.
- Dancing was popular, especially if servicemen were in the neighbourhood.

Key terms

Black market
Buying or selling that is against the law.

Coupons
Vouchers from ration books, allowing people to buy goods.

The impact of the war on women

Pre-1939 it was almost universally accepted that men were the breadwinners: women the homemakers. It followed that most women in paid work were thought to be in a temporary activity prior to marriage and a domestic role. A **marriage bar** affected most public and many private sector occupations. The need to mobilise women for the war effort presented the government with a dilemma: on one side it needed to recruit sufficient female labour to meet production targets; on the other, it had no wish to overturn women's traditional role.

The impact on women: the positive view

By 1943 compulsory recruitment of females into the women's services, civil defence or munitions factories had helped to increase the number of women in the workforce by some 1.5 million compared with 1939. However, the increased female presence in the labour force was due in part to the voluntary entry of married women into employment. Whereas in 1931 only 16 per cent of working women were married, by 1943 the figure had climbed to 43 per cent, a rise that was helped by the provision of state-run nurseries for working mothers. Historian Arthur Marwick claimed that prejudice against the employment of married women was overcome during the war.

Not only did women participate in the labour force in greater numbers but they also did work previously restricted to men. Most of the no-go areas for women, such as iron and steel working, engineering and vehicle building, were opened up. At the same time, the presence of women in traditionally female and lower-paid sectors such as textiles, domestic service and consumer services declined. Arguably this contributed to a gender restructuring of the labour force post-1945.

Despite the barrage of advice from all quarters urging women to return to their traditional domestic role post-1945, a number of surveys suggest that most working women wanted to continue in paid work. It may be that most simply enjoyed the increased affluence the extra income brought. But many also enjoyed the company, working with others as a contrast to socially restricted family life. Moreover, it seems that many women no longer saw the roles of housewife and paid worker as mutually exclusive. They realised that it was possible to go out to work without causing any detrimental effects to family life.

Evidence from social surveys suggests that the new roles, earning power and geographical mobility experienced by women during the war enhanced their self-awareness and self-esteem and made them more confident about their ability to take on new challenges after 1945.

The Royal Commission on Population, established in 1945, declared that marriage partners had more equality of status – a trend accelerated by the war. Although many women left employment after 1945, the sense of independence they developed in the war possibly made them less likely to accept a

Key question
What impact did the war have on women's traditional role?

Marriage bar
A rule whereby women were forced to resign from their jobs once they married.

Key term

subordinate role within marriage. This may help to explain the sharp rise in the divorce rate after 1945. Perhaps women had developed higher expectations of marriage and had greater confidence to break one which was not meeting those expectations.

The impact on women: the negative view

Between 1939 and 1943 the number of women in employment rose from 4.8 million to 6.7 million, reducing to 6.2 million by 1945. In other words, most women doing paid work during the war did not embark on it because of the war. Most were already in paid employment when the war came and the war made little difference to this aspect of their lives. Moreover, after 1945 there was a shift back towards the pre-war situation. By 1951 the proportion of women in the labour force had returned to 1930s' levels.

Importantly, employers and trade unions agreed that that there should be a restoration of pre-war practices when the war was over. Thus, in many jobs, however competent they were, women could not look forward to the prospect of career advancement or even of being retained on the payroll when peace came.

Women received lower rates of pay than men engaged in equivalent work. Although some apparent progress was made towards the principle of equal pay in the engineering industry, it only applied to a minority of women who directly replaced men and were able to perform precisely the same job. In practice, many employers altered the work process slightly in order to keep women's wages below the male rate. Thus, while average earnings for women workers increased during the war, their rates of pay remained substantially below those of males.

The government tried to ignore the issue of equal pay. This stance persuaded women's pressure groups to establish the Equal Pay Campaign Committee. In 1944 its lobbying helped to produce a victory of sorts when an amendment to the Education Bill requiring equal pay for female teachers was passed by 117 to 116 votes. The victory was short lived. The government declared it would resign unless the vote was overturned – as duly happened. The appointment of a Royal Commission on the issue effectively removed equal pay from the wartime political agenda. When the commission reported in 1946, equal pay was less of a concern and its findings were largely ignored.

During the war many married women worked part time. Many continued to do so post-1945 as a useful way of supplementing family income. Unfortunately:

- part-time workers had few rights with regard to job security, training, sick pay, paid leave or pensions
- part-time work tended to reinforce the sexual division of labour and the association of working women with low-paid and low-skilled jobs.

Domestic work continued to be seen as a female responsibility, even after women were conscripted into the labour force. The government's wish to minimise any challenge to gender stereotypes was evident in its propaganda which emphasised that women could take on manual occupations without sacrificing their femininity. Women's magazines also continued to promote the view that home and family were women's main responsibility. Carrying a recurrent theme of 'beauty as duty', they encouraged readers to beautify themselves in order to maintain men's morale.

Post-1945 several major firms (in effect) restored the marriage bar, casting doubt on claims that the war helped to promote more progressive attitudes. Barriers which restricted employment opportunities for married women were given added significance by the post-1945 marriage boom. This was followed by a baby boom. (Over one million children were born in 1947.) Both booms can be interpreted as confirmation of the fact that the war years had neither encouraged nor empowered women to break free from their domestic roles.

Conclusion

In short, the wartime experience of women did not amount to a liberation from their traditional roles or to a significant change in society's attitude to those roles. Survey evidence suggests that most men and women post-1945 thought that men were the main income-earners and that wives should work only if it did not interfere with domestic duties. Nor did the war advance sexual equality in terms of pay and career prospects. Women had to wait until the 1970s before the principle of equal pay was established in law.

The impact of the people's war

During the war a diverse collection of reformers, ranging from Beveridge, Keynes, J.B. Priestley and George Orwell, to the Labour Party and the Tory Reform Group, argued that the common experience of war resulted in pre-war class divisions being set aside in favour of a new social cohesion. This greater sense of collective consciousness in turn created an opportunity to construct a new social and political order on the basis of the acceptance of an enhanced role for the state in people's lives.

> **Key question**
> Did the war lead to a new social cohesion?

Many scholars have endorsed the view that the war produced a heightened sense of public solidarity which resulted in social change. Richard Titmuss, for example, has argued that changed public values helped to produce the egalitarian social policies and collectivist economic measures adopted in part by the coalition government and more fully by the post-war Labour government. Historian Arthur Marwick, while regarding Titmuss's theory of the relationship between war and social change as over-simplistic, agreed that the war led to profound changes in society, caused in part by the collective nature of the war effort.

However, a number of historians have raised doubts about the validity of the war–social change thesis. For example, Titmuss believed that evacuation played a major role in the promotion of social solidarity, claiming that the interaction of previously distant social groups – working and middle class, town and country –

increased awareness of the problems of urban poverty, as reception halls in the country filled up with malnourished, ill-clothed and lice-ridden children. According to Titmuss, evacuation stirred the national conscience and produced important changes in social policy, including the increased provision of free milk and meals in schools and the implementation of the 1944 Education Act. However, Titmuss's interpretation of the effect of evacuation has been challenged. Middle-class social work agencies at the time identified working-class parental failure and 'problem' families as explanations for the poor condition of evacuees, not deep-seated social and economic deprivation. A change in working-class lifestyle and attitudes rather than extensive social reform was their solution to the problem. It also seems that many evacuee families found it hard to reside with their hosts, to the extent that two families sharing the same home often lived virtually separate existences. Middle-class hosts became reluctant to accommodate evacuees while evacuee families were usually most happy when they resided with hosts from a similar background. In short, far from promoting cross-class co-operation and understanding, evacuation confirmed and often deepened class antagonism. The relationship between evacuation and social reform is also problematic. While the provision of milk and meals was widely extended for schoolchildren in wartime, plans to extend this provision had been drawn up in the 1930s. Similarly the 1944 Education Act developed from pre-war plans and contained little that drew directly from wartime experiences.

It does not seem as though British citizenship was reconstructed in any fundamental way as a result of the war. Wartime survey evidence suggests that by 1945 Britons focused on their own needs and those of their families rather than identifying in any strong sense with the state or community. The unhappy story of labour–employer relations (see pages 181–2) clashes uncomfortably with the broad picture of a nation united and committed to the challenge of resisting Nazi aggression.

Nevertheless, the war proved that Britain was a cohesive society. Britons of all classes made sacrifices, worked together and abandoned narrow self-interest in pursuit of the shared goal of defeating the enemy. While class divisions and class attitudes remained, they were no more conducive to the breakdown of society in the war than they had been before it. George Orwell, writing in 1941, said: 'the English sense of national unity has never disintegrated. Patriotism is finally stronger than class-hatred.' The symbol of this feeling, the monarchy, gained popular affection in the war. The fact that the king and queen had remained in London and shared the dangers of the blitz (Buckingham Palace was bombed nine times) was an important explanation for this, together with their insistence on visiting bombed cities to bolster people's morale.

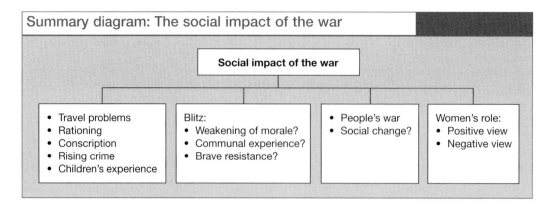

Summary diagram: The social impact of the war

Social impact of the war

- Travel problems
- Rationing
- Conscription
- Rising crime
- Children's experience

Blitz:
- Weakening of morale?
- Communal experience?
- Brave resistance?

- People's war
- Social change?

Women's role:
- Positive view
- Negative view

5 | Morale, Propaganda and Civil Liberties

Given the view that Russia, Austria-Hungary and Germany had collapsed in the First World War because of internal problems, the government realised the importance of sustaining the spirit and commitment of the people. An excess of bad news or circulation of alarmist rumours could act negatively on morale.

The Ministry of Information

A Ministry of Information (MOI) was created in 1939. Its brief was to sustain civilian morale, to give a positive presentation of war news, and to stimulate the war effort. Initially, it failed to find the common touch with the public; its patronising tone and policy of exhortation was irritating rather than inspiring. The situation improved when Brendan Bracken became Minister of Information in 1941. Bracken believed that the MOI should act on the premise that the public were happy to make sacrifices if the need was clearly explained and they knew how things stood. The MOI also wanted to know how things stood with the public. It thus collected information about civilian opinion via Home Intelligence and the Wartime Social Survey. This information, passed on to relevant departments, enabled the government to act knowledgeably to counter potential threats to morale.

Morale

Fears that British morale would be unable to sustain a long war proved groundless. Despite defeats in 1940 defeatism was never rife. People supported the war effort in the dark days of 1940 because there was really no alternative. There was a loathing for Hitler's Germany and a strong sense that the British way of life was worth preserving. Churchill's role in sustaining morale was also important. His speeches, bearing and actions personified defiance. (Labour leader Attlee once said, somewhat unfairly, that Churchill's contribution to winning the war was mainly to talk about it!) The 'Dunkirk spirit' – part reality, part myth – was first evoked by Churchill in his uncompromising 'we will fight on the

Key question
How effective were the government's efforts to sustain civilian morale?

Key question
Did the government need to be so concerned about British morale?

beaches' speech on 4 June. His words matched the stubborn, national mood.

By October 1940 the fear of invasion had abated: instead people had to cope with the blitz. Morale held up well. The stereotype of civilians braving the bombing with resolution, comradeliness and undimmed cheerfulness was no mere propaganda construct. Mass Observation and Home Intelligence reports suggest that its basis was essentially true. After 1941 apathy and war weariness were seen as greater threats than panic and defeatism. The MOI's hardest task was persuading civilians not to become complacent.

Morale-boosting aids

Propaganda experts knew that action was more effective than words. Churchill's government thus attempted to raise the material standards of life for the poor. Full employment and greater purchasing power were powerful aids to feelings of well-being and determination to see the war through to a successful conclusion.

The government recognised the importance of tobacco and alcohol for morale purposes. Unaware of the health risks, most adults smoked. For many it was a way of 'calming the nerves'. Cigarettes were never rationed and scarce shipping space was reserved to ensure supplies got through. By 1943 tobacco imports were higher than in 1939. The comforting effects of alcohol were also acknowledged. The War Cabinet included several members (not least Churchill) whose daily consumption suggested that they at least felt it helped them to cope with the stress of work. Thus beer stayed off ration. Consumption rose by 25 per cent during the war.

The provision of entertainment became an important part of the government agenda. There was a realisation that light relief helped to counter the dispiriting effects of austerity. Professional entertainers were thus permitted, and indeed encouraged, to entertain. Cinema and radio were good for morale. The government also supported:

- ENSA (the Entertainments National Services Association), which provided light entertainment for servicemen and factory workers
- CEMA (the Council for the Encouragement of Music and the Arts), whose aim was to sustain more highbrow cultural activity.

Between them ENSA and CEMA took to the public a wealth of cultural diversion ranging from George Formby and his ukulele to the London Philharmonic Orchestra.

Morale: conclusion

From March 1941 the MOI produced a chart that recorded the course of public morale, according to Home Intelligence weekly reports. The chart shows sharp fluctuations, usually in relation to wartime events. But overall the picture is clear: there was much grumbling, some bitterness and occasional despair, but most

Britons were determined to see the business through. While the Dunkirk spirit was a short-lived phenomenon, fading away as the invasion threat receded, there was never any doubt that national solidarity was real. The government's – at times obsessive – efforts to raise morale may have had only a marginal effect. There was always a sound-enough base of commitment to defeat Hitler.

The national press

Full freedom of the press could not survive the outbreak of war: censorship in some form had to be employed if only because of the need to safeguard information which might be of value to the enemy. Defence ('D') notices prevented newspaper discussion of a host of military matters. This made sense. The problem for the press was the tendency of the service ministries to interpret censorship guidelines in the most restrictive way possible. Journalists, unable to meaningfully discuss the progress of the war, vented their frustration on the shortcomings of the MOI.

In May 1940 the coalition government extended controls over the press, allowing the Home Secretary to act against material which in his view was calculated to foment opposition to the war. Attlee told the Commons that criticisms of the government or military leadership endangered the war effort by threatening to undermine public morale – a moot point. Restriction of free comment conflicted with the official portrayal of the war as a defence of democracy against totalitarianism. This consideration helps to explain why ministers tried to regulate press coverage wherever possible by discreet approaches to newspaper proprietors and editors. This enabled the government to influence newspaper comment in private while maintaining in public a commitment to press freedom.

There were occasions when more direct methods of censorship were used. Charged with undermining public morale by its criticisms of the government, the communist *Daily Worker* was suppressed from January 1941 to August 1942. Arguably its suppression exaggerated the paper's significance (it accounted for less than one per cent of total national daily circulation) and allowed British communists to present themselves as martyrs. Churchill, who was highly sensitive to press criticism, loathed the *Daily Mirror*, a paper which pilloried ministers, military leaders or industrialists who it saw as letting down the national cause. In March 1942 he supported the *Mirror*'s suppression following the publication of a cartoon which implied that the government was allowing petrol companies to profit from oil shortages caused by shipping losses. A Special Committee decided against suppression but agreed that Home Secretary Morrison would issue a public warning, threatening the *Mirror* with closure if it continued to print 'unwarranted and malignant' criticism. Some MPs and most newspapers rallied to the defence of the *Mirror*, pointing out that freedom to criticise the government was more likely to help

Key question
To what extent was the national press censored?

rather than hinder the search for victory. No sanctions were applied to the *Mirror* or any other major paper after Morrison's warning, possibly reflecting a more circumspect approach by editors. Alternatively, the voices raised in defence of the *Mirror* may have persuaded ministers that attacks on press freedom would be counterproductive.

It was in the government's interest to maintain cordial relations with the press, especially as the demand for war news pushed newspaper sales above their pre-war level. Four out of five men and two out of three women read at least one paper each day, despite higher prices and a reduction in size, resulting from the shortage of newsprint. Fortunately for the government, all the major papers supported the war effort and most journalists were prepared to follow the official line, acting more as cheerleaders and propagandists than independent reporters.

Key question
How did the BBC
help the war effort?

The BBC

The government had more control over the BBC than it had over newspapers. It had final authority over broadcasting policy and controlled the content of BBC's political statements and news coverage. The output of the BBC was confined to radio: TV broadcasting was suspended throughout the war. Given that less than five per cent of the population had a TV in 1939 this had little impact. By contrast there were some nine million radio sets. BBC broadcasts helped the war effort in several ways:

- They disseminated information to a mass audience. This information ranged from ministerial announcements, to news from the battlefield, to advice on matters such as food preparation.
- They reflected the hopes and fears of ordinary people, whose voices were carried across the airwaves in programmes from factories and army barracks.
- They functioned as a common reference point for civilians and soldiers alike, bringing people together as they listened to the same programmes.

Reliant on information from various government departments, the BBC did not always provide accurate news (for example RAF losses in the Battle of Britain). But it did not broadcast deliberate falsehoods and generally earned the trust of its audience.

The BBC leavened serious output with a liberal dose of light entertainment. The critical development came in 1940 with the start of the Forces Programme, the output of which was designed specifically for soldiers seeking entertainment. This was a departure from the high-minded tradition of broadcasting that had characterised the BBC's pre-war output. The BBC was now providing what (it thought) people wanted, not necessarily what it thought they needed.

Cinema

Recognising the role that films could play in the maintenance of morale, the MOI created a film division. It functions were to:

- liaise with commercial studios, independent producers and newsreel companies
- commission work and help with the logistics of film-making (for example, releasing artists from the armed services)
- decide which messages and themes should be emphasised.

Key question
Why were films an important medium for propaganda purposes?

A range of genres was used to convey propaganda to cinema audiences. The MOI believed newsreels were the most effective form of film propaganda, so these were given priority in the allocation of film stock. The MOI also made its own short films which exhorted the public to greater effort or which carried specific messages or instruction. Some 1400 of these were produced or sponsored by the MOI and given free to cinemas to include in their programmes. Feature films, dramatising episodes of the war or paying tribute to ordinary servicemen, were an effective medium of propaganda: the best could integrate messages and themes into an interesting story.

Civil liberties and the power of the state

By 1941 state interference had made Britain the most regimented society in Europe. This, inevitably, led to an erosion of civil liberties. In certain areas the extension of state power was uncontentious, for example, conscription. Relatively few males (some 60,000 in total) registered as conscientious objectors, despite the fact that conscientious objection was now accepted on grounds other than religion. Most were conscripted to do civilian work.

Internal censorship

In 1940 the authorities began to censor internal mail and to make snap checks on telegrams and telephone calls, particularly monitoring communists and other dissidents. Censorship of postal and telegraphic communication ultimately involved a network of offices and the employment of over 10,000 civil servants.

Alien internment

In September 1939 there were 75,000 Germans and Austrians living in Britain. While most were refugees who had fled Nazi persecution, the authorities feared that some might be Nazi sympathisers. The main suspects were immediately interned. The rest were passed before tribunals that classified them according to one of three types:

Key question
Was the internment of aliens a misconceived policy?

- Class A aliens who were to be interned
- Class B aliens who were to have their freedom of movement restricted
- Class C aliens who were to be exempt from restrictions.

By early 1940 only about 600 were classified as Class A. Over 64,000 were regarded as Class C. However, in May 1940, some newspapers campaigned for the internment of all aliens. After the fall of France and the entry of Italy into the war, in an atmosphere bordering on panic, everyone of German and Italian descent was regarded as a potential enemy. The 1939 security checks were set aside and all aliens were rounded up and herded into makeshift camps. Families were separated and internees suffered deficiencies in food, medical provision and sanitation facilities. Five internment camps were eventually set up on the Isle of Man (where conditions were not much better). Within the camps, pro-Nazis were held alongside leading anti-Nazis and German Jews, some of whom had spent time in Hitler's concentration camps before fleeing to Britain. These refugees had more reason to fear a German invasion than most Britons. Yet they were held as security risks.

In July 1940 8000 internees were shipped to Canada and Australia. Nearly 700 died when their ship was sunk by a U-boat. This helped to spark a backlash against the treatment of aliens. Home Secretary Anderson spoke of 'the most regrettable and deplorable things' which had happened. Although most of the internees were released, it was a slow process, and 70,000 spent the winter of 1940–1 as prisoners.

Internment of British nationals

British nationals deemed a security risk because of their pro-fascist views were arrested, including Sir Oswald Mosley, leader of the British Union of Fascists. Government emergency measures allowed for indefinite detention of suspected subversives. Most were held on the Isle of Man. Each of the 1800 individual cases was eventually reviewed and by mid-1941 most had been freed. (Mosley was released in 1943.)

Conclusion

Civil liberties were infringed in the war but within a framework of law and consent. The internment of aliens was a blot on the government's record but amends were made, in part, because of the continuing existence of freedom of expression. The government had the power to silence those speaking against the national interest. The fact that it so rarely used its powers testifies not only to its restraint but also to the generally co-operative attitude of the media. In return for the retention of the right to express opinion, media leaders, generally, were more than willing to endeavour to maintain national morale. Press, radio and cinema played their part in victory, assisted by a MOI whose performance improved the longer the war continued. The audience also played its part. Government messages were not simply carried via the media to a passive public: the audience helped to shape the message by making their preferences, values and attitudes known, for example in surveys conducted by the MOI or simply by making decisions about which newspaper to buy or which film to watch.

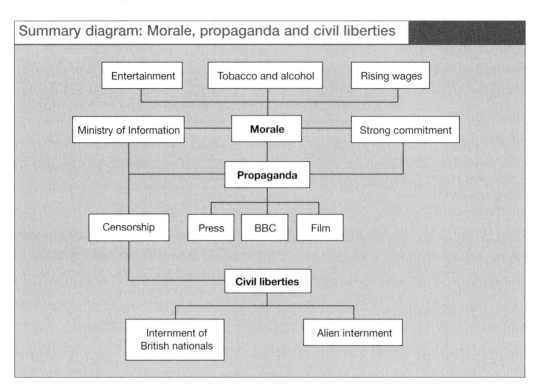

Summary diagram: Morale, propaganda and civil liberties

6 | Britain Post-1945

In 1945 there were two strong and contradictory trends. Many wanted to return to the good old (pre-war) days. Others, hoping for a better quality of life, looked forward to change. In 1945 the people had the chance to vote about Britain's future course.

The end of the coalition government

For five years Britain's political leaders had suspended party rivalry for the higher call of defending the nation. The compromises which coalition government entailed proved painful for many within the Labour movement, particularly as the party's reform programme was continually frustrated. In 1944 the Labour Party made it clear that it would only support the coalition until the end of the war in Europe. That came in May 1945. Given the choice by Churchill of either an immediate election or one after the defeat of Japan, Labour plumped for the early election. Churchill thereupon resigned on 23 May as head of the coalition and formed a 'caretaker' government until the result of the election, to be held on 5 July, was known.

Most Conservatives thought the 'Churchill factor' would win them the election. However, the evidence of by-election results and opinion polls suggested otherwise. Under the terms of the 1939 electoral truce, the three main parties had agreed not to nominate candidates for vacant constituencies against the candidate named by the party holding the seat. This did not prevent independents standing or small parties putting forward candidates. While Labour candidates were invariably returned,

Key question
Why did Labour triumph in the 1945 election?

End of war in Europe: May 1945

Labour victory in general election: July 1945

Key dates

Conservative candidates often struggled, losing 12 by-elections after 1940. Most of the victorious independents supported Labour reconstruction policies. Opinion polls, moreover, had given Labour a lead of at least 10 per cent from 1943 onwards – a lead it retained in 1945. However, many pundits regarded by-election results as unreliable and had little faith in new-fangled opinion polls.

Labour strengths in 1945

The Labour Party had several advantages after the end of the war in Europe:

- Some people blamed the Conservatives for mishandling economic and foreign policy in the 1930s.
- Unlike the Conservatives, Labour could not be blamed for the outbreak of war or for the early military failures. But when Britain began to secure victories after 1942 Labour, now a major partner in the coalition, took a share of the credit.
- The coalition provided Labour leaders with an opportunity to prove themselves in office. By 1945, Labour was known and trusted as a responsible party of government, its chief men dominating home front affairs.
- Labour had been able to distance itself from the coalition whenever it was unpopular because Labour backbench MPs still formed the official opposition.
- Many Britons admired the wartime performance of the USSR – a fully fledged socialist state.
- The war had helped to increase support for Labour policies. During the war virtually all aspects of social and economic life had been controlled centrally. In the same way that the state mobilised its resources for war, so Labour claimed, it should use its powers in peacetime to promote economic efficiency, greater equality and social justice.

The campaign

The campaign proper, launched by Churchill with a radio broadcast on 4 June, was an ill-tempered contest. Churchill set the tone by claiming that a Labour victory would result in a *Gestapo*-like state: 'Socialism is inseparably interwoven with totalitarianism and the abject worship of the state'. The Conservative campaign relied on a negative anti-Labour message, combined with a personal appeal to support the man who had led Britain to victory. The strategy was probably mistaken:

- Portraying Labour as a party of extremists was never likely to prove effective. Labour ministers such as Attlee, Bevin, Morrison, Dalton and Cripps had served loyally under Churchill and were respected national figures.
- Opinion polls suggested that while a large majority (some 80 per cent throughout the conflict) had a high regard for Churchill as a war leader, only a minority regarded him as a suitable peacetime Prime Minister.

Key term

Gestapo
The Nazi secret police force.

After years of immersing himself in global strategy, Churchill understandably focused on international issues. But his sense of priorities was at odds with most of the electorate who were mainly concerned with issues such as housing and employment. While the Conservative manifesto did commit the party to Beveridge-style reform, Churchill's wartime attitude towards reconstruction meant that such declarations lacked credibility. Moreover, it was difficult for the party to reconcile its commitment to an enhanced role for the state in welfare provision with its frequently articulated fears about the development of an over-mighty state.

The central theme of Labour's campaign was a positive one: in post-war Britain public welfare should take precedence over private interest. Nevertheless, the Labour manifesto stressed the practical rather than the ideological rationale behind its proposals. Thus, public ownership was justified as a strategy for increasing the efficiency of specific industries, rather than as a matter of socialist principle whereby the needs of the community should replace the profit motive.

The result

The election results, delayed for three weeks because of the need to collect the service vote, were announced on 26 July. Labour won 393 seats, the Conservatives 213 seats, and the Liberals, for whom Beveridge failed to win a seat, 12 (see Table 6.1). Churchill immediately resigned and Attlee formed a new government.

Clement Attlee pictured in his office in 10 Downing Street, London, in 1946.

Labour had overthrown a Conservative majority of over 200 and now held power with an overall majority for the first time. While the new government's core support was in the industrial cities, it won success in southern suburban England and in some rural areas. Polls and surveys suggested that Labour made significant gains among skilled workers. It also won the support of most service personnel and younger voters. Labour's victory, which brought to an end a period of Conservative power which had lasted (apart from two brief periods) since 1918, seemed to mark a major shift of popular political attitudes towards the left. However, this shift should not be exaggerated. Evidence suggests that only a minority of voters supported Labour for ideological reasons. Most were not interested in nationalisation. They simply believed that Labour was more likely to build houses, maintain employment and implement a Beveridge-style welfare scheme.

Table 6.1: General election results 1945–59

	Votes	No. of MPs	Share of vote (%)
1945			
Conservatives	9,988,306	213	39.8
Liberal	2,248,226	12	9.0
Labour	11,995,152	393	47.8
Communist	102,780	2	0.4
Common Wealth	110,634	1	0.4
Others	640,880	19	2.0
Total	25,085,978	640	100.0
1950			
Conservatives	12,502,567	298	43.5
Liberal	2,621,548	9	9.1
Labour	13,266,592	315	46.1
Communist	91,746	0	0.3
Others	290,218	3	1.0
Total	28,772,671	625	100.0
1951			
Conservatives	13,717,538	321	48.0
Liberal	730,556	6	2.5
Labour	13,948,605	295	48.8
Communist	21,640	0	0.1
Others	177,329	3	1.0
Total	28,595,668	625	100.0
1955			
Conservatives	13,286,569	344	49.7
Liberal	722,405	6	2.7
Labour	12,404,970	277	46.4
Communist	33,144	0	0.1
Others	313,410	3	1.1
Total	26,760,498	630	100.0
1959			
Conservatives	13,749,830	365	49.4
Liberal	1,638,571	6	5.0
Labour	12,215,538	258	43.8
Other	142,670	1	0.4
Total	27,859,241	630	100.0

Britain's world position in 1945

In 1945 most Britons believed that their country remained a great power. Its forces, five million strong, were stationed all over the globe. Although losing 370,000 people, this was only half the number the country had lost in the First World War and less than one-fiftieth the number of Soviet dead. The scale of destruction in British cities bore no comparison with much of Europe. Britain had escaped the rigours of enemy occupation and its economy seemed far ahead of most war-shattered European economies. Moreover, Britain had come out of the war with its Empire intact. Victory seemed a vindication of the empire's strength and solidarity.

However, Britain could not compare in strength with the USA and the USSR:

- The USSR possessed huge conventional forces and ruled a massive land mass.
- The USA was the richest country on earth, producing half the world's manufactured goods in 1945. It had large conventional forces and was the only country able to manufacture atom bombs.

Key question
Was Britain still a great power in 1945?

British economic and financial problems

The economic/financial cost of the war was huge. The destruction of housing, factories and shipping had cost the country a quarter of its national wealth. In 1945 British exports totalled £350 million (one-third of the pre-war figure) while imports had reached £2 billion. Valuable markets had been lost, mainly to US competitors. Britain was also in debt to the tune of over £3.5 billion and had been forced to sell many of its overseas assets and investments. In 1945 it seemed possible that Britain would run out of hard currency and be unable to import the supplies of food, fuel and raw materials on which its economy depended. US assistance was vital. But in August 1945, following Japan's surrender, the USA announced the end of Lend–Lease. Hugh Dalton, the new Chancellor of the Exchequer, said Britain faced 'total economic ruin' if more US financial aid was not forthcoming. British negotiators, headed by Keynes, persuaded the USA to provide a loan of $3.75 billion over 50 years at two per cent interest. In return, Britain agreed to dismantle its system of imperial preference and to promise that all holders of sterling should be able to convert their pounds into dollars in 1947. While many MPs resented these terms, they were in fact remarkably generous. The US loan, along with a Canadian loan of $1.25 billion, gave Britain some breathing space.

Key question
Why was Britain's economic and financial situation so dire in 1945?

The main political developments 1945–60

The Labour and Conservative parties dominated post-1945. The Liberal Party was rather irrelevant, with just six MPs for most of the 1950s. The Welsh and Scottish Nationalist parties were even weaker while the Unionists in Northern Ireland were allied with the Conservatives.

Key question
Why was the British political system so stable in the two decades after 1945?

Attlee's government

In 1945 Attlee's government faced serious problems at home and abroad: the threat from the USSR, Indian demands for independence, a balance of payments crisis, the transition from a wartime to a peacetime economy, and a housing problem. It was also committed to introducing large-scale reform. While introducing the Welfare State and nationalising some important industries, it did not introduce full-blooded socialism. Only a small section of private industry was brought under public control, and there was no all-out attack on wealth and privilege.

In 1950 Attlee called a general election, stressing Labour's achievements and proposing more nationalisation. Labour won 315 seats, the Conservatives 298 seats (see Table 6.1 on page 201). Attlee's government now had a majority of just five. Many voters were tiring of government controls and high taxation, preferring the Conservative cry of 'set the people free'. Attlee found it hard to govern in 1950–1. Facing a balance of payments crisis and a divided party, he called another election in October 1951. The result was a Conservative victory. They won 321 seats to Labour's 295 seats (see Table 6.1). Attlee resigned as Prime Minister and Churchill returned to power.

Churchill's government 1951–5

Churchill was 77 years old in 1951 and in poor health. He had already suffered two strokes and experienced another in 1953. But he coped reasonably well with the demands of office, leading his party 'with great vigour and flair towards the middle ground of politics', according to Paul Addison. Churchill's political outlook and that of his government was conciliatory and undogmatic. There was a general continuation of Labour's welfare and employment policies, although this was tempered by a greater emphasis on the role of the market. Rationing finally ended in 1954.

Anthony Eden 1955–7

In April 1955 Churchill resigned and was replaced as Prime Minister by Anthony Eden, who called a general election in May. Eden was respected and popular, there was rising prosperity and the Labour Party was divided between right and left. The Conservatives won 344 seats, Labour 277 (see Table 6.1). The **Suez crisis** destroyed Eden's premiership. His health broke down and he retired as Prime Minister in January 1957.

Harold Macmillan 1957–63

Harold Macmillan, the new Tory leader, quickly restored the self-confidence of his party after the Suez débâcle. With rising prosperity, he called an election in 1959. 'Life is better under the Conservatives' was the Tory slogan, 'Don't let Labour ruin it'. Although the Labour Party was now more united owing to the reconciliation of Bevan and Gaitskell, there was no compelling reason for the electorate to shift to Labour. The Conservatives thus won 365 seats, Labour 258 seats (see Table 6.1).

Key term

Suez crisis
In 1956 British and French forces occupied the Suez Canal, which had just been nationalised by Egypt. The attack provoked intense political controversy in Britain and widespread opposition abroad. In the end Britain and France had to recall their troops.

Consensus

Many historians, following Paul Addison, claim that there was considerable 'consensus' between the two main parties after 1945. Addison argued that as a result of the wartime experience, Tory and Labour leaders came to adopt similar attitudes with regard to the mixed economy, the welfare state and full employment – attitudes were very much influenced by the economic ideas of Keynes and the welfare principles embodied in the Beveridge Report. There was thus little difference between the main parties. Voters plumped for either Labour or Conservative because of the persistence of class-feeling or because of their estimate of which party would best deliver a very similar social and economic package.

Key question
To what extent were the main parties essentially the same after 1945?

Addison's thesis is not accepted by all historians. Ben Pimlott, for example, has rejected the notion of consensus as a 'myth'. He claims that wartime unity masked 'deep ideological conflicts' and has argued that Labour's post-1945 programme was 'fiercely resisted and furiously resented' by the Tories. Nevertheless, many scholars insist that a broad consensus can be discerned, particularly among the governing élites of the two main parties. This does not mean that there was an absence of party disputes, nor that all Conservative and Labour party members approved of the consensus. But it does suggest that the more extreme views on both sides were contained.

The mixed economy

Attlee's government carried through a major programme of nationalisation, covering the Bank of England (1946), coal (1947), civil aviation (1946), electricity (1948), inland transport (1948), gas (1948) and iron and steel (1949). There was little Conservative opposition to Labour's initial programme. This was partly because many of the proposals concerned public utilities, such as electricity, where state enterprise had always played a significant role. Nor was it easy to oppose the nationalisation of the coal industry, given its backwardness and dreadful labour relations' record. The nationalisation pill was also made easier for the Conservatives to swallow by the generous compensation provided – too generous by far for most Labour supporters. Coal owners, for example, received £164 million for their half-bankrupt industry.

If the first phase of nationalisation was carried through in a relatively peaceful fashion, this was not true of the last item on Labour's agenda – iron and steel. Here, for the first time, the state would be taking over a manufacturing industry and one which had a reasonable productivity record. Even Attlee's cabinet was divided over the issue. Morrison, who feared it would be unpopular with the voters, opposed the measure. Bevan, on grounds of socialist commitment, was the main supporter. The bill to take over the larger iron and steel firms was fiercely opposed by the Conservatives.

By 1950 more than two million workers were employed in nationalised industries. However, 80 per cent of British industry remained in private hands. Thus, Attlee's government had not gone far down the socialist road. Conservative governments of the 1950s, apart from denationalising iron and steel and road haulage, made no attempt to uproot the rest of Labour's nationalisation programme. 'It is only where we believed that a measure of nationalisation was a real hindrance to our island life,' said Churchill, 'that we have reversed the policy'. In Dutton's view, the Conservatives' acceptance of the mixed economy in the 1950s was 'the most notable feature of the whole period'.

Full employment

While both parties were committed to maintaining full employment, they disagreed about how this was to be achieved. Whereas the Conservatives emphasised the virtue of private enterprise, Labour stressed the importance of state management of the economy. Ironically, the general conditions of high demand post-1945 were more important than government policy. The economic boom – and near full employment – continued for a quarter of a century.

The Welfare State

Key dates

National Insurance Act: 1946

Establishment of the National Health Service: 1948

The 1946 National Insurance Act was one of the foundation stones of the Welfare State. It applied universally to all paid employees and most of the self-employed, and their dependants, and provided comprehensive cover against sickness, unemployment and old age. The National Health Service (NHS), which began in 1948, accepted the fundamental principle of a free and universal service, directly financed by the state. There was little Conservative opposition to Labour's national insurance legislation. Although the Tories were critical of some aspects of the NHS scheme, Churchill's government made no attempt to dismantle it. In fact expenditure on the social services increased both in real terms and as a percentage of total public spending under the Conservatives. Thus, both major parties supported the Welfare State, even though Conservative rhetoric still stressed the benefits of thrift and self-reliance while Labour praised the virtues of equality and social justice.

Education

The 1944 Education Act laid the framework of a new secondary system. Conservative and Labour MPs supported the measure. The school leaving age was raised to 15. There were to be three types of schools – secondary modern, grammar and technical. (Fee-paying private schools also continued.) The results of an 11-plus examination would determine which school a pupil attended. Grammar schools provided the route to the best jobs. Secondary moderns were the route for most working-class children. Thus, although the potential for mobility through the education system was greater than it had been in the 1930s – more working-class children did go to grammar school – the whole system tended to replicate the division of the social structure into working, lower-middle, upper-middle and upper classes. No real debate on the organisation of state education took place until the 1950s. Only then did Labour begin to consider the merits of a comprehensive system of secondary education.

Attitudes to the trade unions

The major trade unions were an integral part of the Labour Party, dominating much of its decision-making machinery and providing the bulk of its income. As a result the trade union movement gained much from the Labour government after 1945: the 1946 Trade Union Act, nationalisation, and the appointment of many trade union representatives to committees and boards at both national and local level. The Conservatives had denounced parts of the 1946 Trade Union Act, including the '**closed shop**'. But after 1951 they made no real effort to change the status quo and challenge trade union power and privileges. Conservative Ministers of Labour pursued a policy of conciliation in industrial disputes.

Conclusion

In a famous article in 1954 the *Economist* invented the term 'Butskellism' to describe the similarities between the economic policies of Butler, the Conservative Chancellor of the Exchequer, and Gaitskell, his Labour shadow. Although Gaitskell dismissed the term as a 'silly catchword', Butler was perhaps nearer the mark when he later wrote that 'both of us, it is true, spoke the language of **Keynesianism**', although he added 'with different accents and with a differing emphasis'. In many other respects, Conservative and Labour governments spoke the same language, with slightly different emphasis. While Conservative and Labour ideas and values often seemed fundamentally at odds, there was broad agreement over many aspects of policy after 1945.

Key terms

Closed shop
An establishment in which only members of a particular trade union will be employed.

Keynesianism
The economic ideas of Lord Keynes.

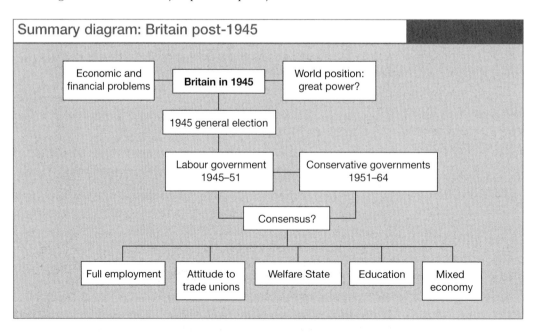

Summary diagram: Britain post-1945

7 | Key Debate

Was the social and economic impact of the war on Britain positive or negative in the years 1945–60?

The Second World War has evoked nostalgia and pride in Britain for over 60 years. Those who experienced the war at first hand have tended to emphasise the heroic nature of the war effort: Britain alone (at least in 1940–1), fighting the good fight against Nazi Germany. Many historians have argued that the war produced a sense of social solidarity at home which in turn led to a commitment to welfare reform and a drive to improve social conditions both during and after the conflict. As well as a 'people's war', the conflict is still generally seen as a 'good' war. But did the war actually benefit Britain? Leaving aside the fact that Britain was no longer a great power (and its Empire was soon to collapse), what were the main positive and negative effects of the conflict with regard to Britain's socioeconomic development?

The negative effects

Over 370,000 people were killed: 272,000 in the armed forces, 35,000 in the merchant navy and 63,000 civilians.

The economic/financial cost of the war was huge (see page 202). Moreover, it took time to convert a wartime economy for peacetime. Britain thus faced serious economic/financial problems post-1945. In 1947 a severely cold winter led to a fuel crisis, declining production, a dramatic fall in exports and a balance of payments problem. In 1947 Cripps, the new Minister of Economic Affairs, introduced strict import controls, limiting both the quantity and the range of goods available. Rationing of most basic foodstuffs (including bread) lasted until 1950. Shortages had to be accepted for the sake of the export drive. Even so, in order to stave off bankruptcy Britain still needed, and received, huge amounts of **Marshall Aid** from the USA.

Many of Britain's 'old' industries were in a bad way in 1945. While the war had checked a long-term decline in the shipbuilding and textile industries, there had been little change to operational methods.

Despite growing affluence, Britain entered on a period of relative economic decline after 1950, falling behind its main rivals. Between 1951 and 1964 industrial production grew three times faster in France, four times faster in West Germany and 10 times the British rate in Japan. During the same period, Britain's share of world trade in manufactured goods slumped from 25.5 per cent to 13.9 per cent. Historian Corelli Barnett, in a provocative book, *The Audit of War* (1986), claimed that the origins of Britain's economic decline lay in the wartime consensus. It was then, he argued, that Britons were beguiled by a largely leftish political and intellectual establishment into expecting a 'New Jerusalem' after the war: economic security and mounting prosperity, effortlessly achieved and sustained by handouts from the state. Barnett was particularly critical of

Key term

Marshall Aid
In 1947 the US Congress supported US Secretary of State George Marshall's plan to give economic aid to Europe. Sixteen nations in Western Europe received $13 billion in grants and loans between 1948 and 1952. Britain received $2693 million.

Attlee's government which tried to put this ideal into practice, creating an expensive Welfare State. What Britain should have been doing, Barnett believed, was concentrating on the modernisation of its industry and producing a better educated and more efficient workforce.

Trade union power, which had grown considerably during the war, is often blamed for Britain's economic malaise. After 1945 British industry was beset by over-manning, demarcation disputes and unofficial strikes.

The war exacerbated a pre-war housing shortage: nearly 500,000 homes had been destroyed or made uninhabitable by bombing. Many more needed repair. Only 300,000 houses had been built during the war. Two million wartime marriages had added to the shortfall of homes needed. In 1945 Labour committed itself to build 200,000 new houses a year. It failed to meet its target, building one million houses by 1951. Most were council houses for the working classes to rent.

The educational system in 1945 was short of everything, including teachers. A large building programme was needed to accommodate not only 200,000 pupils whose schools had been destroyed by bombing but 400,000 added by the raising of the school leaving age.

The university sector had shrunk during the war. By 1945 it had only two-thirds of the number of staff and three-quarters of the number of students that it had in 1939.

Britain's pretensions as a great power post-1945 resulted in crippling defence spending – nearly 18 per cent of gross national product in 1947 – far more than any of its European competitors. National service for 18-year-old males was instituted in 1947. This took hundreds of thousands of men from economic production.

The role of women had not changed much (see pages 188–90).

The positive effects

Devastating though the war deaths were, they did not seriously damage Britain's industrial capacity. During the war, Britain's total population grew by 1.4 million.

The rate at which Britain recovered economically after 1945 was impressive, helped by US loans and by the fact that Germany and Japan, two of Britain's chief industrial rivals, were laid low. By 1950 Britain had a healthy balance of payments surplus.

The war had a beneficial effect on a number of important industries:

- Massive inputs of space, machine tools, research and labour enabled the aircraft industry to increase output and to develop new inventions like the jet engine.
- The motor industry was booming in 1945 with production lines ready for conversion from wartime to peacetime vehicle production.
- Engineering industries had benefited from the spread of modern methods of mass production and management, and scientific development.

- The petrochemical industry, with its offshoots in artificial fibres, fertilisers, synthetic rubber and plastics, had expanded.
- Government policies to increase food production had helped to modernise farming (see pages 178–9).

Many wartime developments, inspired by military objectives, had economic (and social) repercussions post-1945:

- Nuclear power was adapted to generate energy for civilian purposes.
- Radar was adapted to meet the needs of commercial air transport.
- The (successful) search for new antibiotics and the use of penicillin (a pre-war discovery but exploited during the war) revolutionised medicine post-1945.
- The war led to breakthroughs in computing.

Depressed areas (for example, south Wales and north-east England) had benefited through large government investment in armaments during the war.

The expansion of industrial welfare during the war affected millions of workers. By 1945 most large factories had canteens and washrooms, and there had been improvements in lighting and ventilation.

Barnett's view of the origins of Britain's economic decline is not supported by most historians. His criticism of Attlee's government underestimates the constraints under which it operated and understates its attempts to modernise Britain's industrial base. Barnett's claim that expenditure on social welfare had debilitating consequences for the British economy can also be challenged. Many Western nations which overtook Britain economically post-1945 devoted a higher proportion of their domestic product to welfare expenditure than Britain. It is unlikely that in Britain alone such provision inhibited economic growth.

In 1945 the average citizen enjoyed a slightly higher standard of living than in 1939. This was the result of full employment and the availability of overtime work. Britain continued to enjoy virtually full employment for two decades after 1945.

The war had witnessed a narrowing of income differentiation as unskilled wages rose more than skilled wages and wages in general rose more than salaries.

New standards of pensions, child allowances and the introduction of the NHS all helped to eliminate the grosser forms of poverty and ill-health which had blighted the lives of so many families pre-1939.

The nation's health had improved, which was a remarkable fact given that medical services were overstretched for most of the war. The improvement owed much to government intervention such as free vaccination schemes, school meals, subsidised milk for young children and expectant mothers, and the distribution of orange juice and cod-liver oil.

The housing situation slowly improved. In 1951 Churchill pledged to build 300,000 houses a year, a target Minister of

Housing Harold Macmillan successfully achieved in 1953. While most houses belonged to the public sector, the proportion of private houses gradually increased. An important part of the housing programme was the building of 'new towns' in the countryside such as Crawley and Basildon.

The dedication of teachers and administrators had managed to keep the education system going after 1939. The number of children staying on at school after the age of 14 increased during the war, as did the number successfully taking public examinations. The 1944 Education Act raised the minimum leaving age to 15.

The role of women had changed to some extent (see pages 188–90).

Attlee's government did much to improve the conditions of life of the working class and to provide a more just and humane society. As Peter Hennessey writes of the period 1945–51: 'It is largely the achievement of these years – and the wartime experience – that 1951 Britain, certainly compared to the UK of 1931 or any previous decade, was a far, far better place in which to be born, to grow up, to live, love, work and even to die.' In the 1950s living standards continued to rise at a rate faster than at any time in British history. In real terms, consumer expenditure rose by 45 per cent between 1952 and 1964. People spent money on a range of consumer goods such as televisions, cars, washing machines and fridges. 'Let's be frank about it: most of our people have never had it so good', said Macmillan in 1957.

Some key books in the debate

P. Addison, *The Road to 1945* (Pimlico, 1994).
C. Barnett, *The Audit of War* (Macmillan, 1986).
D. Childs, *Britain Since 1945* (Routledge, 2006).
Peter Hennessey, *Never Again, Britain 1945–51* (Vintage Paperback, 1993).
D. Kynaston, *Austerity Britain 1945–1951* (Bloomsbury, 2008).
R. Mackay, *The Test of War: Inside Britain 1939–45* (UCL Press, 1999).
A. Marwick, *British Society Since 1945* (Penguin, 1996).
R. Middleton and J. Black, *The British Economy Since 1945* (Palgrave Macmillan, 2000).
K. Morgan, *Britain Since 1945* (Oxford University Press, 2001).
A. Sked and C. Cook, *Post-War Britain* (Penguin, 1992).

Study Guide: A2 Question

In the style of Edexcel

Study Sources 1, 2 and 3. How far do you agree with the view that economic policy and performance in the years to 1951 was dominated by the negative impact of the Second World War? Explain your answer, using Sources 1, 2 and 3 and your own knowledge of the issues related to this controversy.

Source 1

From: M. Lynch, Britain 1945–2007, *published in 2008.*

The six years of government-directed war effort, during which Keynes was an influential figure at the Treasury, helped to give strength to his arguments. What is interesting is that, although Keynes thought in terms of limited government action, it was the notion of government being an essential part of economic planning that became widely accepted. This new conviction had the effect of giving added legitimacy and justification to the economic reform programme followed by Clement Attlee's Labour governments after 1945.

Source 2

From: D. Murphy (editor), Britain 1914–2000, *published in 2000.*

Twenty per cent of British industry, much of it suffering from years of neglect and underinvestment, was nationalised [by Attlee's government]. In many industries – coal, electricity, gas and the railways – it made sense to establish a national monopoly rather than the patchwork of municipal and private companies that had existed before the war. Yet looking at the subsequent history of these industries it is easy to query the reasons behind nationalisation. The government was often uncertain about what the nationalised industries should do, except act as non-profit-making utilities. It was hoped that nationalisation would encourage efficiency and investment as well as improve working conditions. Critics such as Correlli Barnett in *The Lost Victory* (1995) have claimed that 'nationalisation turned out in all respects to be not so much a revolution as the prolonging of the *ancien régime* by bureaucratic means'. In nationalising industries, the government was generally content to leave existing managers in charge. Attempts to plan the economy were also less than successful. Ministers adopted a voluntary approach towards industry, which had been commonplace during the war, encouraging rather than directing effort.

Source 3

From: P. Addison, Now the War is Over, *published in 1985.*

Between 1945 and 1951 British industry staged a spirited recovery. By 1951, industrial production was up 50 per cent on 1946 and exports were up 67 per cent. The standard of living, deliberately held back in order to free resources for industrial growth, was little changed but full employment had been maintained. Presented as curves on a graph, the industrial record looks impressive. It compared well at that time with the rates of recovery achieved by the other nations of Western Europe. Not until the 1950s was it apparent that British industry was advancing at a more sluggish pace than its competitors.

Exam tips

The cross-references are intended to take you straight to the material that will help you to answer the question.

There are different aspects to explore in this question:

- Whether both policy and performance were dominated by the legacy of war.
- Whether that legacy was entirely negative.

Begin your planning by analysing the sources and identifying the issues they raise. From Source 1 you can identify the increased acceptance of central government planning as one legacy of war. Cross-referring to Sources 2 and 3 you can show that this strengthened the economic reform policies of Attlee's government by adding 'legitimacy and justification' which in turn contributed to the government's carrying through of the nationalisation policies. Acceptance of government planning would also contribute to the government's ability to hold back the standard of living 'in order to free resources for industrial growth'.

Other relevant issues raised by the sources are:

- Nationalisation effected only limited changes, 'prolonging the *ancien régime* by bureaucratic means'.
- Attempts to plan the economy were met with limited success partly because of the continuation of the 'voluntary' approach adopted during the war.

However:

- Industrial production 'staged a spirited recovery'.
- Industry before the war had suffered from neglect and underinvestment.

You can add to and extend these issues using the material in Chapter 6. The highest marks are gained for the effective integration of material from your own knowledge with material from the sources. You should consider:

- The extent of Britain's economic problems at the end of the war, and how far these had been exacerbated by the war (pages 207–9).
- Whether the 'wartime consensus' engendered attitudes conducive to or harmful to post-war economic recovery (pages 207–9).
- How far the impact of war influenced the economic policies of Attlee's Labour government and the extent to which this influence was negative (pages 202–4).
- How far the effects of war were beneficial and contributed to an impressive period of post-war recovery (pages 208–10).

Before coming to a final conclusion about the claim stated in the question, you should also take note of the indication in Source 3 that, by 1951, Britain's post-war economic record began to compare unfavourably with its competitors. But how much of that can be directly attributed to a negative legacy of war?

Glossary

Admiralty   The government board that administered the Royal Navy.

Alliance system   Before 1914 Europe had been divided into two armed camps: the Triple Entente (Britain, France and Russia) against the Triple Alliance (Germany, Austria-Hungary and Italy).

Anschluss   The union of Austria and Germany.

Anti-Semitic   Anti-Jewish.

Appeasement   A policy of making concessions to another nation to avoid war. The term is primarily associated with British and French foreign policy in the 1930s.

Armistice   A truce: the suspension of hostilities.

Axis   The term Axis Powers was used to describe Germany, Italy and Japan.

Balance of payments   The difference between a nation's total receipts from foreign countries and its total payments to foreign countries.

Balance of power   British governments had long tried to ensure that no nation was so strong that it could dominate Europe and thus threaten Britain.

Baltic States   Lithuania, Latvia and Estonia.

Banking house of the world   Britain had surplus capital (money) to invest in projects around the world in the nineteenth century.

Battle of the Atlantic   The name given by Churchill in 1941 to the struggle to protect the merchant ships bringing supplies to Britain. The chief threat came from German U-boats.

Battle of Britain   The aerial conflict fought over Britain between the RAF and the *Luftwaffe* from July to September 1940.

Big Three   Lloyd George (Britain), Clemenceau (France) and Woodrow Wilson (USA) dominated the peacemaking process. They represented the strongest countries that had defeated the Central Powers.

Black market   Buying or selling that is against the law.

Blank cheques   In diplomatic terms, it means complete freedom to act as one thinks best.

Blitz   A shortened form of the German word *blitzkrieg* (or lightening war). The term was used to describe the bombing of British cities by the *Luftwaffe* in 1940–1.

Bohemia   A major province in Czechoslovakia.

Bolshevism   The Bolshevik Party seized power in Russia in November 1917. Led by Lenin, the Bolsheviks supported communism. The word 'Bolshevism' became a derogatory term for communism.

Buffer state   A neutral country lying between two others whose relations are, or may become, strained.

Cabinet   Senior ministers of the government who meet regularly to discuss policy.

Capital ships   Warships of the largest and most heavily armoured class, for example, battleships.

Caretaker government   A temporary government. The French political situation was highly unstable. Coalitions of various parties formed governments but then quickly fell. The result was weak government.

Cash and carry   Britain was now able to acquire US weapons, provided it paid for them and they were transported in British ships.

Central Powers   Germany, Austria-Hungary, Turkey and Bulgaria were known as the Central Powers in the First World War.

Closed shop   An establishment in which only members of a particular trade union will be employed.

Coalition government   Government by a combination of allied political parties. A coalition government is sometimes called a national government.

Colonial war   An overseas conflict in defence of Britain's imperial interests. It could be action against insurgents seeking independence or war against a hostile power.

Comintern   Communist International (also known as the Third International), founded in 1919 in Moscow, in an effort to co-ordinate the actions of communist parties globally.

Communism   A social theory according to which society should be classless, private property should be abolished, and the means of production and distribution should be collectively owned and controlled.

Conscientious objectors   People who refuse to fight for reasons of conscience.

Conscription   Compulsory enrolment for military service.

Constitutional monarchy   Government where the powers of the monarch are defined and limited.

Coup d'état   The overthrow of a government by force or subversive action.

Coupons   Vouchers from ration books, allowing people to buy goods.

Decolonisation   The process of bringing about the end of colonial rule.

Demilitarised   Not occupied by military forces.

Dominions   Countries within the British Empire that had considerable – in some cases almost total – self-rule.

Dunkirk spirit   The determination of the British people (after Dunkirk) to resist Nazi aggression whatever the cost.

Economic sanctions   Refusing to trade with a particular country.

Europe first strategy   The strategic notion that the Allies should focus on defeating Germany (and Italy) before Japan.

Fascist Party   A nationalist, authoritarian, anti-communist movement developed by Mussolini in Italy after 1919. The word fascism is often applied to authoritarian and National Socialist movements in Europe and elsewhere.

Five-Year Plans   In the late 1920s Stalin embarked on ambitious efforts to make the USSR a major industrial power. Every industry had a five-year target.

Fourteen Points   Wilson's peace programme, the Fourteen Points, was announced to the US Congress in January 1918.

Franchise for women   The right of women to vote.

Free collective bargaining   Negotiation on pay and conditions of service between one or more trade unions on one side and an employer or association of employers on the other.

Free trade   The interchange of all commodities without import and export duties.

French Indo-China   Pre-1954 Vietnam, Laos and Cambodia were ruled by France. The whole area was known as Indo-China.

General Staff   The body which administers the British army.

General strike   When workers in all industries refuse to work.

General Strike of 1926   In May 1926 British workers, from a variety of industries, went on strike in support of the coal miners. In the face of resolute government action, the TUC called off the strike after nine days.

German militarism The German army had been a major force in Europe since 1870. German generals had exerted great political influence, particularly during the First World War.

German problem Since 1871, Germany had been the strongest nation in Europe. The Treaty of Versailles reduced but did not destroy Germany's potential power. The German problem was essentially Germany's power.

Gestapo The Nazi secret police force.

Grand Alliance Churchill's term for the wartime alliance between Britain (and its Empire), the USA and the USSR. (Roosevelt called it the United Nations.)

Great purges In the late 1930s Stalin imprisoned or executed millions of people who were suspected of disloyalty. Many of the USSR's chief generals were killed.

Gross domestic product The total value of goods and services produced within a country.

Habsburg Empire Until 1918 the Austro-Hungarian Empire, ruled for centuries by the Habsburg family, had controlled much of Central and Eastern Europe.

Hyperinflation A huge increase in the amount of (almost worthless) money in circulation, resulting in a massive increase in prices. In Germany in 1923 an egg cost hundreds of millions of marks.

Imperial preference Britain tried to ensure that countries within the Empire traded first and foremost with each other.

Industrial Revolution The economic and social changes arising out of the change from industries carried on in the home with simple machines to industries in factories with power-driven machinery.

Inflationary pressures Problems arising from the rise in the price of goods and the general cost of living.

International Brigade A left-wing military force made up of volunteers from a number of different countries.

Iron Curtain The imaginary frontier between Soviet-dominated Europe and the West.

Isolationist One who supports avoiding political entanglements with other countries.

Kaiser Wilhelm II German Emperor, 1888–1918. When it was clear that the First World War was lost, he abdicated and fled to the Netherlands.

Keynesianism The economic ideas of Lord Keynes.

League of Nations A global organisation, set up in 1919, to resolve international disputes.

League of Nations Union A British organisation set up to support the League.

Lebensraum 'Living space': Hitler hoped to expand Germany's territory in the east, at the expense of Poland and the USSR.

Left Those who want to change society and who might incline to socialism or communism.

Luftwaffe The German air force.

Maginot Line French defensive fortifications stretching along the German frontier.

Mandates The system created in the Peace Settlement for the supervision of all the colonies of Germany (and Turkey) by the League of Nations.

Manhood suffrage The right of all men to vote.

Marriage bar A rule whereby women were forced to resign from their jobs once they married.

Marshall Aid In 1947 the US Congress supported US Secretary of State George Marshall's plan to give economic aid to Europe. Sixteen nations in Western Europe received $13 billion in grants and loans between 1948 and 1952. Britain received $2693 million.

Martial law The suspension of ordinary administration and policing and the imposition of military power.

Means testing The method by which the government determined whether people should be given allowances and how much they should be paid.

Mixed economy An economic system where there are nationalised industries and private businesses.

Monarchists In terms of Spain, those who supported the return of a Spanish king.

National debt Money borrowed by a government and not yet repaid.

Nationalisation State control of an industry.

Nationalist A person who favours or strives after the unity, independence or interests of a nation.

Nazi Short for National Socialist German Workers Party.

Neutrality Acts A series of Acts passed by the US Congress between 1935 and 1939 prohibiting the US government giving loans to belligerent nations and placing embargoes on shipments of arms.

New Economic Policy (NEP) In 1922 Lenin backed down from the notion of total communism. His NEP allowed some private ownership.

New order Japan's aim for Asia, ending European imperialism and uniting Asians in an alliance (led by Japan) free of Western taint.

Newsreels Short news programmes shown between feature films at cinemas.

Nuremberg rally Hitler held major annual Nazi Party meetings at Nuremberg.

Operation Sealion The German code name for the invasion of Britain.

Ottoman Empire Ottoman rulers controlled Turkey and much of the Middle East.

Paper tiger Something that is far less strong than it might appear to be.

Passive resistance Deliberate refusal to co-operate with the authorities. Those who support such action adopt peaceful, not violent, protest.

Peace settlement This term comprises all the different peace treaties, including the Treaty of Versailles.

Periodicals Journals or magazines that are usually published weekly or monthly.

Plebiscite A vote by the people on one specific issue – like a referendum.

Plenipotentiary A special ambassador or envoy with full powers to negotiate.

Pogrom An organised attack on Jews.

Policy of rapprochement To renew or improve relations with someone.

Polish Corridor A stretch of land which gave Poland access to the Baltic Sea but which cut off East Prussia from the rest of Germany.

Protectorate A territory administered by another, usually much stronger state.

Putsch An attempt to seize power, usually by force.

Quotas Limits of goods allowed in the country.

Radar The use of high-powered radio pulses for locating objects (for example, enemy planes).

RAF The Royal Air Force, formed in 1918, was the youngest of Britain's armed services.

Reconstruction The rebuilding and reorganisation of a society after a great upheaval.

Reds Bolshevik supporters.

Reparations Compensation paid by defeated states to the victors.

Revisionist Keen to change or overthrow the status quo.

Rhineland The part of Germany to the west of the River Rhine.

Right Those who are inclined towards conservatism or who are strongly nationalist.

Rome–Berlin Axis A term first used by Mussolini in 1936 to describe Italy's relationship with Germany. He envisaged

European affairs being determined by, or revolving around, Italy and Germany.

Satellite A country that is subordinate to another.

Scapa Flow A major British naval base in the Orkney Islands.

Second Front The term used to describe an Allied invasion of northern France.

Secret diplomacy Negotiations taking place behind closed doors.

Seditious activities Actions against the state which are intended to cause disorder and trouble.

Self-determination The right of people, usually of the same nationality, to set up their own government and rule themselves.

Service ministries The ministries responsible for the army, navy and air force.

Socialism A social and economic system in which most forms of private property are abolished and the means of production and distribution of wealth are owned by the community as a whole.

Spartakist rising An attempt by communists to seize power in Germany over the winter of 1918–19.

Sphere of influence A state under the control of another, more powerful, state.

Status quo The existing condition.

Sterling area A group of countries (many within the Empire/Commonwealth) with currencies tied to the British currency.

The Straits Comprising the Bosphorus and the Dardanelles, these form the outlet from the Black Sea to the Mediterranean.

Suez Canal The canal, which ran through Egyptian territory, joined the Mediterranean to the Red Sea. It was controlled by Britain.

Suez crisis In 1956 British and French forces occupied the Suez Canal, which had just been nationalised by Egypt. The attack provoked intense political controversy in Britain and widespread opposition abroad. In the end Britain and France had to recall their troops.

Surtax An additional tax payable on incomes above a high level.

Territorial army Britain's voluntary military force.

Third Reich Hitler's Germany from 1933 to 1945. (*Reich* meaning Empire.)

Totalitarianism A form of government that controls everything under one authority and allows no opposition.

Trades Union Congress (TUC) The main organisation of the British trade union movement.

Treaty of Versailles One of the peace treaties that ended the First World War.

Ultimatum A final offer or demand.

United Nations An association of states formed in 1945 to promote peace and international security and co-operation, taking over many of the functions of the dissolved League of Nations.

USSR The Union of Soviet Socialist Republics.

Wall Street Crash In October 1929 share prices on the New York Stock Exchange (on Wall Street) collapsed. Many US banks and businesses lost money. This event is often seen as triggering the Great Depression.

War Cabinet A small inner group of chief ministers who are mainly responsible for co-ordinating the war effort.

War on two fronts From Germany's point of view, this meant a war in the east (against Poland) and a war in the west (against France and Britain).

White papers Government-produced statements for the information of Parliament (and the country).

Whites Various opponents of the Bolsheviks.

Women's Land Army An organisation of some 80,000 women employed to work on the land.

Workshop of the world Britain had produced most of the world's industrial goods before 1870.

Index